*A Philadelphia Family*

*Henry Howard Houston in 1884, aged 64. Oil on canvas, by David John Gué. Dallett collection.*

# A Philadelphia Family / The Houstons and Woodwards of Chestnut Hill / DAVID R. CONTOSTA

FOREWORD BY E. DIGBY BALTZELL

*Best wishes,*
*David R. Contosta*

𝓊𝓅𝓅

UNIVERSITY OF PENNSYLVANIA PRESS
*Philadelphia*

Library of Congress Cataloging-in-Publication Data

Contosta, David R.
   A Philadelphia family: the Houstons and Woodwards of Chestnut
Hill / David R. Contosta; foreword by E. Digby Baltzell.
      p.   cm.
   Bibliography: p.
   Includes index.
   ISBN 0-8122-8136-5
   1. Philadelphia (Pa.)—Biography.   2. Houston family.   3. Woodward
family.   4. Philadelphia (Pa.)—Social life and customs.   I. Title.
F158.25.C66   1988
974.8′1104′0922—dc19
[B]                                                                    88-21596
                                                                          CIP

# Contents

# Acknowledgments

I AM INDEBTED TO an unusually large number of men and women who generously assisted me at every stage of this project. Above all I wish to thank Mrs. Charles Woodward for proposing this book nearly three years ago, as well as for a generous stipend that permitted a reduction of my teaching obligations during the major period of research and writing. I also thank her for providing photographs and newspaper clippings and for granting two long interviews. Her daughter, Quita Woodward Horan, lent several photographs, sat for an interview, and cheerfully answered what must have seemed like an endless stream of questions.

Stanley Woodward, Sr., graciously invited me to spend four days with him at Northeast Harbor, Maine, in July 1986. We passed long but relaxing hours talking about his parents and his own years in the diplomatic service. A lengthy correspondence with Mr. Woodward has proven both informative and enjoyable. He, too, has lent a number of family photographs.

On the Houston side, the late Eleanor Houston Smith allowed me unrestricted use of her extensive family archives, in addition to extending special permission to examine the Houston Estate Papers at the Pennsylvania State Archives in Harrisburg. She gave two long interviews and never tired of my many telephone calls and casual questions as we worked together through her collections. The wonderful tour of Roxborough that she gave me provided new and frequently humorous insights into the family's development of that section. Her daughter, Sallie Smith Kise, kindly showed me around Druim Moir, supplied additional facts about her parents, and made helpful comments on several portions of the manuscript.

I am also indebted to her sisters Eleanor Smith Morris and Meredith Smith Smith for their readings and constructive comments. An interview with Cornelia Dodge Fraley provided much information on the Henry family. She also allowed me to use her papers on the Cherokee development and lent several photographs for publication.

Historian and archivist Francis James Dallett shared his enormous knowledge of the Houston family with me, provided some of the best photographs in the book, and made a thorough criticism of the manuscript that saved me from a number of embarrassing errors. His wife, Charlotte Houston Dallett, has likewise supplied valuable information about the family. Mark F. Lloyd, archivist of the University of Pennsylvania, was extraordinarily forthcoming with his vast knowledge of Germantown and of Henry Howard Houston's years there. He also guided me through the relevant materials in the University archives in addition to lending photographs from his own collection.

Many other archivists and librarians were kind and accommodating. These include Dr. Helen Hayes of the Chestnut Hill College Library, along with staffs of the Philadelphia Free Library, the University of Pennsylvania's Van Pelt Library, the Bryn Mawr College Library, the Historical Society of Pennsylvania, the Pennsylvania State Archives, the Hagley Library, the Clarion County, Pennsylvania Historical Society, and the Chestnut Hill Historical Society. Christ Church, Philadelphia; St. Peter's, Germantown; and St. Martin-in-the-Fields, Chestnut Hill, all provided documentation from their parish records. The Philadelphia City Archives supplied various statistics on family members. The *Pennsylvania Magazine of History and Biography* gave permission to use segments from my article "George Woodward, Philadelphia Progressive," which appeared in the issue of July 1987.

Longtime friend and colleague John Lukacs read large portions of the manuscript and offered his characteristically perceptive suggestions. Professor Lloyd M. Abernethy of Beaver College read the manuscript and made several helpful suggestions, as did Professor Emeritus E. Digby Baltzell of the University of Pennsylvania. I am particularly grateful to Professor Baltzell for his constant encouragement during some of the most difficult moments. Indeed, without his wholly spontaneous assistance, this volume might never have found a suitable publisher. I am thankful to Mary Wickham Bond, a lifelong resident of Chestnut Hill, for sharing her unequaled knowledge of the community and her memories of George Woodward, Jr.

Zachary Simpson, my editor at the University of Pennsylvania Press, never lost faith in the book and ultimately brought all our negotiations to a fruitful conclusion. I must thank him, too, for his judicious advice on illustrations and revisions. Others to whom I am indebted at the University of Pennsylvania Press are Ruth Veleta, Carl Gross, Jean Sue Johnson, and Mary Deininger.

Finally, I want to thank my wife, Mary, for understanding my need to hide away in the study for hours and even days on end, for her excellent work as a proofreader, and for her always cheerful companionship.

*Whitemarsh Township, Pennsylvania*
*January 1988*

# Foreword

ALEXIS DE TOCQUEVILLE, in his classic study of the causes of the French Revolution, contrasted the English aristocracy with the French nobility as follows:

> The English aristocrats were haughtier by nature than the French and even less disposed to demean themselves by hobnobbing with persons of lower rank; nevertheless no sacrifice was too great if it ensured their power.
> The French nobility, after having lost its ancient political rights, had ceased more than any other country of feudal Europe to govern and guide the nation. . . . It not only preserved but considerably enlarged its pecuniary . . . advantages.

Following Tocqueville's lead in my first book, *Philadelphia Gentlemen,* I concluded that "Philadelphia provides an excellent example of a business aristocracy which has all too often placed the desire for material comfort and security above the duties of political and intellectual leadership." In a later book, *Puritan Boston and Quaker Philadelphia,* I showed how the Calvinist-Puritan culture of Boston produced an aristocracy in the British style, while the Quaker-turned-Episcopal gentry of Philadelphia followed in the footsteps of the French nobility.

Additional insight into any generalization or rule is usually provided by exceptions, or, as the saying goes, the exception proves the rule. The Houston–Woodward clan is a fine and instructive exception to the general Proper Philadelphia rule of *noblesse* without *oblige*. And David R. Contosta has written a very good book showing how this extended family has contributed to the political and civic life of Philadelphia, the state of Pennsylvania, and the federal government for three generations since the family founder, Henry Howard Houston (1820–1895), came to the city in 1847. Houston worked for the Pennsylvania Railroad and soon became the leading transportation expert in the nation. In the 1880s he brought the Pennsylvania Railroad to the Philadelphia suburb of Chestnut Hill and built one of the earliest planned communities in America in what is now St. Martin's, two stops before the end of the line. The community centered around an Episcopal Church, St. Martin-in-the-Fields, the Philadelphia Cricket Club next door, and the old Wissahickon Inn (now home of the Chestnut Hill Academy) down and across the street from the Cricket Club. He also built eighty houses that he rented to young professionals and business managers at reasonable rates.

Henry Howard Houston's son-in-law, Dr. George Woodward (1863–1952), built almost 200 more houses in St. Martin's and devoted his life to civic and political reform in Philadelphia. He served as a Republican in the Pennsylvania state senate for seven consecutive terms (1919–1947). Two of his four sons followed in this tradition of civic service: Stanley Woodward 1899–    ) in the federal government and Charles H. Woodward (1904–1986) as a philanthropic developer and preserver in Chestnut Hill, as well as in Charleston, South Carolina, and Northeast Harbor, Maine. Finally, Eleanor Houston Smith (1910–1987), granddaughter of the family founder, devoted her life to the Episcopal church, to civic improvement, and to conservation, donating park lands in both Philadelphia and Maine.

While the Houstons and Woodwards were Episcopalians in Philadelphia, they were deeply rooted in the Calvinist faith which, of course, is almost the exact antithesis to Quaker belief. Henry Howard Houston was born in Wrightsville, downstream from Harrisburg and in the heart of Scotch-Irish Presbyterianism. Woodward came to Philadelphia from Wilkes-Barre, Pennsylvania. Like the families of Governor William Scranton and Governor Gifford Pinchot (two of the best in Pennsylvania history), Woodward's ancestors were deeply rooted in Connecticut and Massachusetts Puritanism. The point is that, while the Houston–Woodward clan was an exception in Quaker-turned-Episcopal Proper Philadelphia, they were definitely following the Calvinist-Presbyterian and Calvinist-Puritan lines of their Scotch-Irish and Yankee ancestors.

This book, then, is a fine history of one of Philadelphia's finest families. It is also of more general interest as a contribution to the sociology of religion, as well as the city planning and conservation movements in twentieth-century America.

*E. Digby Baltzell*

# Preface

IN COUNTRIES where there are or have been hereditary aristocracies, it is not unusual for numerous generations of the same family to achieve great distinction. But in democratic societies like the United States, there is little to guarantee that the sons and daughters of notable parents will become either prominent or successful. There have been exceptions, of course: Adamses, Du Ponts, Rockefellers, and Kennedys have all maintained a high level of personal achievement and social recognition over several generations.

Although Philadelphia has been one of the nation's largest cities since the colonial period, it has produced fewer families of great distinction than most other cities in its class. Boston First Families, for example, are more renowned for their scholarship and philanthropy than their Philadelphia counterparts, while New Yorkers are far better known for their business and financial acumen. Social historian E. Digby Baltzell has attributed Philadelphia's patrician lethargy to the city's atmosphere of Quaker egalitarianism which, in his opinion, has bred a reluctance to seek leadership positions on either the local or the national level.[1] Instead, as Sam Bass Warner has also noted in his well-received study of Philadelphia, members of the city's upper class have typically been more concerned with pursuing their private interests than with serving the community or nation at large.[2]

Although the Houston and Woodward families, connected through marriage in the second generation, have shared certain characteristics of Philadelphia First Families, they have been unusually civic-minded. For more than a century, three generations of these closely allied families have done much to mold the city of Philadelphia and the nation at large: economically, politically, and even demographically. Family founder Henry Howard Houston was one of America's greatest nineteenth-century entrepreneurs. He became a top executive and trustee for the Pennsylvania Railroad, then the largest and most powerful corporation in the country, as well as a leading speculator in oil, mining, shipping, and other railroad ventures.

In the latter half of his life Houston also invested heavily in Philadelphia real estate. He eventually acquired over 3,000 acres of land in the northwest section of the city, comprising much of Chestnut Hill and Upper Roxborough, along with a sizable chunk of adjoining Montgomery County. On the west side of Chestnut Hill, Houston began perhaps the most attractive and unique suburb in the United States. His son Samuel would maintain and extend these building projects—especially in Roxborough. But it was the elder Houston's son-in-law, George Woodward, who did the most to further the family's housing experiment in Chestnut Hill, thus completing a planned community that has attracted the attention of numerous scholars and urban planners in the decades since.

Woodward was also a major progressive reformer, whose career as a reform politician extended from the late 1890s to the early years of the Truman administration. His half-century crusade for better housing and more efficient government accordingly provides an important example of how the progressive impulse lasted well beyond the Progressive Era itself. Woodward's son Stanley went on to become assistant chief of protocol under President Franklin Roosevelt, chief of protocol under President Truman, and ambassador to Canada. Serving at the very moment of America's emergence as the world's greatest power, Stanley worked to facilitate better personal relations among now legendary leaders. Still others in the Woodward, Houston, and Henry branches have been in the forefront of conservation and historical preservation, among them the Charles Woodwards and the Lawrence M. C. Smiths. Inspired by the example of parents and grandparents rather than through direct admonition or moral preachment, members of each generation have succeeded in carrying on the good works of their forebears while often carving out new paths for themselves.

Although both Henry Howard Houston and George Woodward came from old and prominent families in Pennsylvania—Houston from the Columbia-Wrightsville region and Woodward from Wilkes-Barre— they were not immediately absorbed into the inner sanctum of Philadelphia society. Yet within two generations, and without really trying to put themselves forward, they or their children were in the mainstream of the city's social elite. By the second generation, family members had been invited into the most prestigious Philadelphia clubs, while the grand-daughters of Henry Howard Houston made their debuts along with the daughters of other Philadelphia First Families.

Despite the families' rapid acceptance by Proper Philadelphia, their relatively recent arrival in the city perhaps saved them from falling into the local habit of complacency and resistance to reform. (The elder Houston did not arrive in Philadelphia until 1847, with George Woodward settling in the city nearly fifty years later in the mid-1890s.) Nor did all of them follow the political custom of most other wealthy and socially prominent Philadelphians of becoming conservative Republicans. Henry Howard Houston was a lifelong Democrat and his son-in-law George Woodward was one of the most liberal and reform-minded Republicans of his day. In the third generation Stanley Woodward became a staunch Democrat and Roosevelt supporter, while another in-law, Lawrence M. C. Smith, was a New Deal lawyer and later head of the Philadelphia chapter of Americans for Democratic Action.

The families' religious roots may have been another factor that saved them from the kind of social complacency so often associated with Phila-delphia's upper class, for both the Houston and Woodward families had originally belonged to Calvinist denominations (in this case Presbyterians and Congregationalists) that traditionally placed great emphasis on the wealthy and capable individuals' duty to guide and inspire others. It is, in fact, this Calvinist elitism, according to Baltzell in his *Puritan Boston and Quaker Philadelphia,* that has produced so many national leaders from Boston, while Philadelphia, with its tradition of Quaker egalitarianism, nurtured relatively fewer men of great distinction. It was also, perhaps, this Calvinist ancestry that made members of both the Houston and Woodward families into powerful spokesmen for the social gospel, with its goal of ap-plying Christ's teachings to community life. In any case, religion would remain a powerful motivating force behind the family's good works for several generations.

In other respects the Houstons and Woodwards clearly have shared many characteristics of Proper Philadelphians, including a distaste for per-sonal publicity. They have likewise reflected the local preference for quiet entertaining at home, combined with a high regard for family stability and well-being. Thus in both their conformance to and their divergence from the typical upper-class pattern, the Houstons and Woodwards offer impor-tant insights into the formation of a Philadelphia First Family.[3]

But beyond their good works and individual accomplishments, the record of these two closely related families should remind everyone that

American history has been lived by real people and their families. Like others, too, the Houstons and Woodwards have not been untouched by wars, depressions, and popular currents. Nor have they been immune to the joys and sorrows and misunderstandings of other Americans. In this sense, their history is the story of every family.

Finally, the scope of this family history has been determined to some extent by the positions occupied by various individuals and by the sources that have survived. Much attention, for example, has been paid to the wide activities of George Woodward. This is partly because he was one of the most ambitious and accomplished members of the family, but also because he left ten volumes of his own writings and generated a mountain of newsworthy material for the local press. On the other extreme, little has been said about Henry Howard Houston's descendants on the Henry side. This is largely because few documents about that side of the family have survived. In addition, many Henry descendants have left Philadelphia and therefore have not provided the same continuity of generations on the local level as have their Houston and Woodward cousins. With these limitations in mind, the reader will, I hope, gain new insights into the Philadelphia family, as well as into the rare phenomenon of noteworthy achievement over several generations.

*A Philadelphia Family*

# CHAPTER 1

# *Beginnings*

THE RISE OF HENRY HOWARD HOUSTON (1820–1895) was swift and impressive. By age forty-five he had become the Pennsylvania Railroad's leading transportation expert. He had also amassed enough capital to become one of the most successful entrepreneurs of the post-Civil War period. Investments in railroads, mining, oil, shipping, and real estate would make him a multimillionaire at his death, providing great wealth as well as special opportunities for his descendants. He was also a pioneer in suburban development and is best remembered today for the unique community that he created on the west side of Philadelphia's Chestnut Hill.

Yet surprisingly little is known about this family founder. The only documents to survive are a handful of letters, several business ledgers, passing references in corporate and public records, brief newspaper reports, a few biographical sketches, and a collection of family traditions.[1] Houston apparently felt little need to explain his actions or to leave a fuller account for future generations. He was also well known for avoiding publicity. If he kept a diary, it has long since disappeared, while all but a few fragments of his correspondence were probably discarded when his son cleared out the family offices just before his own retirement during World War II. Houston's marriage at age thirty-five also may have meant that his children were not old enough at their father's death to appreciate his accomplishments fully or to ask detailed questions about his path to success.

Despite many gaps in the record, something of a life can be reconstructed for Henry Howard Houston. His Houston ancestors, originally from Scotland, came to America from northern Ireland in the early eighteenth century and were related to the forebears of several other Houston families in the future United States. The northern Houstons settled on land in the Pequea valley of Lancaster County, Pennsylvania, where their descendants acquired substantial holdings over the years and prospered with large families. Like most other Scotch-Irish immigrants, the Houstons remained loyal to the Presbyterian faith, with several generations of Houston men becoming leaders of the local church. Susanna Wright Houston donated land for a Union chapel in Wrightsville, while others in the family contributed generously to church building projects, an example that would be followed by their Philadelphia descendants.[2]

Henry Howard's grandfather, Dr. John Houston, became the first in the family to obtain a college education. He studied under the famed Adam Smith at the University of Glasgow and then earned a medical degree at the University of Pennsylvania. Settling in York County, he was elected in 1774 to the local Committee of Observation and Correspondence, which had the task of enforcing economic sanctions just voted by the First Continental Congress in Philadelphia. And when the American Revolution broke out, he served for a while as a surgeon attending Continental soldiers.

Dr. Houston's marriage to Susanna Wright was also an excellent choice. Her father, John Wright, owned the only ferry at an important crossing of the Susquehanna River between Columbia and Wrightsville.[3] The Wrights not only gave their name to this small settlement on the west bank of the river, but they also were well known in the area as judges and local leaders: John Wright was sent to the Pennsylvania colonial Assembly several times.[4]

Besides her reading and writing, Susanna (known as "the Duchess") managed to bring up nine children. The youngest of these, Samuel Nelson, would become Henry Howard Houston's father. Samuel studied pharmacy and medicine in Philadelphia, but left school before completing his degrees on account of temporary ill health. It also appears that he was not so successful a provider as his father, relying on occasional sales of timber from his property for the bulk of his modest income. Known for his powerful physique and good looks, he became an excellent rider and joined Captain Shippen's cavalry troop during the War of 1812. Also in the troop was future president James Buchanan who became a lifelong friend and fellow Democrat.[5]

Samuel returned to Wrightsville after his military service and in 1817 married Susan Strickler, daughter of a former state legislator. Henry Howard, their second son and the second of five children, was born three years later on 3 October 1820.[6] Just what may have molded Houston during his childhood years will never be known. He would inherit his father's Presbyterian faith, along with his devotion to the Democratic party. There was also much about the area that might have impressed a future expert on transportation. Henry must have learned from family sources, if not from his own powers of observation, that the secret to Wright's ferry had been its location at a crucial break along the main road from Philadelphia to the west. Nor could he have missed hearing about how the first bridge across the Susquehanna between Columbia and Wrightsville had doomed the ferry just a few years before his birth. He witnessed yet another dramatic change in the mid-1830s when both a railroad and canal were completed through the town, greatly improving its strategic position and providing additional insights into the importance of transportation.[7]

Perhaps it was a fascination for canal boats and railroad locomotives that convinced Henry to leave the local school at age fourteen with only an elementary education. Or perhaps he just did not share his father's and grandfather's drive for higher education. It may be that his father simply could not afford to send him to college. Whatever the case, Henry soon found a job at John S. Futhey's general store in Wrightsville.

Futhey carried an enormous variety of goods, enabling Houston to learn about all kinds of merchandise, as well as to pick up valuable skills in bookkeeping and the transport of goods. Futhey also gathered local laborers and handled supplies for the canal and railroad building projects in and around the town. Houston's part in this effort may have been slight, but it must have given him some idea of building logistics.[8]

By 1840 Houston was doubtless ready for larger challenges. That year he landed the position of clerk for the Lucinda iron furnace in Clarion County, a facility owned by his father's friend, James Buchanan.[9] The furnace itself was almost 250 miles from Wrightsville in a remote area of northwestern Pennsylvania where Houston often felt homesick. In one of his few surviving letters, written from Lucinda in March 1843, he offered a dismal account of his life there. The furnace, he declared, "is 9 miles from no particular place surrounded by woods which abound in deer and bear." Snow had been on the ground since November and was now about two feet deep. Worst of all, he wrote, was the "want of Fair Sex to occupy us in our rides [through] this neck of the woods." Tired of his isolation and reminded of friends and family back home, he promised to get away as soon as he could for a good, long visit.[10]

The winter weather had no doubt made Lucinda seem worse than usual. Most of the time Houston had more than enough work to distract his thoughts from home. The iron furnaces of the time were much like industrial plantations, with numerous tasks carried out right on the site. In addition to producing iron in tall stone blast furnaces, employees mined ore, burned charcoal, and hauled supplies as well as finished "pigs" in and out of the facility. Most furnaces also ran a company store and tried to produce as much of their own food as possible, including feed for the draft animals. A successful furnace thus required numerous workers, from charcoal burners and woodcutters to teamsters and furnace tenders.[11]

It was Houston's job as clerk to keep all the records, run the store, order supplies, handle the company correspondence, pay accounts, extend credit to workers, and make up the payroll. The typical salary for a clerk was $300 a year, in addition to room and board. And as clerk Houston was entitled to a room in the "big house," a name commonly given to the manager's residence at the furnaces.

From all accounts the Lucinda Furnace was one of the largest and most productive of the thirty-one iron facilities in Clarion County. With a stack about thirty feet high, it turned out around 1,200 tons a year. The pig iron was then hauled by wagon to Clarion City where it went by flatboat down the Clarion and Allegheny Rivers to Pittsburgh.[12]

Houston remained at Lucinda until 1843. Then, with his three years of experience in the iron business, he joined with a man named Edmund Evans to rebuild and manage the Horse Creek Furnace in neighboring Venango County.[13] As managers, Houston and Evans occupied the big house from which they superintended the whole operation. Besides coordinating all phases of manufacturing, the manager made sure that there was enough food and raw materials; hired, fired, and disciplined workers; and served as the company's principal salesman. All things considered, running a furnace could be a difficult and risky business, with frequent bankruptcies. According to the brief accounts of Houston's years at Horse Creek, he and his partner did very well under trying circumstances.[14]

For unknown reasons Houston left Horse Creek Furnace for Wrightsville in January 1845 and soon thereafter embarked on an extensive tour of the southern and western states. Whether the trip was for pleasure or was connected to some kind of business venture is unclear. He returned home in December 1846, only to leave for Philadelphia the next year to take a job with David Leech and Company, a leading canal and railroad transportation firm. There Houston was responsible for moving both passengers and merchandise throughout Pennsylvania and adjoining states in what turned out to be his final preparation for a lifelong career in various transportation enterprises.[15]

The move to Philadelphia itself was also crucial to Houston's rise. He entered a city on the eve of its most rapid industrialization, poised to become the most important manufacturing center in America. It was also the nation's second largest city, with a population of 287,000 in the soon to be consolidated city—up a full seventy-five percent from ten years before. Much of this growth arose from Philadelphia's location at one of the major crossroads of trade. Its seaport was second only to New York's, and it was already a terminus for the pioneering Reading Railroad. In a few years it would also be served by the newly chartered Pennsylvania Railroad, destined to become the largest, wealthiest, and most powerful railroad in the land.[16]

In fact, the rationale for building this railroad, with which Houston would be associated for much of his adult life, was to give Philadelphia a better access to crucial western markets. The city's link to the West had been challenged earlier in the century by the Erie Canal and then by the Baltimore and Ohio Railroad. The state had responded with a system of canals, railroads, and inclined planes (the latter being used to haul canal boats by cable over the steep mountains of central Pennsylvania). Known as the Main Line of Public Works, this route proved costly, inconvenient, and time-consuming. The obvious alternative was a railroad across the entire state from Philadelphia to Pittsburgh.

Chartered by the legislature in the spring of 1846, the Pennsylvania Railroad would eventually become a vast network of rails that extended as far west as Chicago, Saint Louis, and Kansas City. Enormous profits would accumulate for its stockholders, while the railroad assured Philadelphia a prime role in the nation's expanding economy. The Pennsylvania also emerged as a model railroad. Its managers and directors refused to issue massive quantities of "watered" stock like most of their competitors, consistently bought the latest equipment, and regularly reinvested half its profits in the railroad itself. Throughout the nineteenth century and beyond, the Pennsylvania Railroad set the standards for managerial skill and fiscal responsibility.[17]

Houston's association with the Pennsylvania came just four years after he arrived in Philadelphia, when his apparent success at David Leech and Company caught the attention of Colonel William C. Patterson, then president of the railroad. Patterson hired Houston as general freight agent in January 1851, assigning him the task of organizing the company's freight business on the yet uncompleted railroad.[18]

Houston's rapid success as freight agent, combined with regular increases in pay, must have been a great source of personal satisfaction. It also afforded him regular increases in his standard of living. Although Houston's residence during this period is not known, he did acquire his first piece of Germantown real estate, as an investment, in 1853.[19] By age thirty-five he clearly felt prosperous enough to marry and start a family.

His intended was twenty-seven-year-old Sallie Sherrerd Bonnell, the daughter of Samuel and Cornelia Clarkson Bringhurst Bonnell, who then lived at (old number) 136 North Front Street. According to the *Philadelphia Directory* for that year, her father was the cashier of the Globe Insurance Company.[20] Bonnell's father, Charles, had been a Quaker who was "read out of meeting" when he was married at St. Peter's (Episcopal) Church, as his co-religionists put it, "by an hireling priest."[21]

The rector from Christ Church married Henry Howard Houston and Sallie Bonnell at the bride's home on the evening of 8 April 1856.[22] Almost exactly a year later Houston formally joined his wife's church, leaving the Presbyterian faith of his Scotch-Irish ancestors.[23] Like many converts, Houston would remain a vigorous and devout Episcopalian for the rest of his life, giving generously to its missions and contributing two new churches to the local diocese.

Marriage also meant a new address for Houston and his bride, who moved into 1537 Chestnut Street after the wedding.[24] The fifteen-hundred block of Walnut would have been more impressive socially, but their block was certainly a respectable one for the time. And if the Houston residence resembled others nearby, it was a three-story, red-brick townhouse designed in a late Federal style, with attic dormers, green louvered shutters, small-paned sash windows, and four or five white marble steps leading down to a red brick sidewalk. From home, Houston's office at 13th and Market was only a three-and-a-half block walk through the parklike Penn Square, now the site of Philadelphia's massive City Hall.

It was here at 1537 Chestnut that the Houstons' first two children were born. Cornelia, arriving in February 1857, died a month later. Childhood and infant deaths were regular occurrences in the mid-nineteenth century, but the loss must have been difficult for both parents. A son, born in October 1858, undoubtedly softened the blow. They named him Henry Howard Houston, Jr., and called him Howard.[25]

After a year and a half, parents and baby left 1537 Chestnut Street for Germantown, moving sometime during the summer of 1860. In the previous decade or so this once rural village, six miles from downtown Philadelphia, had been transformed into a fashionable suburb. Formerly a separate community, Germantown had been brought within the municipal boundaries when the city and county of Philadelphia merged in 1854. But it was the coming of the Reading Railroad into the region during the early 1830s that made Germantown ripe for development. Within a decade it became the first real suburb in Philadelphia, if not in the entire country.[26]

In a wider sense, nineteenth-century suburbanization stemmed from several related factors. One was the romantic belief that more natural surroundings were good for both body and soul: the fresh air of suburbia would invigorate the health, while the mind and spirit would be uplifted by the sight of flowers, trees, and hills. The suburbs were also viewed as an escape from mounting urban problems: dirt, crime, disease, and over-crowding. And in Philadelphia particularly, owning "a place in the coun-try" had remained a sign of genteel status since the Colonial period—a continuation of the English ideal of a landed gentry.[27]

Whatever the reasons, well-to-do Philadelphians wholly approved of moving to Italianate or Gothic-revival "villas" in scenic Germantown. Even the snobbish and often hypercritical diarist Sidney George Fisher wrote in August 1857 that he was "much impressed in [his] drive with the beauty of the country, the universal aspect of wealth and comfort and the difference a few years have made in Germantown." Germantown had al-ways been "a respectable, substantial village," he went on, "but [it is] now adorned with elegance and supplied with all the conveniences of a city—shops, gas, [and] waterworks." Best of all, there were "none of the an-noyances of town, but quiet, country scenery, [with] gardens and trees everywhere." "So manifold are its advantages," he concluded, "that the wonder to me is how any can now bear to stay in town."[28]

The Houstons first settled into this semirural paradise with a rented house—the east side of a double now numbered 223 West Tulpehocken Street.[29] Then, at a sheriff's sale in December 1863, they bought a large Ital-ianate house (now demolished) on an acre and a half lot at the northwest corner of Wayne and Tulpehocken Streets.[30]

Initially it was only the two parents and Howard who settled in Ger-mantown. Then in November 1860 came Sallie Bonnell, followed by Eleanor Anna in May 1863. (Eleanor would die in early 1875, at age eleven, from scarlet fever.) The last two were Samuel Frederic, born in August 1866, and Gertrude, born in June 1868.[31]

Tulpehocken Street was, in fact, an ideal place to rear five children. Up and down the street were large and attractive houses with ornate iron fences surrounding their well-kept front yards. Author and University of Pennsylvania professor Cornelius Weygandt, who spent part of his child-hood two doors up from the Houstons, remembered that Tulpehocken was the "last street in Germantown. Our back yards looked out on open country, where [there] were farmlands and estates, . . . pastures and pad-docks, wheat . . . and cornfields, . . . gardens [and] orchards."

"As for the neighbors themselves," Weygandt wrote in his *Phila-delphia Folks,* "there was a railroad executive [obviously Houston himself], an agent for a great tobacco firm, the widow of an iron founder, a patent-medicine man, a street-railway director, a man retired from business, . . . and a banker." The adults were not particularly intimate with one another,

he added, "but the children were in and out of all the houses."[32] A favorite
gathering spot for the youngsters was a play house in the Houstons' backyard, and for the boys there were impromptu cricket matches on the long
back lots. Over on Germantown Avenue—the main thoroughfare—there
were several favorite bakeries and ice cream parlors to delight young and
old alike.[33]

There is no record of just how the elder Houstons filled their hours in
Germantown. Sallie was clearly busy with a growing family, though she
certainly had the help of several servants, including her own coachman, as
her husband had his. Henry Howard commuted daily on the train to his
downtown office at the Pennsylvania Railroad and, later, to his own office
at 308 Walnut Street.[34] The nearest train station was some distance, however, at Germantown and Price Streets. Although he certainly could have
walked the eight or nine blocks, most of the commuting husbands from
Tulpehocken Street were met by family carriages at the end of a long day
downtown. In summer the family spent several weeks at Bedford Springs,
Pennsylvania. Houston was reportedly terrified of water, making this resort far away from the seashore in central Pennsylvania quite to his liking.[35]

Houston seems to have been a very private man whom others did not
befriend easily. Yet once he became a friend, no one could be more delightful or loyal. In his unpublished "Memoirs," Frank J. Firth, who was
one of Houston's younger friends and associates on the Pennsylvania Railroad, wrote of him: "He was not an easy man to become intimate with,
but he was a great hearted, able, generous gentleman. I count it one of the
great privileges of my life time to have enjoyed his intimate friendship and
to know I had his confidence and regard." As to Houston's qualities as a
businessman, Firth added, "He was a patient, even tempered man with an
amazing tenacity of purpose."[36]

Powerful and important though Houston was becoming, he did not
enjoy all of Philadelphia's flourishing club life, telling his son Sam one day
as they walked past the elite Philadelphia Club that he hoped never to see
him walking through "those doors."[37] Perhaps his own reticence, combined
with a fear of being rejected by the most prestigious clubs, prompted this
bit of paternal advice. It may also be that he objected to the Philadelphia
Club because of its reputation then as being run by a "fast" and "sporty"
crowd. However, Houston was elected to the Art Club, the third most important club in the city at that time. He was also a manager of the Charity
Ball and a member of the Germantown and Philadelphia Cricket Clubs,
the Musical Fund Society, the Pennsylvania Academy of the Fine Arts,
Academy of Natural Sciences, Pennsylvania Horticultural Society, Historical Society of Pennsylvania, Museum of the University of Pennsylvania,

Sons of the Revolution, Fairmount Park Art Association, and the Hibernian Society. But Houston's greatest single honor was his election to the American Philosophical Society in 1887.[38] If he did not belong to the most prestigious clubs in Philadelphia, Houston clearly was becoming one of the city's most prominent citizens during his years in Germantown.

CHAPTER 2

# Railroad
# Entrepreneur

ALTHOUGH THE MOVE to Germantown must have been a happy
time for the Houston family, it was one of mounting crisis for the nation
at large as secession and civil war threatened to destroy the Union. As both
a patriotic American and a successful businessman, Houston must have
looked with horror on the prospect of war between North and South. Yet
the war would bring many new opportunities for Houston and the Pennsylvania Railroad, permitting him to lay the basis for a large personal fortune. Meanwhile Houston would watch his children grow into young
adulthood.

Just when Houston grew alarmed at sectional conflict can never be
known, but he had a unique opportunity to sense the danger firsthand
during an excursion of Pennsylvania Railroad directors and their families
to inspect various "connecting lines" in October 1859. The special train
took them to St. Louis and back, with stops at Pittsburgh, Chicago, Cincinnati, Baltimore, and other towns in between. In mid-October, when returning East, their train was forced to stop just outside Harper's Ferry,
Virginia. At that very moment John Brown and his men were trapped inside the federal arsenal following their failed attempt to seize arms and
start a slave rebellion. While Houston and the others were still on board
the train, Colonel Robert E. Lee and the Virginia militia managed to force
Brown and his raiders to surrender. When the train finally moved through

Harper's Ferry the next day, the excursionists could see the body of one of Brown's men lying on the ground not far from the tracks, as militiamen milled about or passed the time "shooting target."[1]

The election of Abraham Lincoln just a year later provided the final spark for secession and war. Again there is no account of how Houston felt about these terrible events, but as a lifelong Democrat and friend of outgoing president James Buchanan, it is probably safe to say that he had not voted for Lincoln in November 1860. As a businessman and transplanted Philadelphian, he had plenty of other reasons for regretting the sectional strife.

Philadelphia had maintained strong ties with the South since colonial times. The city's bankers, shippers, and insurance brokers enjoyed a flourishing trade with the South at the same time that there had been considerable intermarriage with southern families—especially between Philadelphians and Charlestonians. Civil war could only divide families and sever carefully nurtured business relations to the detriment of both sides.[2] In the last analysis, Houston probably shared the fears of J. Edgar Thomson, then president of the Pennsylvania Railroad, who predicted that civil war would prove disastrous for the railroad and for business as a whole.[3]

Instead, war gave the Pennsylvania more traffic than it could handle at first. With the Baltimore and Ohio running through territory of uncertain loyalty, the Pennsylvania was the closest and most reliable rail line for supplying the vast Union armies. And as a further guarantee of company prosperity, Secretary of War Cameron—himself a powerful politician from the Keystone State—had made Pennsylvania Railroad vice-president Thomas A. Scott his chief assistant.[4]

The wartime boom was thus a period of unparalleled prosperity for the Pennsylvania. In 1860 alone it shipped ten times as many cattle as the year before, with the road constantly clogged with fifty to sixty carloads of freight in excess of daily capacity. In time, facilities caught up with demand and the railroad ended the war with twice as many cars as before. Net earnings also soared, nearly doubling from $2.3 million in 1860 to $4.2 million in 1865. Dividends to stockholders averaged 18 percent from 1862 through 1865.[5]

Houston's salary also rose handsomely during the conflict, but it was his decision toward the end of the war to join with several other entrepreneurs to form a "fast freight" line that became truly lucrative. Although such lines were already operating on other railroads like the New York Central, the Pennsylvania had long resisted this sort of semi-independent operation. But to compete with the express services being offered elsewhere, the board succumbed to the idea in December 1863.[6]

The result was the Union Freight Line, with Henry Howard Houston, William Thaw, William H. Barnes, and Joseph D. Potts as the principal stockholders.[7] It was a common practice of the day to give a large block of stock to certain individuals in exchange for their expertise; and it may be that Houston acquired a substantial interest in this way. Whatever the financial arrangements, Houston became a central figure in the new venture, organizing the Union Line with the same skill as he had used to establish the Pennsylvania's freight department more than a decade earlier.

An essential feature of these fast freight lines was "through bills of lading" for all merchandise. Regardless of how many different railroad connections were involved in the shipment, it was not necessary to make individual negotiations and go through the attendant paperwork with each separate railroad, thereby avoiding much confusion and delay. The whole enterprise was also very profitable for Houston, especially in the early years when the Union Line handled large military shipments. When the war began, for example, his yearly income was about $5,000; by 1863 it had risen to only $5,800. Then in 1864 it soared dramatically to $22,000 and in 1865 to an astronomical $114,000.[8]

Thus at the end of the Civil War Houston found himself with well over $100,000 to invest as he chose. Meanwhile the country was about to embark on the greatest period of industrial growth in its history, with Houston in an ideal position to take part in it from the very beginning. His and other large investments would soon transform the United States into the most important industrial power on earth.

Personally, however, Houston's own future must have been clouded by concerns over his health as the war ended. In a letter to Pennsylvania Railroad president J. Edgar Thomson written in June 1867, he explained that ill health had forced him to resign as general freight agent. Although not explaining the exact nature of his illness, he told Thomson that he had decided to "place myself at once in charge of the Surgeon in New York by whom I was successfully healed four years ago, and from whom I can now expect great benefit, if not permanent cure."[9] Whatever the nature of these two operations, the procedure was obviously a success, for Houston would live nearly thirty years more and enjoy generally good health.

Despite whatever may have plagued him, Houston continued his ambitious program of investment. Not surprisingly, most of his ventures in the boom years during and just after the Civil War involved transportation enterprises in one way or another, virtually all of them supported by the mighty Pennsylvania Railroad. Most of these railroad-sponsored undertakings grew out of attempts to consolidate and expand the Pennsylvania's commanding position in American transportation.[10] One of these was the

Pennsylvania Steel Company in Harrisburg. Owned largely by Pennsylvania Railroad managers and investors, including Houston himself, the firm specialized in steel rails, which were sold to the parent firm at advantageous rates. He was also president for a short time of the William Butcher Steel Works, forerunner of Midvale Steel. Meanwhile, Houston became a major investor in the American Line, a Pennsylvania subsidiary that was established in November 1865 to provide the first regular steamship service between Philadelphia and Liverpool.[11]

This steamship venture was clearly aimed at siphoning off rail transportation from the port of New York, for, if successful, the new shipping line would provide a direct link between Great Britain and Pennsylvania Railroad customers. It is also clear from the Pennsylvania board minutes that the American Line was expected to give top priority to the parent company. On 21 October 1868 the directors approved an agreement whereby the steamship line promised to "convey all freight and passenger traffic over the Pennsylvania Railroad at their minimum rates of transportation." The American Line also promised not to discontinue service without expressed permission from the railroad.[12] Just two years later the railroad threw its support behind another steamship line with which Houston had become heavily involved. Called the International Navigation Company, it established the Red Star Line to provide regular service between Philadelphia and Antwerp.[13]

Meanwhile, the Union Fast Freight Line was expanded and absorbed into a larger concern called the Empire Transportation Company, established in early 1867. Its president was Joseph D. Potts, and Henry Howard Houston was its treasurer.[14] Besides using the Pennsylvania and its connecting lines, the Empire also owned and operated twenty steamships on the Great Lakes through a subsidiary called the Erie and Western Transportation Company. The ships carried grain, timber, and other commodities. And to receive and store grain, the Empire operated its own elevators at strategic points.[15] The Empire also became a pioneer in the shipment of crude oil from western Pennsylvania fields, where the first wells in the United States had been drilled just before the Civil War. In order to transport petroleum from the wells to the nearest railroad depot, the Empire bought or built several oil pipelines, eventually consolidating them as the Union Pipe Company. It then used especially designed tank cars, belonging to yet another subsidiary called the Green Line, to haul the oil to its own terminal facility in New York.[16]

The Empire Company and its farflung activities proved highly successful, but the Pennsylvania Railroad had never felt entirely comfortable about its semi-independent freight lines. In the summer of 1873 the Pennsylvania bought the Empire Transportation Company, paying for it in various railroad securities. Houston himself made a tidy profit from the transaction, receiving 7,191 Pennsylvania shares worth $359,550 compared with the $305,000 that he had originally invested in the Empire—a $54,000 increase over six years.[17]

In addition to producing handsome profits for its owners, the Empire also brought the Pennsylvania Railroad into a fierce battle with John D. Rockefeller's rising Standard Oil Trust, and at the same time convinced Houston that there was a great deal of money to be made in oil. The open clash between Rockefeller on the one side and the Pennsylvania-owned Empire Company on the other was a long and complex affair that Rockefeller eventually won. In the end the railroad agreed to sell its oil interests for $3.4 million. That Houston directed this unsuccessful battle for the Empire's oil interests is clear. According to his young friend Frank Firth, "[he] was the master mind in our struggle with the Standard."[18]

Although defeated in this bout with Rockefeller, Houston would invest in various oil ventures over the years that would later account for the bulk of his descendants' wealth. As early as November 1865 he bought $1,000 worth of stock in the Great Eastern Rock Oil Company, and in 1873 he received 1,540 shares of the Garland Oil Pipe Company, whose president was the ubiquitous Joseph Potts. Houston also invested heavily in oil storage facilities. Between 30 June and 1 September 1864 he put $11,250 into the F. W. Greene Company of Red Hook, New York, which was later bought out by the National Storage Company, a subsidiary of the Empire group.[19]

But Houston's single most important oil investment—indeed the most significant purchase of his whole life, as it turned out—was in the Atlantic Refining Company of Philadelphia, founded in early 1870 by William G. Warden. On 19 February of that year Houston bought 400 shares in the new enterprise at $100 each. Atlantic quickly became the largest refinery in Philadelphia and one of the most important in the nation, with extensive properties just below the city along the Delaware waterfront. In October 1874 Warden joined Rockefeller's Standard Oil Trust, becoming one of the earliest of the large refiners to do so. Atlantic Refining would remain among the most productive installations in the Standard Oil group for decades to come.[20] Exactly how many shares Houston received in the Standard Oil Trust is unclear, but they would eventually become the greatest earners in his portfolio and afterwards the centerpiece of the entire Houston estate. His original investment of $40,000 in Atlantic Refining (unless there were other, unrecorded purchases of Standard Oil companies) would be worth nearly $90 million by the early 1960s.[21]

Yet in his own age, before the automobile, when most petroleum was made into kerosene for lamps, Houston certainly had no inkling of how profitable his oil investments would become, doubtless believing that his other stock purchases were just as valuable, if not more so. His personal account book for the years 1864–1880 shows that he bought large amounts of railroad stock, especially in the Pennsylvania's various "connecting" lines to the West. In addition to acquiring sizable chunks of Pennsylvania stock, Houston bought into the Union Pacific, the Texas Pacific, the Kansas Pacific, the Pittsburgh, Cincinnati, and St. Louis, the Cleveland and Pittsburgh, the Denver and Boulder Valley, the Grand Rapids and Indiana, the Alexandria and Fredericksburg, and the Southern Railroad, among many others. He invested in several stockyard companies that of necessity depended on rail transportation to move cattle or other livestock to market; and he also put substantial sums into Ohio and Pennsylvania coal lands, as well as into gold and silver mines out West. Finally, he placed moderate amounts into bank stocks in Philadelphia and other cities with which he was acquainted through business contacts.[22]

Very few of Houston's investments failed to pay off, in part because many of them had the backing of the Pennsylvania Railroad. By the early 1880s these investments had made Houston one of the richest men in Philadelphia. The Dun and Bradstreet *Credit Ledgers,* which evaluated the holdings of wealthy men as a service to potential creditors, reflected his rise during the two decades following the Civil War. In July 1869, when his name first appeared in the *Ledgers,* Houston's wealth was estimated at about $100,000. Thirteen years later, in 1882, it was put at $250,000 (though the writer admitted that it had been extremely difficult to evaluate Houston's holdings). The last entry in 1886 placed his personal worth at $3 million.[23] By Houston's own accounting, these figures were gross underestimations. In January 1884 he listed his total holdings at $6,753,000, from which he had derived $327,000 in income during the previous year.[24] Still more recognition for Houston's growing financial importance was apparent in his election in March 1881 to the Pennsylvania Railroad board of directors, without question the most prestigious board position in America at the time.[25]

Unfortunately, Houston left no record of his motives for accumulating such vast wealth. It may be that he simply loved to build, create, and otherwise impose his will on the world around him. Or it may be that he wanted to protect himself and his family forever from the sort of straited circumstances into which his own father had fallen. In the end, it is impossible to say just what motivated Houston, the entrepreneur.

On the family front, meanwhile, the oldest of Houston's children were growing into young adulthood. They clearly had enjoyed advantages that their father could not have imagined at a similar age. Although he had become spectacularly successful with an "eighth-grade" education, Houston was not taking any chances with his own sons. Their schooling would be second to none, giving them entrée to both worldly success and wide social acceptance. Both Howard and Sam went to the prominent Episcopal Academy (of which several of their maternal ancestors had been founders and trustees) and then to the University of Pennsylvania.

After college it was customary for the sons of wealthy parents to spend a year abroad on "the grand tour," where they could absorb something of Old World culture and languages while "rounding out" their educations in a pleasant, informal way. Howard embarked on such an adventure just a few days after his graduation from college in June 1878. Accompanying him were Penn professor Charles Thompson and Howard's uncle, Charles Russell Bonnell, who was an Episcopal clergyman.[26]

Crossing the Atlantic in one of Henry Howard Houston's steamers from the American Line took eleven days (20 June to 1 July) from Philadelphia to Liverpool. To pass the time, Howard noted in his diary, they played "horse billiards," quoits, and ring toss. In the evening the first-class passengers engaged in a number of debates and other verbal exercises. On 26 June, for example, there was a discussion on the "position of women." Two days later they held a mock breach of promise suit. On Sunday morning there were religious services led by Uncle Charles and several other clergymen on board—including an Episcopal bishop—followed by hymn singing in the evening.[27]

After docking in Liverpool on 1 July, Howard, Uncle Charles, and the professor took a walk around town, eventually wandering into one of the city's teeming slums. Instead of blaming such conditions on economic exploitation, the democratic-minded young American laid them squarely at the feet of monarchical government.[28]

From Liverpool the three were off to London, spending part of the Fourth of July at a service in Westminster Abbey.[29] (Uncle Charles would haul them off to services in scores of churches before the trip was over.) August found them in Scotland, with visits to Edinburgh and Glasgow, followed by a leisurely tour of the Scottish lakes and to Renfrewshire, where they visited the ancestral house of the Houston clan.[30] Then it was back to London where they signed up for a Cook's tour of Belgium, Germany, and Switzerland.[31] Howard fell in love with Cologne, a "very dream" and the "sweetest city" he had seen since leaving Philadelphia.[32]

A letter to his parents from the city of Constance on 15 September found him in a sentimental and nostalgic mood, perhaps recognizing for the first time that the earliest phase of youth had now passed. "One year ago today," he reflected, "I entered upon my last year at 'Old Penn' little dreaming that the next opening [of classes] would be spent at the foot of Lake Constance."[33]

A week later in Zurich such sentiments turned to a sort of melancholy, with overtones of youthful romance. He had climbed atop a small mountain to a pilgrimage chapel, he related: "It was a glorious day. . . . The whole surroundings were as quiet as if no one was within a thousand miles and I felt a soft, quiet, irresistible feeling steal over me. . . . It seemed as though Peace, for one, rules supreme. I wandered over the hill for over an hour. Now it would be as still as though nothing existed. Then the breeze would come softly through the pines. . . . It is at such times that one thinks of home. I . . . feel so happy at these times that my feelings relax and the repose makes tears come to my eyes."[34]

With this transcendental experience behind him, Howard and the other two were off to Paris for a complete change of scenery and mood, their principal goal to visit the 1878 Exposition before it closed that fall. Howard loved to sit in the sidewalk cafes on the warm October afternoons "where you can take your lunch and watch the passers by."[35] But a trip to the renowned Grands Magasins du Louvre, Paris's chief department store, left him less than enthusiastic. As with most first-time travelers, the way things were done at home was his only frame of reference; and he was sure that the Magasins could not begin to compare with John Wanamaker's famous emporium back in Philadelphia.[36]

Even at the Exposition Howard could not let go of his native pride. He exulted in the fact that a Philadelphia brewer had won a grand prize and that Whitman's Chocolates, another home-town operation, had received a silver medal. Neither the French nor the British, he thought, appreciated the quality of American products and accomplishments. "The more I see [of] the English people," he wrote home, "the more heartily I hate them. The more I see of the French, the more I hold them in contempt." But Germans were altogether different. The more Germans he met, "the greater resemblance" he saw "between them and the Americans."[37] These warm feelings toward Germany would later be shared by his brother Sam—at least until World War I ended the family's love affair with German culture.

With the Exposition ready to close, Howard and his companions traveled by rail to Spain and from there to North Africa. In Egypt they took a thirty-five-day boat trip down the Nile to see the ancient palaces and tombs.[38] Howard's letters became less frequent at this point, his missive of 28 January being the last to survive. From Egypt they appear to have gone to the Holy Land and then on to Greece and Italy. Somewhere along the way, Howard contracted typhoid fever and died in Rome on 13 May 1879, not yet twenty-one years old.[39]

His parents must have been devastated, especially after having lost eleven-year-old Eleanor only four years before. Howard had clearly been a bright and sensitive young man whose future held much promise. Although deeply saddened, Henry Howard Houston would soon launch the last of his great ventures.

CHAPTER 3

# A Planned
# Community

WHILE HOWARD had been wandering about Europe, North Africa, and the Near East, his father was already laying plans for a unique suburban development just north and west of Germantown in the Chestnut Hill section of Philadelphia, located approximately nine miles from the city's business district. Houston's nearly two decades in Germantown had afforded him many lessons on how to mount such an enterprise, with much of what he later accomplished in Chestnut Hill growing out of his Germantown experiences. These included his first venture in church building during the early 1870s.[1]

Houston's decision to build a second Episcopal church in their Germantown neighborhood grew out of a move to expel the rector of Christ Church which was located at the corner of Tulpehocken and McCallum Streets. It had been built on land donated by developers who hoped that an Episcopal church in the immediate vicinity would do much to attract residents. The Houstons joined Christ Church shortly after their arrival in Germantown: their younger children were baptized there, and Houston was soon elected to the vestry and as its lay delegate to the diocesan conventions. When the rector resigned in 1869 Houston was instrumental in securing Dr. Theodore S. Rumney to fill the vacancy. Within a year, a number of parishioners, not including Houston, who would remain one of the rector's staunchest allies and friends, were complaining that Rumney had instituted a host of "high church" practices, all in callous disregard for the congregation's established preference for "low, evangelical" forms of worship.[2] Although there is no record of Rumney's innovations, it is clear that he and his congregation were caught up in the complex "ritualism" controversy that divided the Episcopal church during the third quarter of the nineteenth century. While some clergy and laymen saw themselves as essentially Protestant, others leaned toward the more Catholic roots of their Anglican faith, with an emphasis on the Eucharist and its ancient liturgy.[3]

When Rumney refused the vestry's invitation to resign in April 1871, the case went before a diocesan panel for adjudication. Rumney was eventually cleared of all charges and permitted to remain as rector of Christ Church.[4] Despite their victory, Houston and other well-wishers concluded that continuing hostility against Rumney would make it extremely difficult for him to stay on and function effectively as parish priest. Under the circumstances they thought it best to organize a new church (to be known as St. Peter's, Germantown) for their embattled rector. Houston donated a large lot at the corner of Wayne Avenue and Harvey Street and engaged George W. Hewitt as architect for the building. Breaking ground in May 1873, the contractors were able to complete the structure in time for Christmas. The next year Houston assumed the church's $30,000 mortgage, forgiving the entire sum in November 1880. Houston also became rector's warden for St. Peter's. In the years to come he and his family would contribute generously to the church through monetary gifts, as well as through improvements to the physical plant.[5]

Besides learning how to build a church from the bottom up during his years in Germantown, Houston was also surrounded by an excellent example of suburban development. He could observe how enterprising men like John Fallon had bought up long agricultural strips on either side of Germantown Avenue that had been laid out by settlers in the late seventeenth century. Because these strips were of ample width, it was easy for developers to cut new streets down the middle of each plot, laying out building lots on either side.[6]

Houston himself imitated this practice as early as August 1865 when he paid $8,500 for seven acres near Wayne Avenue and Washington Lane. Four years later, in February 1869, he spent $2,166 for a lot measuring 100 × 440 feet near Wayne and Walnut Lane, and in May 1870 he bought a similar strip nearby for $4,583. Then in June 1872 he paid $34,000 for thirty acres of land around Wissahickon Avenue and Walnut Lane. In the years ahead he and his heirs would divide these properties into building lots, some of which they sold to individuals who wished to build on them. Houston and his estate also erected a number of houses on these tracts and then rented them, a practice that he and other members of the family would continue in Chestnut Hill.[7]

By the 1870s there were few undeveloped parcels left in Germantown, forcing Houston to think about buying in less accessible areas to the north and west. According to family tradition, he had long been struck by the wild and rolling beauty of the Wissahickon gorge as it plunged through the far west side of Chestnut Hill. Frequently climbing to the cupola atop his Germantown villa, he vowed to secure the entire domain for himself.[8]

Just north of his Germantown holdings, however, Houston confronted an obstacle in Phil-Ellena, the large estate of George W. Carpenter, which extended all the way to Allen's Lane and included most of the present West Mount Airy. Houston accordingly had to "jump" beyond this acreage to continue his purchases. Once across Allen's Lane, he would eventually acquire about 3,000 acres, amounting to nearly four and a half square miles of territory. These holdings would extend through the northwest corner of Philadelphia and on into Montgomery County. Paralleling both sides of the Wissahickon Creek, they would occupy almost the whole west side of Chestnut Hill, as well as much of Upper Roxborough on the opposite bank. It was in the Chestnut Hill segment of this vast domain that Houston and his heirs would create one of the most attractive and unique suburbs in America.[9]

Like Germantown, Chestnut Hill had been a separate village before city boundaries engulfed it following the Consolidation Act of 1854. It was in this year, too, that the rail line that had connected Germantown with Philadelphia's business district was extended into Chestnut Hill. This line ran through the east side of Chestnut Hill, and it was here, on the northeast summit of the village, that wealthy Philadelphians began to build Italianate summer houses. Within a decade or so many of these residences were transformed into year-round dwellings for suburban commuters.[10]

Without a convenient railroad connection, the west side of Chestnut Hill had remained undeveloped, making the land available to Houston at comparatively low prices. At the same time it was clear to him that a railroad through the west side of the Hill would have to precede any kind of serious development. Houston accordingly decided to build a line into the area as a subsidiary to the Pennsylvania Railroad. The original idea seems to have been to go well beyond Chestnut Hill into Montgomery and Chester Counties: Houston called his projected route the Germantown, Norristown, and Phoenixville Railroad. Besides Houston, the directors of this new enterprise were James A. Wright, George W. Carpenter, and Amos R. Little, with Henry D. Welsh serving as the corporation's president.[11]

The Pennsylvania directors readily agreed that the extension line would benefit the railroad as a whole, and on 6 August 1879 they voted to support the project financially.[12] Two years later, in July 1881, after making careful surveys of the route and estimates of construction costs, the Pennsylvania authorized the issuance of $1,250,000 in stock plus another $1,250,000 in first mortgage, five percent, forty-year bonds. The Pennsylvania board also agreed to purchase nearly $1.5 million of the new railroad's capital stock, to construct the line "in a first-class manner," and then to lease and manage the completed route.[13] It was not until December 1882, after the idea of going all the way into Phoenixville was abandoned for the time being because of high construction costs, that the name was changed to the Philadelphia, Germantown, and Chestnut Hill Railroad.[14]

Just how much Houston himself invested in the Chestnut Hill line is unclear. Since he donated $500,000 in land for the right-of-way, it may be that his contribution was largely in the form of property instead of cash.[15] Whatever the arrangement, critics have long charged that Houston knew well before the general public that the railroad was going to be built, allowing him to buy potentially valuable land at bargain prices. But available evidence does not support these allegations. To begin with, Houston invited a number of other property owners along the prospective route to join him in petitioning the Pennsylvania directors to build the route.[16] Rumors that such a line might be constructed were reported in the Philadelphia newspapers throughout 1879, while the Pennsylvania board made a public announcement about the projected railroad in early September of 1879, just one month after its decision to support the undertaking.[17] Even more telling was the fact that it was not until early December (more than three months after the press announcements) that Houston began a systematic campaign to buy up parcels of land in Chestnut Hill.

Houston's personal account book reveals just how energetically he went after local property at year's end. On 4 December 1879, he bought 62.5 acres just north of Cresheim Creek for $18,000. That same day at a sheriff's sale he paid $3,150 for a five-acre parcel at the corner of Allen's Lane and McCallum Street. Two and a half weeks later, on 22 December, he picked up 77.5 acres between Allen's and Mermaid Lanes for $12,816. Altogether he acquired 145 acres at an average price of $234 per acre.[18] During 1880 he spent $98,000 on an additional 142 acres of land, at an average price of $689 an acre. Much of this land was closer to the center of Chestnut Hill and therefore more desirable for development purposes. Word of the planned railroad had also had a chance to spread more widely by then, causing owners to demand more for their property. Besides these larger purchases, Houston paid another $11,000 that year for seven smaller plots scattered around Chestnut Hill.[19]

Completion of the railroad four years later unquestionably increased the value of this and other land that Houston subsequently bought in the area. His personal balance sheet for January 1884 lists real estate holdings at $1.8 million. A year later, after the railroad had been completed to Chestnut Hill, essentially the same properties were listed at $2.3 million.[20]

In the meantime, Houston could only hope that everything would work out as projected. Construction of the new railroad began in 1882, as Houston was planning the first of his ambitious building projects on the lower west side of Chestnut Hill, in an area that he eventually named Wissahickon Heights. Just when the plan unfolded in his mind is unclear, but it is obvious that Houston intended Wissahickon Heights to be an "organic" community from the start.

Houston's first project on the Heights was a tourist hotel called the Wissahickon Inn. It was actually the third hotel on the site, the most recent one having been the Park House which had burned down in 1879. All three facilities took advantage of Chestnut Hill's longstanding reputation as a summer resort. Located near the highest point on a range of hills that stretched from Trenton, New Jersey, through the Philadelphia Main Line, Chestnut Hill was one of the coolest spots in the city during the summer months. The scenic Wissahickon valley, which bordered Chestnut Hill on the west, was an added attraction to summer visitors who could stroll through the woods or drive their carriages along the Valley Green Road. Taking full advantage of the setting, Houston's inn would be built just above one of the old wagon roads leading down to the Wissahickon Creek.

As designers for the inn Houston chose the firm of William D. and George W. Hewitt, apparently because he was pleased by George's work for St. Peter's, Germantown. The Hewitts created a large, three-story, U-shaped structure that measured 236 × 227 × 227 feet. There were 250 guest rooms, many with their own fireplaces. Wide wooden porches wrapped around the entire first floor. A ballroom, library, and spacious dining room were also there for the guests to enjoy. The inn was essentially Queen Anne in style, but with fairly simple lines. A locally quarried stone called Wissahickon schist, but popularly known as Chestnut Hill stone, was used on the lower two stories. Wood, made to simulate stucco and half-timbering, covered the third story. Square turrets, with carved wooden sunbursts beneath their windows, set off the corners of the building, while tall chimneys, constructed of alternating bands of red brick and local stone, punctuated the roof line.[21]

Several years after the structure was completed, Houston laid out an attractive arboretum just east of the inn which he called St. Martin's Green. And just below the inn's south entrance he dammed up the Cresheim Creek to create Lake Surprise. There guests could enjoy canoeing in summer and ice-skating during the winter months.

Houston leased the Wissahickon Inn to J. E. Kingsley, who served as its proprietor and manager.[22] The inn opened on Decoration Day 1884, despite unusually late frosts that had damaged crops and gardens throughout eastern Pennsylvania the week before.[23] An article in the Philadelphia *Press* on 1 June described the inn's attractions in some detail: "Pure water is supplied from the reservoir at Chestnut Hill. . . . The Willow Grove [or Wissahickon Heights Station] is a minute's walk from the hotel and twenty minutes [by train] from Broad Street [downtown]." "The vicinity of the hotel," the writer added, "is most romantic and beautiful in its scenery."[24] What the writer failed to mention was that the first train would not arrive in Chestnut Hill until the morning of 11 June.[25] Construction difficulties had prevented the initial run on 1 June, but train service was available early enough for the inn not to suffer during its maiden season.[26] The total cost for construction was about $2 million.[27]

Train service was well in place for the opening of the Philadelphia Cricket Club, which Houston had lured to the Heights with a grant of land just across Willow Grove Avenue from the Wissahickon Inn. Although founded in 1854 during the height of the Philadelphia cricket craze, the club had never known a permanent home.[28] A cricket match with the Orpheus Club, which Houston undoubtedly attended, inaugurated the new grounds on 1 October 1884. There was a dinner and ball that evening at the Wissahickon Inn, where the grounds were illuminated with electric lights for the first time. The dining room was resplendent with American flags and banners from the two teams. The Orpheus Club Singers treated the guests to an after-dinner concert, which was followed by a "grand hop" in the ballroom, with music provided by the Herzberg orchestra. A special train waited at the station to carry partygoers back downtown when the festivities finally broke up around midnight.[29]

In the spring of 1892 Houston brought yet another attraction to the area with the Philadelphia Horse Show, predecessor of the event now held in Devon. Its first location was directly east of the Wissahickon Inn; later it moved across the street near the Cricket Club. The Horse Show brought visitors to the inn, and, additionally, provided an introduction to Wissahickon Heights for the spectators.[30]

Far more important in the long run was the Church of St. Martin-in-the-Fields, named for the famous Anglican church in London. Built and equipped by Houston, the new Episcopal church opened for services in early 1889. Houston's genuine faith was clearly one of his motives for building a church on the Heights. But like the developers of Germantown nearly two generations earlier, he realized that an attractive Episcopal church would help bring prosperous families to the neighborhood. Houston accordingly donated a large lot for the church at the corner of Willow

Grove Avenue and St. Martin's Lane (then Thirty-first Street), engaged the Hewitts to draw up plans, and paid all costs for constructing and furnishing the church, complete with tower, parish hall, and a rectory next door. Although the total price has never been revealed, he must have spent about $100,000 on the combined project.[31] Houston also traveled to different parishes in search of a suitable rector, eventually engaging the Reverend Jacob LeRoy and agreeing to pay his salary of $2,500 per year.[32] Until Mr. LeRoy could assume his duties at St. Martin's, services were often led by the Reverend Theodore Rumney of St. Peter's, Germantown, assisted by the St. Peter's choir.[33]

The church opened formally on Sunday, 2 February. Two days later the Philadelphia *Inquirer* reported that "crowds attended the first service in the new Protestant Episcopal Church of St. Martin-in-the-Fields. . . . The audience room is large, but it was filled to over-flowing. Carriages drew up in numbers and many came by train. The chancel was decorated with growing plants."[34]

In the years ahead Houston's heirs would contribute many improvements to the church: a baptistery in 1899, an extension to the chancel three years later, and numerous financial gifts over the decades.[35] Houston himself did not join the new parish formally, preferring to remain a member of St. Peter's where he continued as rector's warden. But St. Martin's became a family church for his children and grandchildren, the scene of many baptisms, weddings, and funerals.

Meanwhile, Houston had been busy building houses to the north, south, and east of St. Martin's, with the church serving as a sort of anchor for these residential streets.[36] It was to this development that he actually gave the name Wissahickon Heights, plans having been drawn up in June 1886.[37] The area was bordered on the north by Willow Grove Avenue and on the south by Cresheim Creek, with the present St. Martin's Lane and Seminole Avenue forming its other two boundaries. Houston eventually commissioned between eighty and one hundred houses here and elsewhere on the Hill, with the Hewitts designing most of them.[38]

The houses that Houston built in the eighties were of eclectic design. The dwellings on the two-hundred blocks of Moreland Avenue and Mermaid Lane, for instance, were modest-sized single units rendered in a Queen Anne style, with steeply pitched roofs and large front porches. On the south side of the two-hundred block of Springfield Avenue, however, Houston commissioned several double houses that were more mixed in design. These featured mansard roofs and plain, almost neocolonial façades, a motif that was repeated in the double houses on the 8300 block of Shawnee Street.

Near the corner of Seminole and Highland Avenues there were four more singles in a very distinct Queen Anne style, with an alternating use of stone, red brick, and stucco in the façades. Most impressive of all was the flamboyant Queen Anne house at 8205 Seminole Avenue. It boasted a two-story porch in front, steep roofs, multiple, half-timbered gable ends, and banks of casement windows, making it one of the most distinctive Queen Anne houses in America. Then there were several dwellings built in the 1890s—such as those on the north side of the two-hundred block of Springfield Avenue—that clearly reflected the growing popularity of colonial revival motifs. Most of these are in a vaguely Dutch colonial style, typified by double-pitched gambrel roofs.

Although there was considerable variety among Houston's commissions, the use of local Chestnut Hill stone throughout served as a unifying element. By the mid-1890s Wissahickon Heights was a very attractive suburban development that drew many of the same sort of people who had settled in Germantown a generation or so before. For the most part they were not members of Philadelphia's highest class, but were largely lawyers, bankers, businessmen, and industrial managers of upper-middle-class standing. And as if to insure that such families would settle in Wissahickon Heights, Houston continued to own most of the houses that he commissioned, renting them to families whom he knew would appreciate and maintain them. If they were not Episcopalians when they arrived, the convenience of St. Martin's church induced many to convert within a few years.

It is also evident that Houston's primary aim was not to make a great deal of money from these properties. The rents were quite modest, even for those noninflationary times. Numbers 310 and 313 Mermaid Lane, for example, rented for $40 a month, while numbers 303 and 305 Springfield Avenue (both of them twins) went for only $30 a month. Very large single dwellings on Thirty-first Street (St. Martin's Lane) were listed at $135 a month.[39] Houston Estate audits in fact show that Houston and his heirs did not reap considerable profits from these rentals, and in future decades they would often just break even—and sometimes actually lose money on them.[40] Houston's aim was thus to provide attractive housing to the sorts of people who would appreciate living in a place like Wissahickon Heights. In any case, his income of $356,000 in 1884—on investments worth just over $7 million—meant that he could well afford to charge moderate rents in Wissahickon Heights.[41]

But the most striking feature about Houston's Wissahickon Heights was its unity and convenience. It had its own church and recreation centers (the Cricket Club, the Wissahickon Inn, Lake Surprise, and the Wissahickon valley itself), as well as a rapid and dependable means of transportation in the Pennsylvania Railroad's Chestnut Hill Local. The Wissahickon Heights station (renamed St. Martin's after Houston's death) had its own freight siding where even the bulkiest pieces of merchandise could be delivered. And for years department stores and other downtown businesses would send items up on one of the thirty-two trains that ran to Wissahickon Heights every day. Passengers meanwhile could travel the nine miles to "town" in less than half an hour and from there make train connections to anywhere in the country. Or they might take themselves several more blocks to the Delaware River docks and board one of Houston's steamers to Liverpool or Antwerp. Finally, there were several good private schools in the community, including the Chestnut Hill Academy for boys and the Springside School for girls. Houston's descendants would help to maintain and expand these institutions through generous gifts over the years.

With Wissahickon Heights well under way by the early 1890s, Houston was ready to begin developing his Roxborough lands that lay west across Wissahickon Creek from Chestnut Hill. The first step was an extension of the Chestnut Hill rail line over the valley into Roxborough itself. Houston may have intended this route as a second stage in the line that had originally been projected to Norristown and Phoenixville, although there is no documented evidence to prove such a design. Whatever the case, Houston's agents began buying up the necessary land during the summer of 1891.[42] In March of 1892 the Pennsylvania Railroad board approved the venture, provided that the right-of-way could be obtained for $50,000 or less and in June raised the limit to $80,000. In December, however, the directors withdrew their support because of increasing estimates for construction.[43] The economic depression that began in 1893 doomed any prospect of renewal until prosperity returned in the late nineties, and by then Houston would be dead. This initial failure to link Roxborough to Chestnut Hill, along with several other factors, would postpone the development of these lands for another half century and impose a far different fate on Roxborough from what Houston had probably intended.

Houston was far more successful in his plan to construct a bridge across Cresheim Creek at McCallum Street. In July 1890 he agreed to pay the company of Levering and Garrigues the sum of $21,320 for constructing such a span. Following completion, Houston would turn the McCallum Street Bridge over to the city of Philadelphia. The new bridge (replaced by the city in the mid-1980s) would provide a carriage and then an auto route from the present Lincoln Drive into the far west side of Chestnut Hill.[44]

Houston's decision to build the bridge may have been related to his own removal to the western slopes of Chestnut Hill in the summer or autumn of 1886. There Houston broke ground in 1885 for a thirty-room residence for his family, which he first thought of calling the "Crow's Nest." He dropped the designation before the house was finished in favor of "Druim Moir," a Gaelic name meaning great ridge. However he came up with the new name, it was well suited to the house's location high above Wissahickon Creek.[45]

Druim Moir was originally described as Gothic revival in style and, according to one family member, resembled Humewood Castle in County Wicklow, Ireland, designed in 1867–1870 by English architect William White.[46] Whether the Hewitts used it as a model cannot be determined, but Druim Moir did resemble a medieval castle in certain ways. On the south side was a five-story tower with embattlements. Beside the front entrance was an oriel with a steep conical roof and above the Romanesque porte-cochère was another set of embattlements. Inside, Druim Moir looked more eclectic. Mantelpieces varied from Tudor to Jacobean to Italian Renaissance, while wooden columns and pilasters were largely neoclassical in form. Many of the walls and ceilings were paneled in wood and there were parquet floors in several rooms. According to a contemporary description, the front hall and stairs were " in oak; the parlor in butternut; the reception room in mahogany; the library and dining room in quartered oak; the office in cherry; the servants' quarters in white pine; and the principal bedrooms in oak, cherry, and sycamore."[47]

Outside were fifty-two acres of lawn and woodland that included a small deer park. A small stone house from an earlier farm on the site remained. Later Houston built two more dwellings on the property, one stone and one frame, to house employees. Besides these structures, there were a stone entrance lodge, coach house and stables, cow barns, and other outbuildings which together resembled a small village. On the property, too, were vegetable gardens and a small farm with chickens, pigs, cows, and horses, which would continue in operation until World War II. Three greenhouses kept Druim Moir filled with flowers year round and supplied St. Martin's church on Sundays. Houston also bred Irish wolfhounds on the estate. For centuries it had been the habit of Irish landlords to raise these large, shaggy dogs. This particular breed of dogs, and Houston's choice of the Gaelic name Druim Moir for his home, suggest a conscious effort to identify with his Scotch-Irish heritage, as did his later selection of an elaborately carved Celtic cross for his gravestone.[48]

By the late 1880s Henry Howard Houston had become a genuine country gentleman. Once a young transportation agent living in the fifteen-hundred block of Chestnut Street, he had moved to Tulpehocken

Street in Germantown, and then to a country seat in Chestnut Hill. In a little less than fifty years he had gone as far as any man could expect to go in one lifetime.

During these last years in Chestnut Hill, Houston continued his many philanthropies and was particularly generous to the church's missions at home and abroad. Over the decades he had also made numerous gifts and loans to friends or family members in need. Around 1890 he opened Buttercup Cottage, located on the present Cresheim Valley Drive, as a weeklong summer retreat for working girls. Its director was Sister Ruth, a member of the Sisterhood of the Good Shepherd and for many years a deaconess at St. Martin's church. Houston's daughter Gertrude was president of the Buttercup Cottage corporation and his daughter-in-law Edith (Mrs. Samuel F. Houston) was a member of the board. Buttercup was Gertrude's private charity, which she very much enjoyed. Houston also donated the House of Rest for the Aged to the Episcopal diocese in 1891 as a haven for the elderly. It was located on Wayne Avenue in Germantown not far from the former Houston residence.[49]

Other acts of generosity reached well beyond Philadelphia. During the Civil War Houston convinced Union authorities to release the wounded son of Texas's famed Sam Houston into his father's care. In gratitude, the hero gave the Philadelphia Houston, to whom he was not related, a gold snuff box that he had received from Santa Anna after the battle of San Jacinto. (In 1952 the northern Houstons returned the snuff box to Texas and it is now in the museum at the Alamo.)[50]

In 1871 Houston gave $5,000 for relief efforts after the great Chicago fire.[51] He also donated large sums to colleges and universities. In 1873 Houston sent $7,000 to Washington University (now Washington and Lee), where he was later elected to the board of trustees.[52] Over the years he provided substantial amounts for black institutions of higher learning, among them Lincoln University and the Tuskeegee Institute. At Lincoln he donated a building for the theological seminary which was subsequently named Houston Hall, and in 1881 he contributed $10,000 to the university. Yet another school which benefitted from his generosity was the Pennsylvania School for the Deaf to which he gave a large parcel of land for a new campus in Mount Airy; Houston also served as a trustee for the school.[53]

Houston was very generous to the arts in his adopted city. In 1872 he pledged $10,000 toward a new home for the Pennsylvania Academy of Fine Arts on North Broad Street. Meanwhile he became the principal patron of Newbold Hough Trotter, a noted landscape painter. Houston commissioned canvases of animals that were disappearing from the American West, including bison and elk.[54] Trotter did another series of works for Houston on early transportation in Pennsylvania, several of which are now at the state museum in Harrisburg.[55]

All such contributions were dwarfed by his bequests to Philadelphia's University of Pennsylvania, where he served as trustee from 1885 until his death. In 1888, for example, he gave $10,000 for a new campus library.[56] But his most important gift to the university was Houston Hall, the first student center in the country and a prototype for hundreds of such centers across the nation.

The hall was not originally Houston's idea but came from Provost Charles C. Harrison, who realized that Penn students had no gathering place on campus other than what they could improvise outdoors or in their own small rooms. Concerned over the lack of student facilities, Harrison took the train out to Wissahickon Heights one snowy evening in February 1894 to discuss the situation with trustee Houston. Listening intently to what Harrison had to say, his host promised $50,000 for the erection of a student "club house." When it soon became evident that $50,000 would not be enough, Houston pledged another $50,000, which was followed in 1895 by a third donation of $50,000 from the family. At the suggestion of fellow trustees, the new building would be named for the Houstons' son Howard who had died in Rome the year after his graduation from the university.[57]

Built in stone along Tudor-Gothic lines, the students' first indoor meeting and recreation space was modeled after an English club and was, in fact, called the "Houston Club" during its early years. The main rooms and hallway were richly paneled in dark wood. Beyond were a swimming pool, gymnasium, billiard room, lounge, reading room, bowling alley, chapel and meeting rooms.

Ground was broken for Houston Hall on 20 December 1894, an unusually warm day, according to newspaper accounts. Present with the Houstons were Provost Harrison, Rector Rumney of St. Peter's, and Episcopal Bishop Ozi W. Whitaker. There were the usual opening remarks, after which Father Rumney described the "Christian life and example" of the young man for whom the building was being named. Then the Houstons placed some personal "mementos of their son" into the cornerstone, along with a number of objects chosen by the university.[58] In the late 1930s a gift of $350,000 from Houston's three surviving children would pay for the addition of two identical wings on either side of the hall.[59]

Houston's precise motives for such large-scale philanthropy can never really be known. It would be exciting to discover that he was influenced by someone like Philadelphia's Russell Conwell, whose Gospel of Wealth held that it was the duty of Christian men to become rich and to use their bounty to help others. But more likely than not Houston was simply moved by old-fashioned noblesse oblige, combined with simple charity and lingering Presbyterian notions of Christian leadership.

If Houston had any well-thought-out theories of stewardship, his death on 21 June 1895 prevented him from recording them for posterity. That first day of summer had been an uneventful one for Houston. He had spent the morning in town at his office, returning on the 1:14 P.M. train and talking with several friends afterward on the station platform at Wissahickon Heights. At five he went for a carriage ride, stopping for a brief visit at the Pennsylvania School for the Deaf. After dinner he chatted for a while with the family and then went up to bed. Around 1:00 A.M. he awoke with severe chest pains, collapsed shortly thereafter, and never regained consciousness.[60]

Houston's funeral took place three days later on 24 June. It was preceded by a private service at Druim Moir where Father Rumney was reportedly so overcome that he could not make it through his prayer. The funeral cortege then moved slowly up Willow Grove Avenue to St. Martin's church where Bishop Whitaker and Pastor LeRoy presided. The church was filled to overflowing, with about one hundred people standing outside. After the service, family and friends climbed into carriages for the four-mile drive out to St. Thomas's, Whitemarsh, where Henry Howard Houston was buried in the churchyard.[61]

At his death, Houston's estate was worth just over $14 million.[62] His lengthy will left the bulk of his money and property in trust. The income would be divided equally among his wife and three children, with the principal to be distributed among his grandchildren after the last of his own children had died. He also made modest bequests to scores of cousins and other relatives. Another section of the will conveyed St. Martin's church to the parish as a "free gift," adding that future rectors should be acceptable to his family. Having already given large amounts to "educational, religious, and charitable institutions," he did not designate any additional gifts in the will. But he pointedly urged his heirs to "continue the system I have practiced, and recommend that they never allow their donations to fall below one tenth of their income."[63]

The principal of Houston's estate would grow more than tenfold over the next seven decades. Henry Howard Houston had provided well for the future; it was now up to his descendants to continue what he had begun.

*Statue of Henry Howard Houston and dog in Fairmount Park, erected 1900 by the Commissioners of Fairmount Park. EHS collection.*

*Henry Howard Houston in February 1840, aged 20. Daguerreotype by Robert Cornelius, Philadelphia. Library Company of Philadelphia; gift of Dallett family.*

*Henry Howard Houston residence at Wayne Avenue and Tulpehocken Street, Germantown, Philadelphia, ca. 1875. Houston children in goat cart at right. UPA.*

*Bedroom of Mr. and Mrs. Henry Howard Houston at Wayne Avenue and Tulpehocken Street, Germantown, Philadelphia, as it looked in 1886. UPA.*

*Druim Moir, residence of Henry Howard Houston and Samuel Frederic Houston, Chestnut Hill, Philadelphia. Designed by William D. and George W. Hewitt and completed in 1886. EHS collection.*

*St. Martin-in-the-Fields Episcopal Church, corner of St. Martin's Lane and Willow Grove Avenue, Chestnut Hill, Philadelphia. Designed by William D. and George W. Hewitt and Gift of Henry Howard Houston. completed in 1889. Church of St. Martin-in-the-Fields collection.*

Houston Hall (original structure before addition of wings), University of Pennsylvania, Philadelphia. Donated by Henry Howard Houston. Designed by University of Pennsylvania students William C. Hayes and Milton B. Medary and supervised by architect Frank Miles Day. Constructed in 1895. UPA.

*Sallie S. Bonnell Houston (Mrs. Henry Howard Houston) with grandchildren, ca. 1896: Henry Howard Houston Woodward seated on lap. Around them (from left to right) are Henry Howard Houston II, Edith Corlies Houston (Brown), Thomas Charlton Henry, Margaret Corlies Houston (Meigs), Gertrude Houston Henry (Dodge), and Elizabeth Wolcott Henry (Chatfield). SW collection.*

# CHAPTER 4

# A New Generation

ALL MEN AND WOMEN must play a variety of roles in life: child and parent, lover and friend, cousin and uncle, in-law and spouse, among many others. When the aging head of a family dies, his survivors are forced to redefine their place in the family network. In the usual scheme of things the middle generation takes its place at the top, while some of the younger adults begin to feel the claims of middle age. For the children of Henry Howard Houston, who were still relatively young at their father's death, the shift was more abrupt, propelling them into positions of responsibility much earlier than their contemporaries. Sallie, now thirty-five, was the closest to middle age, but Sam was only twenty-eight and Gertrude just twenty-seven when their father died.

Houston had lived long enough to see all of them married: Sallie to Charles Wolcott Henry, Sam to Edith Atlee Corlies, and Gertrude to Dr. George Woodward. He could also envision them comfortably settled on their own estates in Chestnut Hill.[1] Sam would inherit the paternal residence, while Sallie and Gertrude would occupy two large houses immediately to the south of their brother's property: Sallie at Stonehurst and Gertrude at Krisheim.

Although sharing equally in land and moneyed income, the three heirs and their spouses would occupy different niches in both family and community. The Henrys would become the most active in Philadelphia social life, while Sam, as the only son, was in charge of the family trust. His brother-in-law, George Woodward, would greatly extend the real estate developments begun by Houston a generation before, besides adding a new dimension to the family as an outspoken reformer and politician. In both style and substance the members of this second generation were very different, which led at times to misunderstandings and hurt feelings among them. In spite of these occasional clashes, they managed to preserve and extend much of what the family founder had left them.

Sallie's wedding in November 1884 had been the first for the Houston children. Her husband was Charles Wolcott Henry (1852–1903) of Germantown, then head of the lumber firm of Henry, Bayard and Company, a business concern that he had inherited from his father. Elected in 1877 to the city's Common Council from the Twenty-second Ward, Henry served until 1884, when he was appointed to the Fairmount Park Commission. Meanwhile, he joined a number of corporate boards, including the Real Estate Trust Company (RET), which he helped to organize in 1890. It was doubtless Henry's connection with the RET that later led the Houston family to choose it as custodian for their estate. Henry was also a nephew of the former well-known Philadelphia mayor Alexander Henry.[2]

As a wedding present, Henry Howard Houston gave the Henrys some fifty acres of land directly adjoining his Druim Moir property, as well as a large three-story house known as Stonehurst, completed in 1887. Stonehurst was designed by the famous beaux arts firm of McKim, Mead, and White and resembled a French château, with its thick, round towers and massive verticle thrust. Descendants particularly remember the so-called West Room, flooded on winter afternoons with brilliant shafts of sunlight. Other features of the room were its rich Tudor-Jacobean wainscoting and beamed ceiling. It was at Stonehurst that Charles Wolcott and Sallie Houston Henry reared their three children: Thomas Charlton Henry, Gertrude Houston Henry (Dodge), and Elizabeth Wolcott Henry (Chatfield).

Sallie herself, tiny in stature, seems to have been a very proper and conservative woman who, as she grew older, looked much like Queen Victoria, leading employees of the RET to call her "the Duchess of Stonehurst." During her married life, as well as her three decades of widowhood, Sallie was intensely interested in the arts, served on the Women's Committee of the Philadelphia Museum of Art, and donated a number of items to local museums over the years.[3]

Brother Sam had, meanwhile, entered his father's office following graduation from the University of Pennsylvania in 1887. The summer before he had gone on a brief tour of western Europe with a college friend instead of waiting until the next year and taking a grand tour like his brother Howard. Perhaps his father discouraged such a plan, fearful that he might lose another son far from home. But Sam's impending engagement in the fall of 1886 and his marriage a year later may have been the real reason for his truncated tour.

The bride-to-be was Edith Atlee Corlies, a graduate of Miss Agnes Irwin's School. Her father, S. Fisher Corlies, was a prominent Quaker attorney whose large inheritance had freed him from regular legal practice to enjoy his considerable talents as a photographer. The couple was married in the Corlies winter residence at 1717 Arch Street by Rector Rumney of St. Peter's, with Edith converting to her husband's religion. The bride wore a brooch sent by Mrs. Grover Cleveland, who was a friend of the family.[4]

After their honeymoon the newlyweds moved into Brinkwood, a rambling Queen Anne house behind Druim Moir that Henry Howard Houston built for them as a wedding present. Since Sam would one day inherit Druim Moir, it was considerably more modest than Stonehurst next door.[5] Sam may not have been completely enthusiastic about living so close to his parents, but as a dutiful son he accepted the arrangement without protest.[6] Despite these conditions, Sam and Edith enjoyed their early years together very much, as both were active in outdoor sports. Sam was an athletic young man who loved hunting, boating, and coaching. An active member of the Philadelphia Four-in-Hand Club, he was well known for his ability behind the reins. Edith rode, was an excellent shot, and loved canoeing. The couple also enjoyed traveling, and in the summer of 1889 they toured the British Isles.[7]

Sam and Edith were not alone for long. Two daughters, Edith and Margaret, were born in 1888 and 1891, with a son, Henry Howard Houston II, coming along four years later in 1895. The birth of a son who would carry on the family name was a particularly joyous event, but the euphoria was soon shattered when Edith died from complications several days later on 16 April 1895. Upon the death of Sam's father, just two months later, the grief-stricken widower and the three children, who were all under seven years of age, moved across the garden to Druim Moir with Sam's mother, Sallie Houston.[8]

For distraction Sam had his work, his interests in various religious, educational, and philanthropic organizations, and his lifelong love of the sea. Henry Howard Houston had been terrified of water and had accordingly forbidden any of his children to buy boats.[9] Since his death, Sam had taken up boating with genuine zeal, joining both the New York and Philadelphia Corinthian Yacht Clubs.[10]

In February 1898 he, the three children, and the children's older cousin, Corlies Morgan—accompanied by a governess, nurse, and "lady doctor"—embarked on a winter's cruise in the Caribbean. They chartered the Philadelphia-based *Alert,* a three-masted, sixty-eight foot schooner that went on ahead while they traveled to the coast of Venezuela by steamer. Joining the *Alert* at La Guaira, they set sail on 12 February for Trinidad. Numerous sharks were encountered along the way, nine of which Sam and Corlies shot and killed from the deck. After Trinidad there were stops in Grenada, St. Lucia, Martinique, and Dominica. At Dominica they received a telegram from home that warned of the impending war with Spain: they were to return home at once. Leaving the *Alert* at St. Kitts, they managed to crowd aboard a sugar ship headed for Scotland, reeking of "molasses and brown sugar." It took them as far as Bermuda and from there they caught a steamer for New York.[11]

It was also in 1898 that Sam bought Clapboard Island in Casco Bay, just off the coast of Maine at Falmouth Foreside. The following year he built a three-story summer dwelling. Shingled on the outside, the house was executed in a loose Colonial-revival style. It contained seven master bedrooms, three guest rooms, twelve open fireplaces, two full baths, and five maids' rooms. The large boathouse contained several more bedrooms. Outside was a large lawn, flower garden, and tennis court, in addition to woods covered with "pine, fir, oak, beech, and white birch."[12]

Summers at Clapboard Island soon became a permanent part of the family routine, with much sailing on the family's large yachts, manned by Down East crews. The trip up each year was made in a private car, provided by the Pennsylvania Railroad. Even the Druim Moir cows went along, so that the children's digestion would not be upset by unfamiliar milk.

Back in Philadelphia Sam spent a good deal of time on church and university matters. At St. Martin's he was rector's warden, a post he had held since the church's establishment in 1889, in addition to his position as superintendent of the Sunday School. For many years he was also a member of the bishop's Standing Committee. In 1898 the University of Pennsylvania elected him a trustee and in 1905 he was made president of the University Museum.[13]

But Sam's principal task was managing the Houston estate. His father's will had designated four trustees in all. Besides Sam himself, there were his mother, his uncle George B. Bonnell (for decades Henry Howard Houston's confidential partner), and Edgar Dudley Faries, a Philadelphia attorney.[14] The trustees chose the Real Estate Trust Company, the full-service commercial bank in Philadelphia that Sam's brother-in-law, Charles Wolcott Henry, had helped to found several years earlier, to handle the funds. Faries seems to have functioned as a sort of executive secretary for the Houston estate, whose job it was to look after the more routine matters while Sam oversaw the enterprise as a whole.

Shortly after its formation the estate built a number of houses in Germantown, most of them concentrated around the intersection of Wayne Avenue and Harvey Street. The Houston heirs also donated a two-and-one-half-acre tract of wooded land between Harvey Street and West Walnut Lane to the Fairmount Park Commission, near the site of a statue of Henry Howard Houston that was erected by the park commission in 1900. And in Upper Roxborough the estate leased sixty acres to the Andorra Nurseries.[15]

Yet another estate venture was a proposal in 1904 to merge the Episcopal Academy with the Chestnut Hill Academy. Both institutions had intimate connections with the Houston family. Henry Howard Houston's cousin-in-law, the Reverend Roger Owen, had founded the Chestnut Hill Academy and Charles Wolcott Henry had served for many years as a trustee, while Sam Houston and his brother Howard had graduated from Episcopal, where there were ancient family roots. As to the merger itself, the Houston estate would provide the former Wissahickon Inn as a school building, already being used as such by the Chestnut Hill Academy. In addition, it would build a chapel for 400 students and give the combined institutions an endowment of $100,000. Episcopal's trustees rejected the offer, however, fearing that they could not afford to maintain the property and being reluctant to leave their principal field of operation, then in Center City. The Houston estate's insistence that the boys attend St. Martin-in-the-Fields on Sunday mornings also did not sit well with the Episcopal trustees, who felt that the academy would then lose control of the boys' religious education.[16]

When it came to the estate's stock portfolio, Sam believed that he should maintain the family's investments rather than make new ones. His caution in this area, stemming in part from a basically conservative temperament, would cause several family members to complain that he was not realizing the highest possible returns from their investments. Yet in the end his tenacity would pay off handsomely—for everyone concerned.

With his own funds, Sam did buy large amounts of stock in the Real Estate Trust, doubtless because of its connection with the Houston estate. Between May 1897 and October 1903 he put $50,000 into the RET and another $25,000 five years later. He became vice-president of the company in 1903 and president in 1928. Such responsibility was not without its risks, as Sam discovered in 1906 when the current RET president embezzled large sums of money and then shot himself. In order to help save the bank from total ruin Sam had to sell his yacht *Shepherdess,* in addition to putting up other personal funds. Every penny was eventually repaid to the depositers.[17]

Besides running the Houston estate and the RET, Houston became a board member or executive officer of several other enterprises: he held directorships in the Third National Bank, the Trust Company of North America, and the Guaranty Trust and Safe Deposit Company. In addition, he was president of the Nelson Valve and Coastwise Transportation Companies and vice-president of the Pennsylvania Sugar and the Winifrede Coal Company.[18] By becoming a banker and corporate director Houston was also pursuing a well-worn path to social and economic prominence. For in Philadelphia, as in other large cities of the East, inheriting money was often considered more respectable than actually making it. While it was necessary for someone in the family to accumulate a large fortune, it was expected that succeeding generations would serve as conservators of family wealth rather than becoming risk-takers themselves.[19]

Whether Houston was conscious of fulfilling this pattern is unclear, but it is certain that he longed for a fuller family life during those years after Edith's death. In April 1902 the young widower married Charlotte Harding Shepherd Brown. Charlotte had been born on a plantation called Golden Grove, some 150 miles up the Mississippi from New Orleans. After her mother died in childbirth, Charlotte had come to Philadelphia at age four to live with her Uncle George Harding, a prominent patent lawyer in the Quaker city. To some of her family and closest friends, Charlotte was known as "Dixie," a charming reminder of her southern roots. Others called her Lottie, while she signed notes to Sam with the nickname "Shep."

Sam and Charlotte, born just one year apart, had much in common. Charlotte, who had made her debut at the Assembly Ball, had been one of Edith's best friends. She was a bridesmaid at Edith and Sam's wedding in 1887 and was their daughter Edith's godmother. Charlotte was also married in 1887, to Charles Wardell Brown, a resident of Mt. Holly, New Jersey, and like Sam a graduate of the University of Pennsylvania. Brown died a few years after Edith, leaving Charlotte with a son and daughter to rear. In their mid-thirties Sam and Charlotte decided to marry, only to face the difficult task of assimilating their two families.

There were now five children at Druim Moir. Sam's Edith was thirteen, Margaret (called Peg) was eleven, and Henry Howard II (or Hennie) was seven. Charlotte's son Charlie was also eleven, while her daughter, Charlotte, was exactly Hennie's age. Having a new set of siblings to play with was no doubt exciting but also threatening, as the two sets of children had to learn to share toys or worried that they might receive less attention than before from their respective parents. Sam and Charlotte would have to learn how to become good stepparents, while Sam's mother, still living at Druim Moir, had to cope with being a stepgrandmother. Fortunately, the house was large and there were both a governess and a nurse to shoulder part of the burden.[20]

Perhaps to get away from some of the strains at home and to bring the two families together through the novelty and fun of travel, Sam, Charlotte, and the five youngsters embarked on an ambitious tour of Europe and the Mediterranean. Accompanying them was Charlotte's nephew, Angus Crawford, a German governess and German maid, and a personal medical doctor. They left aboard the SS *Zealand* in early December of 1902.[21]

At Christmas they were in Rome, where the energetic entourage attracted considerable attention whenever they went out. "When we go to see anything," Edith wrote to Grandmother Houston back at Druim Moir, "we always collect . . . quite a crowd. . . . Whenever our whole party looks in a shop window other people come to see what we are looking at. We must make quite a sensation. We each have our camera and when we see anything we take them out and then people come to see the cameras."[22] For Christmas they bought a tree and had a turkey dinner.[23]

From Rome the party traveled to Naples and there chartered the steam yacht *Gitana*. They were in Tunis by the end of January where both parents and children enjoyed the colorful bazaars. Then it was on to Malta, Zante, Delphi, Corinth, and finally Athens. There the parents called on Mrs. Schliemann, widow of the famous discoverer of Troy. Both Sam and Charlotte had become fascinated with ancient archaeology, having recently contributed substantial monies to the University of Pennsylvania for a dig on the island of Gornia which they planned to visit later in the trip.[24]

Taking on a Greek "dragoman" (professional interpreter), who would put his knowledge of Greek and Turkish at their disposal, they set sail from Athens to Constantinople. Sam admired the mosques and loved the Turkish coffee. They also drove out to the Sultan's palace one Friday to watch His Highness being driven off to his mosque.[25] But much more exciting as far as Sam was concerned was their visit to Knossos in early April where they were taken on a personal tour of the Palace at Minos by the son of Sir John Evans, the much heralded discoverer of Minoan culture. Soon thereafter they landed at Gornia. There Miss Harriet Boyd, who had been heading up the University of Pennsylvania expedition there, took them on a detailed inspection of the site.[26]

Their Mediterranean cruise ended at Venice in early May. The children had come down with whooping cough and they were turned away from several hotels because of it. Charlotte, who had sat up nights nursing the little ones, was quite exhausted. They finally found splendid lodgings in the Grand Hotel, complete with furniture that had supposedly belonged to Napoleon, with Napoleonic eagles carved into the bedsteads.[27]

Sam went on something of a shopping spree in Venice, buying a large ornamental iron gate for the entrance to Druim Moir, along with two stone lions for the gateposts. He also ordered two smaller lions for the rear entrance to the estate and an elaborately carved stone wellhead for the garden. "Perhaps you think I am buying up the whole place," he wrote his mother, "but I assure you I am restraining myself, or perhaps I should give Charlotte the credit for restraining me. . . . If Druim Moir were building, I think I would charter a ship to send everything I could get here in Venice alone, to make the house and grounds attractive."[28]

They had originally planned to return home at this point, but the parents thought that a summer in Germany would give the children a wonderful opportunity to improve what German they had already learned from their governess. From Venice they went to Munich, and from there to Nuremberg, Carlsbad, Dresden, and Berlin. They were so enchanted with the picturesque medieval towers and quaint half-timbered houses at Nuremberg that they later built a German-style garden house at Clapboard Island and filled it with carved wooden furniture with colorful German sayings on the chairs.[29]

In Berlin, Sam and Charlotte had luncheon with the American ambassador, Charlemagne Tower, who invited Sam to a dinner on 27 June in Kiel, the principal German naval base on the North Sea, where a contingent of American ships was making a courtesy call. None other than Kaiser Wilhelm was to be the guest of honor. In addition, Charlotte and Sam were invited to a garden party, to be given on the afternoon of the twenty-seventh by the Kaiser's brother, Prince Henry.

Recounting the garden party for his mother, Sam wrote, "We all entered the Schloss together, and Mr. T[ower] presented first the ladies and then us men to Prince and Princess Henry. Charlotte and Mrs. T[ower] curtseyed most beautifully, just as if they always curtseyed. I bowed my most formal bow, and what did the princess and prince do but break me all up by shaking hands with each of us."[30] The foursome then walked out into the garden where a string orchestra was playing waltzes. Unfortunately, Sam did not describe the dinner with the Kaiser that evening in any detail. Newspapers reported, however, that the German emperor had responded to Ambassador Tower's toast by praising President Theodore Roosevelt for his "iron will, his devotion to his country, and his indomitable energy."[31] For a great admirer of German culture like Sam Houston, the evening must have been impressive indeed.

The travelers reached home late that summer, doubtless feeling much more like a family than when they left. For Sam, the long and difficult years since Edith's death were at an end. In the meantime, his younger sister, Gertrude, and her husband, George Woodward, were well on their way to creating another large family.

In his own way George Woodward (1863–1952) would make as large an impact on Philadelphia as his father-in-law Henry Howard Houston. Over the years he and Gertrude would continue to build attractive houses in Chestnut Hill. George would also become an important political reformer whose impact continues to be felt in housing, municipal health, state and local taxation, and in the Philadelphia city charters of 1919 and 1951.

Born in Wilkes-Barre, Pennsylvania, on 22 June 1863 to Stanley and Sarah (Butler) Woodward, George Woodward came into the world as Robert E. Lee and his Army of Virginia were poised for a bold thrust into Pennsylvania.[32] The expectant parents worried that their second child might arrive in the midst of a Confederate invasion, but the attackers were repulsed at Gettysburg, the Union was saved, and the baby survived into the nuclear age.

Like all children, George Woodward was shaped by the people and events that surrounded him, and by the historical currents that gave rise to both. By 1863 his family had lived in and around Wilkes-Barre for nearly a century, most of the Woodwards' immediate ancestors having come from Connecticut. Their native state had once claimed the whole northern tier of Pennsylvania and had wrangled endlessly with the Pennsylvanians until the American Revolution united the former colonies and eventually put an end to the land disputes.

Two of Woodward's great-grandfathers had helped to win independence. One was Captain Samuel Richards of Farmington, Connecticut, who kept a wartime diary that Woodward proudly published in 1909.[33] The other was Colonel Zebulon Butler, whose men suffered huge casualties at the hands of the British and their Indian allies during the appropriately named "Massacre of Wyoming." The American Revolution and its officers were thus woven into the fabric of the family's heritage, as were some of the earliest settlers of British North America.[34] Richard Woodward had emigrated to Watertown, Massachusetts, in 1634, just four years after John Winthrop's "errand" into the New England wilderness, while the Butler side of the family could trace itself back to John Haynes, governor of Massachusetts in 1635, and to Gurdon Saltonstall, a governor of Connecticut in the early eighteenth century.

Butlers and Woodwards continued to hold public office after moving into Pennsylvania's Wyoming Valley. Zebulon Butler became the first sheriff of Luzerne County, and in the early nineteenth century Abisha Woodward was a constable, sheriff, justice of the peace, and finally an associate judge of Wayne County—the first of four generations of Woodward judges, each the eldest son of an eldest son. George Washington Woodward, young George's grandfather and namesake, served two terms in the U.S. House of Representatives, was chief justice of the Pennsylvania Supreme Court, and was nominated by President Polk to the Supreme Court of the United States, only to have the appointment blocked by Simon Cameron in the Senate. Both Cameron and the Republican machine that he ruled in Pennsylvania remained objects of everlasting scorn in the Woodward household.

Most of all, Judge Woodward was a fierce defender of states' rights and the Democratic party, and when South Carolina seceded in December 1860 he addressed a large crowd outside Independence Hall in Philadelphia, insisting that the Southerners had a right to leave the Union if they chose.[35] When war broke out he became a Peace Democrat as well as an outspoken opponent of Abraham Lincoln. The president's suspension of habeas corpus in 1862 particularly outraged the judge, and he denounced Lincoln as a tyrant and dictator.[36] In 1864 he ran unsuccessfully for the governorship of Pennsylvania, all the while claiming that the South could be lured back into the Union with assurances that they could keep their slaves. Although the Republicans referred to him and the other Peace Democrats as vicious "copperheads," Woodward was undeterred and continued his verbal campaign against the monstrous regime in Washington until Lincoln was assassinated.[37]

Judge Woodward's son Stanley (and young George's father) practiced law and continued the family's Democratic politics, but failed in his bid for the Pennsylvania state senate and was equally unsuccessful five years later when he ran for the U.S. Congress. Despite his failures to win office, Stanley was regarded as an important leader in Wilkes-Barre. Local citizens often turned to him for advice, and it was he who organized the Wyoming Centennial Celebration in 1878, the high point of which was a parade on the Fourth of July, with President Rutherford B. Hayes riding through the main street of Wilkes-Barre in the Woodwards' family carriage. Finally, in 1879 Stanley was appointed an associate judge of Luzerne County, advancing to president judge eleven years later.[38]

Politics and even presidents were thus part of the scenery as George Woodward grew up, but it was Grandmother Butler who made the most lasting impression. "Of all the members of our happy family," Woodward wrote more than a half century later in his *Memoirs of a Mediocre Man*, "the one I loved the most was my mother's mother."[39] Unlike other women of the day, she was intensely interested in politics and "was a perfect mine of information."[40] She had taught in a Presbyterian Sunday school for fifty years and had an unswerving "New England conscience." Woodward remembered that "she was the only one who ever corrected us and she was so consistent . . . and so consistently right in pointing out to us our mistakes that I had immense respect and affection for her." This Calvinist conscience may also have been reinforced by the Puritan and then Congregationalist faith of his Woodward ancestors, though by his father's generation the family had become Episcopalians. For young George, as for his future Houston in-laws, this strong sense of religious morality would become an important motive in future actions, both public and private.[41]

It was this grandmother, too, who taught Woodward to love good literature. She delighted in reading aloud, and together they read through every novel of Sir Walter Scott. One day when George and his brother, Butler, were sick she read all of *Lorna Doone*, "her voice as good [at the end] as in the beginning."[42] When George went to college she wrote him every week. Rather than waste expensive stationery, she wrote on odd scraps of paper, a lesson in thrift that he never forgot.

Woodward had very little to say by comparison about his parents, describing his father as "quite handsome and with so much charm and bonhomie that he had lots of friends."[43] Neither parent was a strict disciplinarian. "My mother was almost too easy going," he recalled; neither he nor his brother "were ever spanked and were seldom reproved for anything [they] did or said."[44]

Woodward wrote even less about his brother Butler, but both boys must have enjoyed their childhoods immensely. There was skating and rafting on the Susquehanna River and summers with the family at Bear Creek, about ten miles from the house in Wilkes-Barre, a long uphill pull for their horses which took a good half-day to get them there. They lodged in a three-story wooden hotel with wide porches around all three floors. They swam and fished in the lake, jumped across floating logs at a nearby sawmill, and took dangerous rides over the mill dam on sharpened wooden planks.

Winter, of course, meant school. George ran home the first day and had to be taken back in disgrace, but once settled at school, he could be as mischievous as the next boy. One year he and the others stole a number of the neighbors' chickens and hid them in an abandoned stable near the school, plucking the feathers for Indian headdresses and making elaborate plans for their own secret poultry farm until the owners finally discovered their missing fowl and spoiled all the fun. Although his brother went off to St. Paul's school, in New Hampshire, George's school days ended at the Wilkes-Barre Academy and in the fall of 1883 he was ready to enter Yale College.[45]

George should have gone to college two years earlier, but his father could not afford to send two children at once, thus George had to wait until Butler had graduated from Yale before he could take his own place at

New Haven.[46] George left no record of his feelings as he left home at the end of the summer, but like any young man going off to college for the first time, he was no doubt anxious as he climbed aboard the train and waved good-bye to his parents and friends. Yet, he must have gone away with a firm sense of belonging, along with a large dose of social confidence. His family had lived in Wilkes-Barre since the pioneer days and had become highly respected as lawyers, judges, and officeholders. Even the decision to enter Yale was dictated by local tradition: generations of Wilkes-Barre men, including George's father and brother, had gone back to Connecticut for college, and George was happy to continue the line.

When Woodward arrived at Yale, the college was still deeply rooted in the past; it was not yet a great world institution and the elective system was still something of a Harvard heresy. Students took an identical curriculum during their first two years, composed almost wholly of classical languages and mathematics.[47] Woodward hated math and flunked nearly every course he took, but managed to clear the deficiencies by returning early each fall, hiring a tutor, and taking the exams over again.[48] During junior and senior years the courses were more contemporary in content and students had some latitude in selection—though no one could escape President Porter's "Evidences of Christianity." Many of Woodward's classmates took the extremely popular William Graham Sumner for political economy. Woodward did not join them, but in later years he frequently quoted Sumner, and his son Stanley recalls that he spoke approvingly of Sumner's works.[49]

Yale was also intensely religious during Woodward's student days, with compulsory morning chapel and an overall college goal of molding Christian gentlemen for a career of useful service. But what most Yale men remembered was their devotion to college and class. Woodward never forgot the college songs and the tours that he took as leader of the Yale glee club. He played on the freshman football team, rowed with his class crew, and was invited into a number of clubs: the Scroll and Key, the University Club, and the Delta Kappa Epsilon fraternity. Later he remarked that the keen competition for a place in the clubs was excellent preparation for the real challenges that lay ahead.[50]

Woodward clearly loved Yale and was no doubt happy to know that graduation in May 1887 would not mean moving from New Haven immediately—because he had decided to enter the premedical course at Yale's Sheffield School the following autumn. His intense desire to become a doctor, however, went back to childhood and stemmed from his great respect for their family physician. "He healed and comforted and we all worshipped him," Woodward wrote in his *Memoirs*. The family doctor loomed larger than life in a town like Wilkes-Barre, and to Woodward there was "no other career that gives so genuine a sense of power as that of the intelligent and conscientious physician. The statesman, the lawyer, the author, the big business man, even the great churchman," he added, "all must humble themselves in our common dust before this searcher of bodies and minds."[51]

At Sheffield, Woodward studied hard to complete two years of work in just one year, writing a thesis on the role of saliva in the digestive process.[52] He was forced to chew rubber bands all day in order to extract enough of the liquid from his own mouth for the experiments, which led him to claim with some exaggeration that he had been an early martyr to medical science: his "salivary glands were overworked," he remarked, "and never fully recovered."[53]

On the recommendation of professors at Sheffield, Woodward applied to the University of Pennsylvania Medical School, enrolling in the fall of 1888. The Penn Medical School was already highly regarded and could boast being the oldest institution of its kind in the nation, although its greatest days were yet to come. The course of study was still only three years; there were no real facilities for research; and state examinations were as yet only an idea.[54] Nevertheless, Woodward and his cohorts had a number of excellent teachers, among them the celebrated William Osler, who was destined to become one of the great medical educators of his time.[55]

Woodward described Osler as "a perfect teacher and a charming person."[56] He recalled that Osler had a habit of pausing before an important word or phrase in a way that made the students remember the most important points of a lecture. At the same time, Osler was beginning to pursue his lifelong interest in public health by studying hundreds of malaria cases in the Philadelphia hospitals. Later at Johns Hopkins, Osler would launch a highly successful crusade to rid Baltimore of typhoid fever, setting an example that was surely not lost on young George Woodward, who became an effective public health advocate in his own right. Osler remained a model scientist and physician for Woodward, and Harvey Cushing's two-volume biography of Osler occupied an honored place in Woodward's personal library.[57]

The study of medicine fascinated Woodward enough that he gave up his Christmas holidays to study anatomy and histology. He was determined to secure an internship at the venerable Pennsylvania Hospital but had to settle for a position at German Hospital, forerunner of the present-day Lankenau. Before his interview he practiced addressing patients in German and so charmed the medical staff with his descriptions of an earlier visit to Munich's Hofbrauhaus that they forgot to examine him on his medical knowledge. He was surprised to find himself "number 1" on the list of candidates.

Woodward enjoyed the *gemutlich* atmosphere of the German Hospital—from the effusive "*guten morgens*" of the older German doctors to the delightfully sentimental Lutheran nuns. He and the other interns even discovered a sister they could flirt with—until she was finally found out and dismissed by the mother superior. It was during this year, too, that Thomas Eakins asked him to pose for the now famous *Agnew Clinic,* a huge group portrait of Dr. Hayes Agnew operating before an amphitheater filled with medical students from the University of Pennsylvania.[58]

Woodward finished his internship on 4 July 1892 and returned to New Haven, ostensibly to open a medical practice. But he also returned to his alma mater, as he put it, "to be . . . with Yale men."[59] He rented a suite at the corner of College and Crown Streets and nailed up his shingle, an immense sign given to him by an old medical friend named G. W. Daggett. He attracted few patients, however, and mistook a case of typhoid fever, losing the case to a doctor who diagnosed it correctly. Meanwhile he became a clinical assistant in the Yale Medical School.[60]

After a year and a half in New Haven, Woodward took down his sign and moved to Philadelphia. The impetus for leaving was his engagement to Gertrude Houston, whom he had met through a mutual friend at Glen Summit, a resort near Wilkes-Barre. The two courted while Woodward was a medical student at Penn, and he skipped classes on at least two occasions to go walking with Gertrude in Chestnut Hill, later causing him to miss a couple of questions in his oral examinations.

According to Woodward, Henry Howard Houston set down two conditions for his marriage to Gertrude: "1. I must never give my wife allopathic medicine, and 2. I must live in Philadelphia."[61] Houston understandably wanted to have his daughter nearby, but the reservations about his future son-in-law's professional ministrations seem to stem from Gertrude's already strong belief in homeopathy, then a respected system of medical treatment.[62] Despite fatherly strictures, the couple was wed at St. Martin's church on 9 October 1894, and they set out for their honeymoon in a carriage lent by the bride's father. A comfortable trip in one of the Pennsylvania Railroad's private cars would have been easy to arrange, but the newlyweds preferred to go by carriage and avoid the cities, staying in country inns along the way. They drove for nearly three weeks through the changing autumn foliage, following a route along the Delaware River into New York state and back through New Jersey. Love of nature, combined with an early attachment to older ways, doubtless lay behind the decision—values that would remain with both for the rest of their lives.

Returning to Chestnut Hill, the couple settled into a house that Henry Howard Houston built for them on the southwest corner of Willow Grove Avenue and St. Martin's Lane, directly across the street from St. Martin's church. Their yard backed onto the park that Houston had created for guests of the Wissahickon Inn and that was later used as a playing field by the Chestnut Hill Academy, inspiring George and Gertrude to borrow the name St. Martin's Green for their house on the corner.[63]

It was there, on 27 February 1896, that the first of their five children was born. The roads were icy that night and the doctor who had been attending Gertrude arrived well after the event, the father and household cook delivering the child instead, with father-in-law Houston's qualms about George's medical ideas being forgotten for the moment. They named him Henry Howard Houston Woodward in honor of his grandfather. Another son, George, Jr., followed in 1897, then Stanley in 1899, Charles in 1904, and Gertrude (Quita) in 1909. The father confessed that he was never very good with small children, passing on his sister-in-law's remark that "when I played 'hobble de hoy' with my children, it always looked as if I were their stepfather."[64] But he was always a devoted parent and would enjoy them all greatly as they grew older.

Gertrude, of course, had plenty to do looking after their growing household. She also managed to be quite active with the Women's Auxiliary of Episcopal Church on the local, diocesan, and national levels. Her particular interest was the church's Indian missions, prompting her to give thousands of dollars to Indian causes over the decades. It was also Gertrude who named or renamed many streets in Chestnut Hill after native American tribes, such as Seminole, Shawnee, and Navajo. And one of her prized possessions was a genuine Indian, birch-bark canoe. "I think I must be part Indian," she often remarked to family and friends.[65]

Meanwhile, George decided to have another try at general practice by opening an office in the house and again waiting for patients to come. His *Memoirs* are completely silent about this event, but his son Stanley surmised that Dr. Woodward had a hard time competing with the well established and much beloved Dr. Cheston. It also seems that Gertrude feared her own children would become infected by sick patients coming into the house for treatment.[66] Sometime in 1896 or 1897, then, George gave up his shingle and never ventured into family practice again.

Woodward himself has supplied other clues to his early retirement from medicine. He had found many of the cases at German Hospital nerveracking, while his misdiagnosis of the typhoid case in New Haven admittedly had undermined his confidence; in the last analysis he probably did not have the right temperament to be a physician.[67] And next to the achievements of a Judge Woodward or a Henry Howard Houston, a general practice in Chestnut Hill may have seemed small indeed. Whatever his reasons for abandoning practical medicine, Woodward was later quite sure that he had "chose[n] the wrong profession."[68]

Despite his disappointment, Woodward would identify with the medical profession in many ways, signing himself "George Woodward, M.D." for the rest of his life. He continued to admire the best physicians for their successful blend of humanitarianism and science. It was a deep regard for these traits that would help make Woodward into a public-health crusader and progressive politician.

CHAPTER 5

# Progressive Reformer

LIKE MANY OTHER AMERICANS in the early twentieth century, Henry Howard Houston's heirs were deeply concerned about the manifold problems of national life. Many of these difficulties had arisen from the rapid industrialization and urbanization that Houston himself had helped to promote after the Civil War. Philadelphia was no exception.[1] By 1900 its population was just under 1.3 million; in twenty years it would increase by half a million more. This astonishing growth was fueled by Philadelphia's bustling port, still second only to New York in the value of goods passing over its docks, and by the city's prosperous and varied industries, leading Philadelphians to brag that they were the "workshop of the world." Baldwin locomotives, Cramp ships, Stetson hats, Keystone watches, and Fels-Naptha soap, along with scores of textile products, poured out of the city's factories and mills.

Many of the workers were native-born, in a city that still had a smaller immigrant population than most of the other urban centers of the country. Nevertheless, Philadelphia was home to an increasing number of immigrants from southern and eastern Europe. By 1910 there were more than 70,000 Russian Jews in the city and an equivalent number of Italians. Most of them had to take low-paying jobs and live in the most crowded and undesirable parts of the city, with South Philadelphia containing some of the most blighted neighborhoods on the eastern seaboard.

Philadelphia's notorious Republican machine worked hard to organize the new arrivals and get them to the polls. Loyal voters, in turn, could approach their precinct captains and ward leaders for a multitude of favors, ranging from a job on the city payroll to help in getting out of a minor scrape with the law. But the city machine was notoriously deficient when it came to providing clean drinking water or regulating slum housing. And, worst of all, Philadelphians seemed to take the corruption and political lethargy more or less in stride. When the famous muckraker Lincoln Steffens visited Philadelphia in 1903, he found it "the most corrupt and the most contented" city in the nation.[2]

Both George Woodward and his brother-in-law, Sam Houston, were moved by strong religious conviction as well as by a sense of civic duty to join others in trying to alleviate the worst of these modern conditions. While Woodward's concerns would propel him into the political arena, Houston's efforts would remain completely private. In a talk delivered before the Men's Club at Holy Trinity Church in Collingswood, New Jersey, for example, Houston proposed that moral behavior by individual Christians could go a long way toward eliminating poverty and exploitation. "The true Christian," he insisted, "does not employ children when they should be at play or at school! The true Christian does not employ women at hours [when] they should be at home! The true Christian does not grind down the employee! . . . The true Christian does not compel any man to live in what Tennyson called 'the rotten warrens of the poor.'"[3]

Meanwhile Sam had abandoned the Democratic party of his father in favor of the Republicans, citing his approval of their call for higher tariffs. In the years ahead he would also be pleased by the G.O.P.'s more conservative approach to government. But politics aside, both Sam and Charlotte believed that they should help to alleviate urban distress. Charlotte bought and renovated a block of houses on Catharine Street in the heart of South Philadelphia, renting them at low rates to needy families, most of them Italian. Sam and his mother also established and maintained St. Martha's settlement house at Eighth and Snyder, also in South Philadelphia.[4] Such private efforts, Houston believed, were the best and safest way to deal with urban problems, and he regarded any attempt to involve government as a dangerous intrusion into the private sector.[5] In this respect he was in full accord with most other well-to-do Philadelphians who had an extraordinary distaste for government interference, a phenomenon that Sam Bass Warner has explored so tellingly in his book *Philadelphia: The Private City.*[6]

Although George Woodward would share some of this distaste for public solutions, he became an outspoken advocate of political reform and limited governmental regulation at the state and local levels. There was, in fact, much about Woodward's background that inclined him toward political reform, embodying as he did many of the personal traits that historians have come to associate with progressive reformers.[7]

Most important was a strong sense of Christian morality. Like his brother-in-law, Sam Houston, he faithfully attended services at St. Martin's and contributed generously to its charitable programs. He also joined Sam on the vestry, where he served for a number of years as accounting warden. At the same time Woodward had a passion for efficiency, practicality, and science—another distinguishing mark of the progressive reformer—no matter how much it appeared to be at odds with the supernatural bases of religious faith. Like many middle- and upper-class citizens, he also worried that poverty and discontent among workers might prove an ideal spawning ground for socialism and other radical programs. And, like a disproportionate number of progressives, Woodward had strong New England ties, and exhibited that region's long-standing heritage of leadership (which E. Digby Baltzell has contrasted so effectively with the Philadelphia Quakers' distaste for political office or elitism of any kind).[8] Finally, Woodward was no stranger to political life. For generations his family had been embroiled in state and local politics, usually belonging to the minority party in Pennsylvania and often taking unpopular positions on the issues of the day—a heartening legacy for anyone who would attempt to reform Philadelphia politics.

Despite Philadelphia's reputation for political corruption, Woodward was not alone in his desire for better government. Outraged citizens had periodically mounted crusades against the bosses.[9] They had even won elections from time to time, but most were political amateurs or nonpartisan politicians who could not compete with the machine in the long run. Like the Mugwumps of the 1880s, they failed to understand that reformers would have to organize as effectively as the bosses if they were to make any real progress. George Woodward, who had begun his political life as a partisan Democrat, joined this group of genteel reformers in the late nineties; interestingly, his entry also came as an extension of his medical concerns.

After closing his office in Chestnut Hill, Woodward worked for a while as an associate at the University of Pennsylvania's newly built William Pepper Laboratory, determined to become "a laboratory man of science." He did research on milk and published two papers on the subject that landed him a directorship in the Walker-Gordon Milk Company.[10] Fascinating though he found his research at the Pepper Laboratory, Woodward was glad to accept an appointment to the Philadelphia Board of Health in 1897, which was made possible when a medical friend recommended him to the mayor. It was this position more than any other that provided him a springboard into municipal reform.

As a physician Woodward was appalled by the periodic typhoid epidemics in Philadelphia that took as many as a thousand lives a year. It had already been established that the disease was transmitted through raw sewage in the water supply, and Woodward suspected that the Schuylkill River, one of the major sources of water for the city, was the primary culprit. He convinced fellow board members to sample and test the water, borrowed a launch from the Fairmount Park Commission and, with the board's chemist and bacteriologist, took samples from every "sewer and privy discharging into the river" all the way to Reading.[11] They also took numerous photographs with which to document their case. In October 1897 they published their results in a 116-page pamphlet, all bound in "bright yellow paper," and distributed thousands of them to journalists, politicians, and interested citizens.[12] Citing the experience of many European cities, they recommended the construction of filtration plants to purify Philadelphia's water.

A terrible typhoid outbreak in the winter of 1899 permitted Woodward and the board to push their case even harder. At the height of the epidemic the Board of Health was reporting over 100 new cases a day, with 430 citizens dying of the infection between 1 January and 25 March alone. Reform-minded newspapers like *The North American* and *The Public Ledger* joined citizens groups and the Emergency Committee of the Manufacturers Club to demand funds for filtration plants from the two city councils (known as the Select and Common Councils) that then existed in Philadelphia. When the councilmen continued to balk, Woodward asked the Board of Health to declare the Schuylkill River a public nuisance and sue the city for abatement. Mayor Samuel Ashbridge was so furious at the board for embarrassing him and the city administration that he had the state legislature abolish and replace it with a bureau more amenable to mayoral control.

But too much public indignation had been aroused for the mayor and councilmen to avoid the filtration question, and in September 1899 the councils finally authorized the first plants. Unfortunately, the facilities were installed in stages and it was not until March 1909 that the entire water supply was being filtered. There were no more typhoid epidemics after that, thanks in large part to the efforts of George Woodward. It had taken twelve years to rid the city of typhoid, but the hard work paid off in the end. Woodward also learned that public health had as much to do with politics as it did with medical science.[13]

Just two months after the city councils approved the first filtration plants, Woodward himself won a seat on the Common Council, though nothing is known of his activities as a councilman. There can be no doubt, however, about his energetic participation in overthrowing the city's political machine in 1905. At this time the Republican organization was run by state insurance commissioner Israel Durham who, with his loyal assistants, had turned out the vote year after year, insuring large Republican victories through massive election frauds that included bribery at the polls, multiple voting, and stuffing ballot boxes with the names of dead or nonexistent citizens. Durham and his machine amassed huge campaign chests by assessing city employees; in 1903 they collected over $349,000 in this way. They also raised large sums by awarding contracts for construction projects and city services to favored companies in return for generous kickbacks. There was no competitive bidding and work was often shoddy. All of this resulted in a tremendous waste of city funds, amounting to more than $5 million a year by one estimate.

The minority Democrats had no chance whatever of winning municipal elections, and many of the Democratic leaders were actually in the pay of the Republican machine. Under the circumstances, Woodward decided to abandon his inherited allegiance to the Democratic party. Over the next decade he would support several third-party reform movements and eventually become what he called an "independent Republican."

Woodward's first real experiences at municipal reform came in the autumn of 1904, when the city's large vote for Theodore Roosevelt breathed new life into the movement for better local government. Since 1891, most of the reformers had belonged to the Municipal League, now moribund by years of failure and ridicule from the press. In mid-November the league called a citizens' meeting at the Bourse where the assembled multitude heard fiery denunciations of the political machine. At an even larger meeting a month later reformers decided to create a new organization and christened it the Committee of Seventy, with George Woodward among the nine men chosen to serve on its executive board.[14]

Within weeks the Committee organized an independent City party and entered candidates for the elections in February 1905 when Philadelphians would go to the polls to choose councilmen and city magistrates. With the support of Edwin Van Valkenburg's crusading *North American,* and several other independent newspapers like the *Press* and *The Public Ledger,* the City party focused its efforts on wards where reform sentiment was most pronounced. They lost, but their candidates made a respectable showing against the prevailing city machine. The local clergy then came to their aid, forming a citywide ministerial association for better government and holding prayer meetings to enlist the hosts of heaven in their battle.

The machine made a fatal mistake when Durham asked the city councils to give the United Gas Improvement Company a seventy-five-year lease on the municipal gas works. In return the city would receive $25 million for various construction projects. The sum was far less than the city would have made from annual rents over the same period and it was clear to the reformers that much of the $25 million would end up as graft. Mass rallies and protests forced the councils to abandon the gas bill and Mayor John Weaver was pressured into joining the reformers. Voting lists were cleansed of fraudulent names and those who had tampered with them were tried and sent to jail. In November 1905 reform candidates won a resounding victory.

Woodward worked hard for the City party all that year, soliciting campaign contributions and speaking on behalf of its candidates. He also wrote a glowing report of their victory for the 2 December issue of *Outlook* magazine. Special police were sent to guard the polls, he reported, and they made numerous arrests. "The patrol-wagons brought . . . load after load of prisoners, and, driving into the courtyard of the City Hall, discharging their loads into the cells amid the cheering, hooting, and howling of a mob of citizens delighted that the tables had been turned upon the old, arrogant 'gang.'" Their victory that night unleashed the spirit of an old-fashioned revival meeting, Woodward wrote, as "triumphant citizens" marched through the streets singing "Onward Christian Soldiers." In his conclusion Woodward himself seemed to fall under the evangelical spell: "The invincible 'Organization' has been shattered by the uprising of the plain people," he exulted. "David has slain Goliath. Elijah has called upon the God of Israel, and the priests of Baal are slain." [15]

The momentum of reform carried over into early 1906 when Boies Penrose, the Republican boss of Pennsylvania, finally agreed to convene a special session of the state legislature to consider several bills urged by the reformers. Legislation was passed that required personal registration of voters in place of lists drawn up by the parties; mandated uniform primaries for city and county offices; and forbade solicitations among municipal employees. A corrupt practices act required candidates to file reports on campaign contributions and expenditures.

Unfortunately, this legislation gave many reformers a false sense of security and their momentum collapsed as the months passed. Mayor Weaver deserted the reformers when the City party refused to endorse him for the governorship, most of the election reforms went unenforced, and the machine easily won the mayor's office in 1907.[16]

Woodward was not one to give up easily, but he decided to change tactics and concentrate on researching municipal problems, an obvious extension of his belief in careful investigation and dissemination of the facts. In 1908 he organized and largely financed the Bureau of Municipal Research, modeled on a similar organization in New York City. With a staff of specialists, the bureau collected data on specific municipal problems, published their results, and made recommendations to the city government—all the while maintaining a nonpartisan stance. One of their early investigations showed that many goods sold in Philadelphia were inaccurately counted or weighed and these revelations resulted in a Bureau of Weights and Measures, created in 1913. The Bureau of Municipal Research also persuaded the city to adopt promotion examinations for employees, prepared modern accounting techniques for city departments, compiled a digest of municipal health ordinances, and revised the city's police manual.[17]

In the meantime, reform sentiment was building throughout the nation and some of its fervor spilled over into Philadelphia, where local reformers scored a magnificent victory over the city machine in 1911 when they elected Rudolph Blankenburg mayor. A longtime municipal reformer of German background, he was nicknamed "Old Dutch Cleanser." Woodward supported the reform ticket and was greatly pleased with Blankenburg's victory.[18]

The year 1912 brought the three-cornered presidential campaign of Woodrow Wilson, William Howard Taft, and Theodore Roosevelt, but Woodward did not join most of the other local reformers in supporting Roosevelt. By 1912 he appreciated the inherent weakness of temporary third parties and resented Roosevelt's division of Republican ranks. And as later remarks would show, he mistrusted strong executives like Roosevelt, believing that the lion's share of power should rest with the legislature. He accordingly voted for Taft, never forgiving Roosevelt for Wilson's victory that year.[19]

Like many reformers during this period, Woodward did not confine his efforts to fighting in the public arena. There were numerous evils that government in the early twentieth century was not equipped to remedy and, according to the laissez-faire principles shared by Woodward and many others of the day, was not entitled to undertake.

One of these areas was housing. Philadelphia was actually far better off than other major cities in this regard, known even then as "the city of homes." It was not hemmed in by water like Boston and New York and was therefore able to expand to the north, west, and south, providing relatively cheap land and resulting in few high-rise tenements. As any aerial view of Philadelphia will confirm, it was and remains an essentially flat city with miles and miles of row houses spreading out as far as the eye can see. Yet there were plenty of dilapidated dwellings, particularly in the river wards south and east of City Hall. There tiny "bandboxes" had been built in dreary alleyways or on crowded back lots. Many were without indoor plumbing, with nearly 61,000 properties in the city still served by backyard privies—a dangerous source of typhoid fever and other infectious diseases.

Woodward's experiences with the Board of Health and the Bureau of Municipal Research doubtless made him keenly aware of the housing problem, a concern that also ranked high in the minds of other progressives throughout the nation. For them, cramped and unsanitary dwellings were not only a source of disease but also a breeding ground for crime and social discontent. They also continued to share the nineteenth-century belief that the home should be an attractive moral sanctuary where the family could overcome the evils and stresses of modern life through a devotion to traditional, middle-class values. Such sentiments moved middle-class women in particular to visit the slums in an effort to disseminate their own values and in so doing rescue the poor from their miseries. Realizing that sporadic visits were not enough, some decided to found settlement houses in the slums where they could live among the disadvantaged and be a more permanent source of instruction and example, while others concentrated on providing better housing for their unfortunate neighbors. Among those dedicated to finding better housing for the working poor was Philadelphia's Octavia Hill Association, a group that Woodward joined in the early twentieth century.[20]

The Association had been founded in 1896 by several women of the Civic Club and was inspired by the work of Octavia Hill in London. An ardent Christian Socialist, Miss Hill had persuaded her friend John Ruskin in 1864 to purchase three houses, renovate them, and rent them to working-class families at low rents. Although a wealthy man, Ruskin asked for a five percent return on his capital, largely to convince others that investing in slum properties could be both profitable and humane. The idea caught on and Miss Hill found herself presiding over several thousand properties by the end of the century.

Besides providing decent housing for the "deserving poor," Miss Hill also wanted to inculcate middle-class values among her tenants, insisting that they pay their rent on time and refrain from immoral behavior. To carry out this program she made use of "friendly rent collectors" who served as unofficial social workers, keeping watch over the tenants and offering them practical advice. Finally, Miss Hill shared Ruskin's belief in "organic communities" and insisted on acquiring several houses at a time in the same location.

Under the direction of Helen Parrish, the Octavia Hill Association of Philadelphia adopted most of the ideas developed in the London experiment, including the friendly rent collectors. They purchased whole blocks of houses, many of them in South Philadelphia, renovated them, and rented them at low rates. All were wired for electricity and equipped with indoor toilets and water supplies. The association was particularly success-ful in combining small yards and alleyways into sunny courtyards for all the tenants to enjoy.[21]

Woodward was an enthusiastic director of the association from the beginning. He built a model tenement for them at the corner of Seventh and Catharine Streets in the heart of South Philadelphia's Italian section, appropriately naming it the Casa Ravello. Woodward maintained owner-ship of the building, but the association managed it and collected the rents. Casa Ravello was a four-story brick structure containing thirty six-room apartments, designed in an obvious Italianate style, with shops on the ground floor framed in large rounded arches. On upper stories there were balconies that overlooked the street, while the structure as a whole exuded an unmistakable Florentine flavor.

In many ways Woodward's tenement was like a settlement house and apartment building combined. On the large roof there was a play-ground for the children, and in July and August the association ran a sum-mer school there, while on the corner of the ground floor there was a clinic where mothers could bring their babies for examinations and receive ad-vice on child care. Two doctors kept regular office hours and nurses visited homes in the neighborhood.[22]

Casa Ravello was an undeniable success, but the association generally preferred the smaller row houses and single-unit dwellings that were so typical of Philadelphia. Of course, their resources were limited, and most of the city's low-cost housing was beyond their reach. To compensate they mounted a campaign for municipal regulations and inspections. They launched a preliminary survey of their own, hiring Emily Dinwiddie, who had been a housing investigator in New York City, to carry out the project. Woodward was on the committee set up to monitor the plan, and he no doubt contributed substantially to cover expenses.

The conditions described by Miss Dinwiddie were truly horrible. In one house she discovered thirty-three individuals belonging to eight dif-ferent families. She noted a goat in the back room of a first-floor grocery store and three dogs in the rooms upstairs, while in another case she re-ported that ten households were using one alley hydrant for all their water. In many instances yards and alleys were heaped with trash surrounded by stagnant pools of rain water that became an ugly frozen mass in winter. With such evidence in hand, the association put two ordinances before the city councils in 1906 that called for better water facilities in alley houses and the installation of drainage sewers. Both ordinances failed, but in 1907 the councils passed a law providing for the licensing and inspection of tenement houses, and the Octavia Hill Association was asked to give advice to the director of public health and charities on how the ordinance should be carried out.[23]

Neither the licensing and inspection act nor the Octavia Hill Association's attempts to house the working poor did anything for the truly destitute. Woodward was moved to do something for these unfortunates; in 1912, at the suggestion of evangelist George Long, he built a seven-story cement shelter on the 1000 block of Locust Street, an area then known as "Hell's Half Acre." He called the shelter the "Inasmuch Mission," from the verse in St. Matthew, "Inasmuch as you have done it unto the least of these you have done it unto Me," an unmistakable allusion to Woodward's strong religious motivations. His son Stanley remembered the mission well: "The price of an overnight room with clean bed was 25 cents, but the lodger was required to take a shower and was given a pair of cotton pajamas. If the poor man didn't have 25 cents, he was given credit and taken in anyway."[24]

Poor children in the city were yet another group who received Woodward's attention. In 1904 he organized and financed the Child Labor Association of Pennsylvania, an organization that campaigned for child labor laws which finally cleared the Pennsylvania legislature in 1915. From 1913 to 1928 he was president of the Children's Aid Society, a group that raised money to buy clothing and food and to provide medical care for the children of impoverished families. And in the years ahead he would donate land for parks and playgrounds in several areas of the city.[25]

Poverty in the inner districts of Philadelphia had preoccupied George Woodward throughout the first decades of the twentieth century; it was a problem that he would turn to again and again in future decades. But around 1910 he began to focus increasing attention on his own Chestnut Hill in the far northwestern corner of the city.

# CHAPTER 6

# *The Model Suburb*

BACK IN CHESTNUT HILL, in the section that Henry Howard Houston had named Wissahickon Heights, George and Gertrude Woodward had already decided to continue the family's real estate undertakings. Changing the area's name to St. Martin's in honor of the nearby church, they eventually built about 180 houses. And, like Houston before them, they continued the practice of renting rather than selling their residential units.

Woodward's motives and methods for extending the family's building enterprises in Chestnut Hill were in many ways an extension of his progressivism, and thus betrayed some of the same contradictions that had characterized his own reform ideas and those of American progressives in general. For him and many other progressives, the suburb was a way of combatting the manifold evils of urban, industrial life. Since the dirt, noise, crime, and overcrowding of the city seemed overwhelming, the only way to provide a completely wholesome residential atmosphere was to create a new community where a healthy environment could be consciously fashioned and maintained. Such a solution appealed to the scientific side of Woodward and other suburban planners, who could turn their energy and intelligence to molding a complete physical and social environment.[1]

But there was also a large sense in which suburban planners had abandoned the city. Woodward himself had done a great deal through the Octavia Hill Association and his sponsorship of the Inasmuch Mission to address urban housing problems. Yet barring some form of state socialism, which might guarantee decent housing to low-income families, there appeared little that he or others could do to reverse the massive forces of urban decay. Given his later opposition to ambitious social welfare programs, it is understandable that Woodward would seek private solutions to the housing problem in an area of the city where he could actually fashion and control the environment to a large degree. He could only hope that others would follow his example in other suburban or even working-class districts.

There were also reactionary elements in Woodward's and other suburban developers' responses to urban problems. In their desire to escape from the city, they hoped to recapture what they saw as a simpler, more salubrious way of life that many associated with an earlier, rural America. At the same time, many suburban dwellers, the vast majority of them Protestants of British background, felt increasingly uncomfortable with the millions of southern and eastern Europeans who had been flooding into American cities since the last decade of the nineteenth century. Convinced that the alien ways of these newest immigrants were a threat to American values, many prosperous natives sought homogeneous enclaves in the suburbs where they might recapture both the texture and values of pre-industrial village life. This ambivalence that many turn-of-the-century suburbanites felt about the modern world was clearly shared by George Woodward, who called for professional, scientific solutions to modern problems while clinging to many older customs and habits in his personal life.

The sources of Woodward's ideas about suburban development were varied, as they were with most of his contemporaries. The tangible and enduring work of his father-in-law Houston was obviously an important factor. So, too, were his activities on behalf of the Octavia Hill Association. Although far from the slums of South Philadelphia, Woodward would apply several concepts that he had learned through the association to the St. Martin's experiment: in both South Philadelphia and Chestnut Hill he was far more interested in promoting sound and attractive housing than he was in making money. Just as with the Octavia Hill Association, he expected only a modest return on his initial investment. His belief that intelligent professionals like himself could improve society through controlling the environment was an important factor as well.

Woodward may have also been influenced by the aesthetic concepts of men like John Ruskin and William Morris. There is no direct evidence that either he or Gertrude read Ruskin, but Woodward might have been aware of Ruskin's influence on the Octavia Hill Association. Like Ruskin, he preferred natural building materials, nearly always selecting the locally quarried stone. Like Ruskin, too, he believed that attractive housing could uplift its occupants morally and spiritually. Furthermore, the Woodwards owned a volume of arts and crafts essays with an introduction by William Morris, and they certainly shared his insistence on careful craftsmanship, employing skilled Italian stoneworkers and the best carpenters and cabinetmakers of the region.[2] They also belonged to the Arts and Crafts Society of Philadelphia. Finally, Woodward was well aware of the English garden city movement, having been introduced to it at the National Housing Conference Annual Meetings, which he attended regularly from 1911 to 1929.[3]

Woodward's real estate developments in Chestnut Hill began in earnest about 1910, in a neighborhood that was several blocks east of St. Martin's itself. The idea, Woodward reported in his *Memoirs,* came from Sister Ruth, the deaconess at St. Martin's church. Drawing their attention to a collection of dilapidated houses just east of Germantown Avenue, "She persuaded us, my wife especially, to buy these little old houses, pull them down, and build modern semi-detached dwellings, or as we call them, 'twins.'" Located on the present Benezet Street, the new units were "to be rented to working people, . . . at low rentals."[4] Following her advice, they bought the properties and replaced them with a pleasing variety of semi-detached houses. But the plan to put workers in them never transpired, as middle-class residents of the Hill leased the dwellings, in Woodward's words, "before we discovered the working people."[5]

There were, in fact, plenty of working-class families in Chestnut Hill. The east side in particular was home to stone quarriers, bricklayers, chauffeurs, and domestic servants, and many would have been interested in Woodward's new houses. The only mystery is why he did not seek them out. Woodward himself gives a partial answer in the *Memoirs,* describing his middle-class tenants as "exactly the people who pay their bills, and seldom complain. Dependable, self respecting, and quite unexciting, these are now famous as 'the forgotten men' of . . . Professor W. G. Sumner, of Yale."[6] In the last analysis he may have believed that such tenants would prove more dependable than their working-class neighbors. Or perhaps he thought he had already done enough for the working class through his model tenement and other contributions to the Octavia Hill Association. Beyond such explanations, Woodward and his contemporaries saw nothing wrong with separating classes into distinct sections of the city, for one of the enduring appeals of suburbia was its social homogeneity, which made for easy personal relations and a sense of community cohesiveness and warmth. Much of Chestnut Hill was already an upper-middle-class preserve; George Woodward saw nothing wrong with keeping it that way.

In the *Memoirs* Woodward also fails to mention that he had built four sets of twins in the one-hundred block of West Springfield Avenue about six years before. Designed in an early colonial revival style, they were large and bulky in appearance and not at all like the picturesque dwellings that marked Woodward's commissions later on. In this sense Woodward was correct in saying that the small twins on Benezet Street signaled the beginning of his distinctive housing developments in Chestnut Hill.

Woodward hired the firm of Durhing, Okie, and Ziegler to design the new houses. For the north side of Benezet Street they projected seven three-story twins, all in a vague neocolonial style, with certain Tudor-Jacobean details such as stucco and half-timbering on some of the second-story gables. Materials were also varied, the façades alternating between stucco, stone, and brick. There was a living room, dining room, and kitchen on the first floor, three bedrooms on the second floor, and a fourth bedroom on the third floor.

Across from the twins on the south side of Benezet Street Woodward tried a new experiment in suburban building—the quadruple house. It is unclear if either Woodward or his architect, Louis Durhing, invented the idea, but there can be no doubt that Woodward was very enthusiastic about the design. He contributed an article about the quadruple houses to the July 1913 issue of *The Architectural Record* that appeared along with another piece on the Benezet Street project.[7]

According to Woodward, the quadruple house was "a logical development of the semi-detached or twin house."[8] Both the twin and the row had long been accepted by all classes in Philadelphia as an economical approach to domestic building; the "quad" merely extended these economies by housing four units instead of two under the same roof and eliminated the cost of two more exterior walls. Woodward was thus able to rent them for $40 a month. But he also highlighted what he saw as the aesthetic qualities of the quadruple plan. Above all, there were no back lots, back alleys, or backyards, all of which Woodward found unsightly. The quads looked identical on both ends and could be surrounded on all four sides with gardens and trees.[9]

Woodward was equally proud of the quads' interior features. On the first floor there was a large rectangular living room, measuring twelve-and-a-half by twenty-three feet and extending fifteen feet beyond it was a spacious stair hall. A ceiling beam and pilasters formed a visual separation between these two spaces that otherwise appeared to be one long room. Off the living room was a dining area, and beside it a pantry and kitchen. The laundry was in the basement beneath the kitchen and just outside the kitchen door was a drying yard enclosed with latticework. On the second floor there were three bedrooms and a bath, with two more bedrooms and a bath on the third floor. The porches were placed at the corners of each quad so as not to block light into the living and dining rooms, and a sky-light on the third floor helped to illuminate the stair hall. Nevertheless, interior spaces were often quite dark, particularly on the north side or in areas where large trees were allowed to grow up.

The quads' exterior design was eclectic. Their stone walls and small-paned windows gave them a slight colonial air, while the leaded glass case-ment windows in the living rooms, and stucco and half-timbering on exterior bays, lent a Tudor-Jacobean flavor. Both American colonial and English revival styles were then current and Woodward's choice of them was not remarkable. Yet he may have been inspired by a set of photographs that appeared in a publication called the *Brochure Series of Architectural Il-lustration,* five bound volumes of which were discovered in Woodward's library bearing the signature of "Gertrude Woodward" on the flyleaves. The issue for June 1903 contained a well illustrated article titled "English Half Timber Houses." [10] The steep, half-timbered gables and long, rectan-gular bays that appeared in several of the photographs were surprisingly similar to those of the Benezet Street quads.

Woodward was so pleased with the quadruple houses that he commis-sioned three more sets for a parcel of land in nearby Mount Airy between the 200 block of West Nippon Street and Mount Airy Avenue. They were almost identical to the Benezet Street quads, but the façades were more varied than the earlier set, with the units at either end of the street having enclosed upstairs porches and those in the middle lacking the porches.

The quadruple house would even figure in a plan to provide a perma-nent endowment for St. Martin's church. In January 1916 Woodward put before the vestry a plan to build four more sets of quads on West Gravers Lane in Chestnut Hill. He would contribute the land, build the houses, and then turn them over to the church. According to his figures, the parish would realize nearly $2,000 in annual rents, while providing decent, low-cost housing for sixteen families. Perhaps because of the American entry into World War I, the project was never undertaken, but the idea itself was one more example of Woodward's constant mingling of the spiritual and the practical. [11]

Meanwhile, Woodward's development on the lower west side of Chest-nut Hill was well under way. It was on land directly adjoining some of the houses built by father-in-law Houston, and Woodward was quite con-scious of following the family precedent. Those who managed the Hous-ton trust, he observed, "were not disposed to buy more land and build more houses. My wife and I therefore determined to buy and build." [12] Gertrude was a sort of silent partner from the beginning, as son Stanley remembered blueprints spread out on the floor at home, with both parents bending over them and discussing the most recent plans.[13] But it was George who negotiated with the architects, handled all the business details, and appeared in the public eye as the developer. As in most things, Gertrude played the traditional role of helpmate rather than entrepreneur.

Although contiguous to Houston's earlier development, Woodward did not want his own project to be known as Wissahickon Heights. To him it "always seemed a cheap name for [such] a lovely country." In 1906 he launched a successful campaign to alter the name of the whole lower west side of Chestnut Hill to St. Martin's. A logical first step was to change the designation of the Wissahickon Heights station. Wishing to appear "fair and democratic," he petitioned the Pennsylvania Railroad for a name change and asked for suggestions. Fortunately, a sympathetic director from Chestnut Hill pressed Woodward's entry. Not long afterwards, he and Gertrude were delighted to find "brand new signs swinging all around the station with the distinguished name of St. Martin's emblazoned on them." Wissahickon Heights soon faded into memory as most of the neighbors agreed that St. Martin's carried a much more dignified ring.[14]

For architectural purposes, the name St. Martin's also turned out to be a felicitous choice, since Woodward's projects on the west side of Chestnut Hill exuded more of a distinct English flavor than Houston's earlier commissions. In some ways these motifs had their roots in the nation's centennial of 1876 which stimulated a slowly mounting interest in the country's architectural past—American as well as English. The shift in immigration during the 1890s, with the majority of entrants now coming from the south and east of Europe rather than from the northern and western portions of the continent, also made old-stock Americans more conscious of their cultural antecedents. One result was the founding of patriotic and ancestral societies like the Colonial Dames and the Daughters of the American Revolution. Another was the revival of English and colonial designs in architecture. Finally, American architects had grown dissatisfied with the European revivals of the nineteenth century, culminating in the fanciful eclecticism of the late Victorian period. For them the simple lines of an English cottage or colonial farmhouse offered welcome alternatives at a time when neither architects nor their patrons were willing to abandon historical styles altogether. The colonial and English revivals thus seemed practical, tasteful, and patriotic.[15]

In addition to being inspired by these broader forces, Woodward may have drawn his ideas for an English village in Chestnut Hill from more specific sources. Several issues of the *Brochure Series* in the Woodwards' possession contained illustrated articles on English thatched cottages. In the issue for May 1898 there is a streetscape from Bramber Village, Sussex, that looks almost identical to the series of houses that Woodward commissioned on the north side of the 8000 block of Crefeld Street in Chestnut Hill.[16] The Woodwards also took a trip to Europe and the British Isles in the summer of 1914, undertaking something of an architectural tour through the English countryside. And in order to amuse five-year-old Quita while they traveled, her parents "taught her a little about English architecture."[17]

The first and in many ways the best of the large projects that Woodward initiated in St. Martin's centered around the newly created Pastorius Park. In addition to Durhing, he engaged Robert Rodes McGoodwin and Edmund Gilchrist, both young Philadelphia architects. They gathered in Woodward's office once a week: "Each architect had to submit his designs to the other two and myself for criticism." He was struck by how well they all worked together—"a happy, harmonious group working for the common good."[18]

Woodward told *The Architectural Record* that this development had been inspired by his visit several years earlier to the area around London's Hyde Park.[19] Back in Chestnut Hill he decided to buy an abandoned field and donate it to the city as a park. The city had already planned two major roads through the grounds, giving Woodward no choice but to accommodate them in his plans. Lincoln Drive would continue up from Mount Airy, pass through the park, and intersect Germantown Avenue opposite the Bethlehem Pike. A local street called Hartwell Lane would extend east and west through the park, cross Lincoln Drive, and become an important link between Chestnut Hill and the suburbs of the Philadelphia Main Line. For various reasons, the intersecting boulevards were never executed: the city did not get around to surveying the routes until the late 1920s, and by then Woodward had built a number of houses in the area, making it difficult to construct the routes without considerable damage to property. Then the Depression set in and disrupted all municipal projects for several years. Woodward doubtlessly used his political connections to have the roads abandoned. In any case, the park was not landscaped until the mid-1930s under a grant from the WPA.[20]

On several streets around the park the architects created a Cotswold village. According to local tradition, Woodward actually sent his architects to England's Cotswold Hills to prepare themselves for the project. Whether this is true or not, their designs did in fact capture the spirit of a rural English village. Exterior walls were built of rough-cut stone and capped with steep roofs that resembled the English cottages the Woodwards so admired. This Cotswold style was also used later in the design of

Winston Court on the east side of Germantown Avenue near the Benezet Street quads.

Most distinctive of all in the Pastorius group were the two courts. At the northwest corner of Lincoln Drive and Willow Grove Avenue, McGoodwin designed three large stone houses around a central court, with one end open to the street. The exteriors were all slightly different, giving each family a sense of privacy and distinctness. On the opposite corner was Gilchrist's Linden Court, one of the few Woodward commissions executed in red brick. Constructed in a Georgian revival style, its six units face a central courtyard, with two units placed on either end and two in the middle. The court conveyed a spacious look that would have been lost entirely if each dwelling had been built in a row with tiny front yards. This set-back design, with trees and other plantings around each unit, also helped to lend a parklike atmosphere to the whole area around Pastorius Park itself. A sense of privacy and individuality was again achieved by varying entranceways and other exterior details.

A bit further south on Lincoln Drive was another group of six houses, arranged by Durhing in a crescent shape known as the "half-moon group." Directly across the street from these was a replica of Sulgrave Manor, the seat of George Washington's English ancestors that the Colonial Dames had built for the Sesquicentennial Exhibition in 1926. Woodward bought it, had it dismantled, and moved it up to Chestnut Hill.

Some of the houses in the Pastorius Park development departed somewhat from the overall English tone, with obvious references to French architecture. The Woodwards had liked the large stone farmhouses of Normandy, an influence that was quite evident in McGoodwin's court at Lincoln Drive and Willow Grove Avenue, as well as in a group of houses that he executed on the east side of Crefeld Street. Architectural critics have described this combination of English and French elements as the Anglo-Norman style.

Woodward's affection for Norman architecture received a full-scale treatment in the mid-1920s when he built the so-called French Village just across Cresheim Creek in West Mount Airy, only a couple of blocks from the Nippon Street quads. The Houston estate had contemplated a development here as early as 1914 and had engaged the Olmstead Brothers to draw up tentative plans for it.[21] The reasons for abandoning the project are unknown. Eventually Woodward bought the land from the estate and engaged McGoodwin to prepare a master plan. Eight houses were designed for Woodward along Gate Lane. Other lots were sold, with stipulations in the deeds that buyers must build in a French style, and many of them hired McGoodwin to design their houses. Like nearly all of Woodward's other dwellings, those in the French Village were executed in local stone. Especially attractive were the two gate houses at the intersection of Allen's Lane and Emlen Street. There were stone archways over the heavy slate sidewalks, attached on the inside to octagonal towers with steep conical roofs.[22]

Altogether Woodward built about 180 houses in St. Martin's and the immediate vicinity. On the whole they are more attractive than those built by Henry Howard Houston a generation earlier. The reasons for his success lay in the fruitful collaboration of his architects, in his own and Gertrude's good taste, and in their nearly universal use of local stone which gave both the Woodward and Houston houses a unity of color and texture that is unknown in most American suburbs. They also had the good fortune to build at a time when American domestic architecture had entered a settled but highly creative phase.

Important, too, were the institutions, created a generation or so earlier by Henry Howard Houston, that continued to provide a social focus for the neighborhood. St. Martin's was there to serve as a community church for Woodward's tenants, most of whom were already Episcopalians. The Philadelphia Cricket Club—whose original buildings burned down in 1909 and were replaced by a graceful row of red brick, Georgian-revival pavilions—became even more of a recreational center, with its tennis courts, golf links, and, later, a swimming pool donated by the Woodwards. The Wissahickon Inn, on the other hand, had failed by the early twentieth century, as prosperous Philadelphians went farther afield for summer vacations. The Houston estate turned it over to the Chestnut Hill Academy, which transformed it into a boys' school that was heavily subsidized by various members of the family, with George Woodward occupying a seat on the board of directors for many years. Although the academy took a number of boarders in the early decades, it became a convenient and economical neighborhood school—albeit a private one—for the occupants of Woodward's houses. These institutions, together with the nearly 250 residences built by Woodward and Houston together, formed an attractive, organic community that continues to give St. Martin's much of its flavor as a pleasant English village on the far edges of Philadelphia.

Another key to the development's homogeneity was Woodward's decision to follow Houston's example of renting most of his houses. Rents were set at six percent of the original investment, an intriguing extension of the Octavia Hill Association's policy of providing low-cost housing at a modest return for the investor. Woodward also prided himself on having good relations with his tenants, outlining the reasons in an article for *The Survey* magazine of 11 December 1920. Most important of all, he said, was complete honesty between landlord and tenant. His tenants were welcome to come to the office any time to look up the value of their houses and figure out the rent for themselves.

The lease also spelled out very clearly just what was expected of both parties. The tenant was to pay all taxes: if property taxes went up, Woodward passed the exact amount on to his renters, thus making them tax-conscious citizens who "decidedly feel [that] they have a stake in the government."[23] They were also to "take the house as it stands" and were responsible for all "interior replacements"—a one month's rent deposit being required to pay for any repairs not made by a departing tenant. Woodward would maintain the exterior. He also assured residents that they could count on receiving the same terms from year to year, and he made it a practice not to raise rents so long as a family stayed in the house, since it was cheaper for him to have the same parties remain in a house year after year than to stand the expense of preparing the property for new occupants.

In the same article he explained that he had decided to rent most of the houses because he "did not wish to lose control of the personnel," adding that he "always inquired into antecedents."[24] Woodward also prided himself in having a number of interesting or creative tenants. Among them were artist Violet Oakley, a well known mural painter for whom he provided a studio on St. George's Road; Leopold Stokowski, director of the famed Philadelphia Orchestra; Mary Wickham Bond, a poet and novelist; and Woodward's architect, Edmund Gilchrist. And, true to the arts and crafts movement, he attracted the Willet Stained Glass Studios by providing them with a renovated ice house at Springfield Avenue and Lincoln Drive, now divided into several dwellings of an eclectic Italianate style.[25] Not mentioned in the article was the fact that Woodward welcomed young couples with children. He liked to help young men and women of the professional and business class to get a start in life and also feared that increasing real estate prices would exclude young families, thereby making Chestnut Hill into a colony for middle-aged and older citizens.

In many ways the suburban community that Woodward created was unique. As Mary Corbin Sies has pointed out, however, in her excellent study of planned suburbs during the late nineteenth and early twentieth centuries, the combined developments of Henry Howard Houston and George Woodward had much in common with other communities. Among these are Short Hills in New Jersey, Kenilworth in Illinois, and Lake of the Isles in Minneapolis, Minnesota.[26] With the exception of Lake of the Isles, all four communities were created by a single individual or family. The developments were also conceived as a means of isolating largely homogeneous residents from the worst ravages of urban, industrial life. In all four cases, too, the developers used similar techniques to establish and maintain their suburban enclaves: screening prospective residents, reviewing all architectural designs, and either renting their properties or attaching deed restrictions to those that they sold.[27]

Unlike the other developers, however, Woodward was much more of a thoroughgoing reformer, who saw his efforts in Chestnut Hill as part of larger attempts to improve living standards throughout the city, state, and nation. As he made clear in his article for *The Architectural Record*, he hoped that his undertaking in Chestnut Hill would provide an example for other developers to follow, including those who might adapt it for low-cost housing.

Although his example was not imitated as he hoped, Woodward had every right to be proud of his work in St. Martin's and its vicinity, which remains one of the most attractive suburbs anywhere in the country. As he began his extensive development of Chestnut Hill, Woodward also planned a new house for himself and his growing family.

# CHAPTER 7

# At Home in Chestnut Hill

THE WOODWARDS could well afford a spacious and attractive dwelling, as Gertrude continued to share the annual income from the Houston estate with her mother, brother, and sister. In 1910 her one-quarter share was a little more than $200,000.[1] In addition to this income, her father had left her a forty-acre tract at the corner of McCallum Street and Mermaid Lane. Adjoining her sister Sallie Henry's place at Stonehurst, it was the last of three large parcels that Houston had laid out for the family along the great ridge above Wissahickon Creek. He had also left Gertrude $75,000 to erect a house there.[2]

The Woodwards did not build immediately, spending close to fifteen years planting and landscaping the grounds.[3] For architects they turned to the Boston firm of Peabody and Stearns, whose work they had admired very much during a trip one summer to Newport, Rhode Island.[4] The family moved in during the autumn of 1911, before the house was completely finished. Stanley recalled that he and his brother George slept in a room without floors that first night and had to "skip and jump across rafters to get to the bathroom."[5] The official housewarming was on 9 October, George and Gertrude's seventeenth wedding anniversary. The evening's highlight came when they asked each of their oldest friends to light one of the house's twenty or so fireplaces for the first time.[6]

The Woodwards called their house Krisheim, literally "Christ's home," taken from the name of an early German settlement in the valley just below Chestnut Hill in what is now the Mount Airy section of Philadelphia. The house was a massive Tudor-Jacobean structure of thirty rooms, built with a structural steel skeleton covered in local stone. It faced away from the road, overlooking a well-manicured formal garden that was framed by the Wissahickon gorge and the Roxborough Hills beyond.[7] On the McCallum Street side there was a semicircular driveway that began at the gatekeeper's gingerbreadlike cottage and then swung into a small courtyard before bending back out through the north gates.[8] Both rear and front entrances took the shape of shallow Gothic archways. Banks of leaded-glass casement windows created by the Willet Studios pierced the heavy stone walls, and many of the panes were made to look as if they had been mended into irregular colors and shapes.

On the garden side of the house, running the whole length of the wall and just above the windows, was a canticle from the Episcopal *Book of Common Prayer* giving thanks for the beauty of the moon and sun and stars and the ever-changing seasons. Immediately inside the garden entrance was a spacious, two-tiered hallway of terra cotta tile, covered here and there by Oriental throw rugs and inset on three sides with quotations from seventeenth-century accounts of the surrounding countryside. To the left was a large formal dining room, with a long table in the center and a smaller family table in a well-lighted alcove on the garden side. Across the hall was the oak-paneled library, featuring a wide Tudor-Gothic fireplace in the center of the far wall and a collection of several thousand books.

A step into the east hallway led to Dr. Woodward's small office next to the courtyard. Adjoining it to the right was a billiard room containing a huge brick fireplace that filled the whole front wall. Above the hearth was a whimsical mosaic showing two medieval knights on horseback, one male and one female, as they thrust their lances into a writhing serpent. An inscription reading "SS George and Gertrude" left no doubt about the crusaders' identity. The mosaic was a gift from Violet Oakley who wished to show her gratitude for the Woodwards' kind support over the years.

Out and across the east hallway was yet another fireplace with the inviting French phrase, "Au Dieu Foi, Aux Amis Foyer," and around the corner from it an oak-paneled reception room with its own cheerful hearth. An open staircase ascended from the hall itself and included a wide landing and gabled window seat that looked out over the curving driveway. On each of its leaded-glass windows were painted figures of famous English adventurers: Sir Richard Grenville, General Monk, Hawkins, and Walter Raleigh. Sharing the landing, too, was an organ console whose pipes were housed above in a special room with slatted acoustical flooring. And on the bannister posts were wooden figures representing the early peoples of

Pennsylvania—Swedes, Germans, Welsh, English, Scots, Dutch, and Indians, with William Penn himself at the top. On the second floor were the family bedrooms, each having its own unique fireplace; and on the third floor were several guest rooms in addition to servants' quarters.

Stanley Woodward recalled much of the daily routine at Krisheim: "At ten to eight . . . every morning my father rang a large brass mortar and pestle . . . to call us for morning prayers by the organ on the landing. A governess played the organ [and] we all sang a hymn. Father then read the collect for the day from the *Book of Common Prayer,* and we said the Lord's prayer." Then they all went downstairs for a hearty breakfast of "oatmeal, . . . milk, eggs, lamb chops, sausage, and fruit."[9]

The children returned from school for a luncheon that was served precisely at one o'clock. "Father said grace, and if any child were late, the delinquent had to repeat the prayer as punishment."[10] Afterward the boys played football, baseball, or some other game in season, and in the winter there was sledding on the sloping grounds at Krisheim or sleigh rides along the Wissahickon. The boys also liked to play at nearby Casey's pond where a favorite game was "Teddy in Darkest Africa," inspired by Theodore Roosevelt's big African game hunt in 1909. Late afternoons were reserved for homework, and before going to bed in the evenings everyone gathered in the library where they talked or read. And on Sunday mornings, the family drove to St. Martin's in a carriage, pulled by a team of matched roan horses.[11]

Because of their ages, the children divided themselves loosely into two groups. Young Houston, George, and Stanley were all born within three years and thus made ideal playmates for one another, while Charles, who was five years younger than Stanley, was often on his own—at least until Quita came along to provide him company in the nursery. Their chief disciplinarians were the Irish nurse Joyce Blong and coachman Patrick O'Hara, and during the summers in Maine an old family retainer named Captain Hight kept them in line.[12]

Dr. Woodward also fell into a congenial daily rhythm at Krisheim. Most mornings he drove one of his two electric cars to the St. Martin's station where he took the train to his office downtown, first in the North American Building and later in the Girard Trust. He owned two electrics, one a family-sized "phaeton" that held five passengers, and the other a two-seater, both of which he guided with a tiller rather than the now universal steering wheel. Although neighbors humorously referred to the cars as Dr. Woodward's "sewing machines," he kept them long after they had gone out of fashion, preferring the old-fashioned steering and quiet, fumeless ride to the more conventional gasoline models.

In the late afternoons Woodward frequently had a horse saddled and went riding over the countryside. He continued riding throughout most of his life, and on his eightieth birthday bought himself a new horse to celebrate. In the evenings he liked to read, but insisted on using a kerosene lamp. And more likely than not he had spent the day in a pair of comfortable golf knickers and knee-length, woolen stockings. He wore these everywhere—the only exceptions being a wedding, funeral, or other extraordinary event. He was known to create a minor sensation when he showed up at a banquet or meeting dressed for the golf links, but he appeared utterly unself-conscious about it all, determined to be comfortable no matter what anyone thought.[13]

Gertrude, meanwhile, had her hands full supervising their large household staff. Charles Woodward remembered that they had a housekeeper, a nurse, an English butler, a cook and kitchen maid, a downstairs parlor maid, two chambermaids, a laundress, a furnace man, and a night watchman. George and Gertrude each had a chauffeur, and then there were the gardeners, stable men, and a gatekeeper—amounting to a staff of about forty men and women.[14]

Outside the house, Gertrude's chief interest continued to be the church. She presided over the Woman's Auxiliary of the Diocese of Pennsylvania for two terms and contributed generously to church projects, giving $10,000 in 1918 for two churches that were to serve shipbuilders in the Philadelphia area and $5,000 in 1924 for the preservation of sacred places in the Holy Land.[15] And each May for a number of years she hosted a garden party at Krisheim for the benefit of the Germantown Convocation.[16] Another of her religious pastimes, as one child irreverently put it, was "collect[ing] bishops": "On Sundays our mid-day meal . . . was not infrequently graced literally as well as figuratively by a visiting bishop, domestic or foreign."[17] In Chestnut Hill itself she took a great interest in the Community Center, buying and renovating a building at 8434 Germantown Avenue for its headquarters.[18]

Then there were many activities that George and Gertrude also enjoyed doing together. They attended local opera productions and for many years held box number nineteen at the Academy of Music where they attended the Friday afternoon concerts of the Philadelphia Orchestra. They also loved the theater. In the 1930s Dr. Woodward contributed $100,000 toward a municipal theater, hoping that well produced plays might help overcome the popularity of movies. They also collected contemporary American paintings by artists such as Redfield, Schofield, Twachtman, Melchers, Prendergast, Garber, Oakley, and Winslow Homer. Their Homer collection eventually included about twenty-five canvases, many of which they donated to the Philadelphia Museum of Art.[19]

In the early years, the Woodwards spent their summers on Casco Bay just about a mile from the Sam Houstons' place at Clapboard Island. "Herron House," as they called their summer residence, was a large Georgian-revival structure made of wood and painted light yellow, with wide porches where the children rode their tricycles on rainy days. Moving up to Maine for the summer was a major production. "We were all packed off," Stanley recalled, "family, cook, maids, horses, carriages, coachmen, . . . a sweet grandmother, and . . . Miss Blong." [20]

Then, beginning in 1916, the Woodwards spent summers near Jackson Hole, Wyoming, where, as Gertrude wrote, the children could "see the West before it was too greatly changed." [21] At first they lodged at the Bar B-C Ranch, but soon built their own camp, Bar None, on Leigh Lake. "We lived out of doors day and night," Gertrude reminisced; "Our dining table was under a tent fly, and only when it rained were our sleeping cots pulled into the tents or lean-tos." [22] The children were free to bring multitudes of friends who stayed up late around the campfire telling tales or singing college songs. There were also ten-day pack trips into the Teton Mountains. In the "Krisheim News," a mimeographed letter that Dr. Woodward sent to their extended family and close friends, he gave a particularly colorful description of one foray in the summer of 1926:

We left Camp Washout between showers. There was no trail but we headed for a gap in the mountains. . . . One pack horse nearly rolled down the mountain side, one cinch broke and had to be repaired on a 45-degree angle. The view almost repaid us for the half hour of waiting. There were not only ranges and peaks of the Rocky Mountains showing snow patches, but also two or three hail storms playing around us. We rode over the first top in the rain, looked down into the canyon of Flat Creek, then struck across another top and encountered a driving hail storm. We were well bundled and slickered up, but in spite of sweaters and oil skins it was extremely cold. The clouds shrouded the peaks about us and made stunning pictures of a wild mountain pass. We rode over broken granite on the lowest possible point and then turned the corner of a big cliff and Glory Be! we were on the leeward side of the peaks. Then we dropped, leading our horses in a zig zag into the valley of Granite Creek. There was no wind, the sunshine broke through the clouds, there were gentle slopes, green and flowery meadows, patches of tall balsam and spruces. Down we rode along the trail and came rather late to a bunch of tall water spruces along side an icy stream of clear water. There we pitched our tent, hobbled our horses and watched the big stars come out. We were in a narrow valley, with magnificent granite mountain sides. One mountain was carmine red to set off the general grayness. The sun turned all the low clouds and tall peaks into gold. It grew cold and dark, until the moon suddenly broke into the open sky and flooded the meadows with silver. [23]

On the Sam Houston side of the family, meanwhile, there were many changes. Hennie joined his stepbrother, Charles Brown, at the University of Pennsylvania in the autumn of 1912, and the following November Sam's mother died. In 1914 his daughter Edith married Dr. Henry P. Brown and a year later his daughter Peg married a young engineer named Robert Rogers Meigs. After World War I would come the marriages of Sam's two stepchildren, Charlotte Brown to W. West Frazier III and Charlie Brown to Gladys Klapp Williams.[24]

But the biggest change of all had come in the summer of 1910 when Sam and Charlotte had a daughter of their own. They named her Eleanor— after Sam's sister who had died at age eleven from scarlet fever. The parents themselves, who by now were in their mid-forties, could not have been more surprised when they learned that a baby was on the way. Charlotte had a difficult delivery, with the baby arriving at Druim Moir, prematurely, on 21 July. The whole ordeal must have frightened Sam badly, having already lost one wife in childbirth. All turned out well in the end, however, with the parents delighted to have a living link between the two families.[25]

With brothers and sisters so much older than she—the youngest being fifteen when she was born—Eleanor often lacked playmates. But Druim Moir was a little world of its own, with plenty of places to explore and people to talk with. Eleanor liked to get up at six o'clock in the morning and go out to help bring the cows in from pasture.[26] And, unknown to her parents, who surely would have disapproved, she also learned to milk the cows. There were always treats to be had in the kitchen, and long talks with the cook. But her favorite was their English butler, Stephen Gilmore, who always took time to show Eleanor the most interesting articles in her father's newly arrived copy of the *London Illustrated News*. In nice weather there were impromptu visits from a "three-instrument" German band or "the Italian lady" with her accordion—both of whom walked into Druim Moir knowing that they could count on a reward for their trouble.

Eleanor's best friend was her cousin Quita Woodward, just one year older, who came over from Krisheim to play. The girls started a bird club, and to encourage them further Eleanor's father made them both life members of the Audubon Society. They could also get into mischief—such as the time they sneaked into the greenhouse without the gardener's permission and cut a huge bouquet of flowers as a Mother's Day present for Eleanor's "Mummy." Then there were the days when Eleanor went over to Krisheim to play. It made both her and Quita quite furious when the maid greeted her at the door as "Baby Eleanor"—even after she was eleven or twelve. Nor did she like it much better when Uncle George teased her about calling her mother "Mummy," a name that he said was more suitable for "an Egyptian dead person." Quita's brother Charlie could also be a tease, often calling her "Smell-anor." But the cousins all had a good time together, putting on magic shows in the billiard room and swimming together over in Aunt Sallie Henry's pool at Stonehurst. The swimming was loads of fun, but they dreaded having to go over each spring to ask if they could use the pool for the coming season.

For Eleanor, Sunday was a day to be taken very seriously. Sunday newspapers were forbidden in the house, while Eleanor was expected to amuse herself with things like "Bible cards." On Sunday evenings the family and guests gathered around the piano in the drawing room to sing hymns, a custom that had begun in the time of Henry Howard Houston. The Houstons were also strict teetotalers, who never served alcohol of any kind. To the dismay of the Woodward boys, Sam had even gone so far as to dispose of his father's excellent wine cellar.[27]

If Sam Houston did not drink, he did enjoy fine boats and automobiles. In addition to his enormous sailing yachts, he owned four large powerboats in succession, each of them named *Dixie* in Charlotte's honor. The *Dixie III* was a fifty-eight-foot power launch that easily slept eight passengers.[28] One of their earliest cars was a Pierce Arrow, purchased in 1907. During most of the twenties they drove a French-made Simplex, and in 1929 they bought a Rolls Royce.[29]

Sam also derived much pleasure from singing with the Orpheus Club and belonging to both the Rittenhouse and the Union League clubs and an unending number of hereditary-patriotic societies, several of which elected him president. By then he and Charlotte (as well as the Woodwards and Henrys) were attending Philadelphia's well-known Assembly Balls. Charlotte also had her favorite charities and clubs and found herself in *Who's Who Among American Women*.

The Houstons enjoyed frequent house guests, some of them well known in international circles. In February 1922, General John Joseph Pershing, who was in Philadelphia to be honored by the University of Pennsylvania and the First City Troop, stayed at Druim Moir. Other distinguished guests included William Cecil, Lord Bishop of Exeter, and, many years later, the Most Reverend Geoffrey Fisher, Archbishop of Canterbury. (In the pastime of "collecting bishops," Sam had clearly trumped his sister Gertrude.) Yet other expected guests did not materialize, as when Sam and Charlotte offered Druim Moir for a convalescent hospital at the end of World War I, a gesture that was declined by the Army because of logistical problems. They offered to give over their house at Clapboard Island for the same purpose, but were also turned down by military authorities. After the war, however, they were able to help unemployed veterans by hiring them to excavate beautiful new gardens at Druim Moir. But far

more than anything else, Sam and Charlotte simply enjoyed being together at home.[30]

Of course, life for the Houstons and Woodwards was not without its
sorrows. The war that had broken out in Europe in 1914 seemed a long
way from Chestnut Hill at first. Before it was over, the whole family would
be plunged into grief by the death of two young sons.

CHAPTER 8

# Two Cousins

BY EARLY 1917 both George Woodward and Sam Houston thought their country had no choice but to enter the war against Germany. Sam, in particular, who would be active in the English Speaking Union all his life, was an ardent Anglophile, and, like most other well-to-do Philadelphians, had sympathized with Great Britain from the very beginning of hostilities. He and George Woodward also shared the outrage of most other citizens at continuing German submarine attacks on American ships. They had similarly grown impatient with President Wilson's diplomacy and were relieved when Congress finally declared war on 6 April. But for Sam, who was such an ardent admirer of German culture, the declaration meant both anger and regret: like a bitterly disappointed lover, he tried to blot out every trace of former affection. All the charming German phrases were removed from the garden house at Clapboard Island, while their Dresden china was stacked aboard one of the boats and tossed overboard into Casco Bay.[1] His fury against Germany would reach a crescendo in 1918 when his only son, Hennie, and the Woodwards' oldest boy, Houston, were killed on the western front. For both fathers the war would remain a touchstone, shaping their views of the world at large for the rest of their lives.

By the time the United States had entered World War I, the two cousins, Hennie and Houston, were already in France as volunteers of the American Ambulance Service. Each had belonged to militia companies before going overseas as ambulance drivers, and each would join combat units once their own country went to war. Hennie's military service had begun when he enlisted with battery C of the First Pennsylvania Artillery in June 1916, the same day that he graduated from the University of Pennsylvania. Later in the month his unit was called up, along with 150,000 other militiamen, to take positions along the Texas and New Mexico border in response to Pancho Villa's recent raids from Mexico. Hennie did not see any action during the punitive expedition under General John Joseph Pershing, but he was much impressed with the huge massing of troops for a formal review in mid-September. With obvious pride he wrote to his father about having been in the "biggest review of U.S. troops since the Civil War." "Over 26,000 participated," he added. "It was really impressive seeing all those men gathered together and being one of them."[2]

Hennie and his unit were back in Pennsylvania by Thanksgiving. In Europe, meanwhile, the war raged on. Despite two years of appalling slaughter on both sides, none of the belligerents had been able to break the stalemate that had settled over the western front shortly after the fighting began. The summer of 1916 had been particularly murderous. There were more than a half million casualties at Verdun and more than a million during the battle of the Somme, most of them sustained as troops charged across no man's land into the face of ruthless machine-gun fire that mowed them down like so many blades of grass. As demoralization swept through the ranks on both sides of the trenches, it seemed to beleaguered Europeans that the war would never end.

But for Hennie, as for many young Americans, war could still seem like a great adventure. Anxious to do whatever he could to help the Allied cause, he joined the American Ambulance corps in January 1917. Once overseas, he was prepared to exult in everything French, much as his father and his Uncle Howard had earlier admired Germany. On 3 February he confided to his diary, "France epitomizes civilization." The same day he was delighted to hear that President Wilson had finally broken diplomatic relations with Germany, and only hoped that war would soon be declared.[3]

After enjoying the sights of Paris for several days, Hennie and his comrades left on 8 February for their first rendezvous at Bar-le-Duc. They spent nights along the way in stables or in their own Ford ambulances. Arriving after three days on the road, Hennie practiced his French with the natives whenever he got the chance and passed his evenings with the other men singing songs in a local café.[4] He found the bathing facilities at "Bar" quite crude, consisting of a "basin of Ford warmed water placed in a sunny and sheltered corner of the church yard." There was absolutely no privacy, as Hennie tried to get used to "the way the kids gather to watch one perform his toilette."[5]

By late February Hennie and his unit were stationed near Verdun, with the cellar of a partly ruined château as their home for the time being. They often had to drive right up to the trenches to pick up wounded French soldiers and were constantly under fire. One of the first days out, Hennie realized that they were in plain view of the enemy. "It was not fear," he later wrote in his diary. "It was something like the feeling that comes after one has left [his] horse and before [he] has hit the ground."[6]

Everywhere there was death and destruction: "Mud pervades everything," Hennie told his diary. "It is impossible to imagine such utter desolation. The houses are all smashed, shell holes line the road. . . . At one place a dead horse sticks his head out of a pile of rubbish. At another there is a French ambulance at the bottom of a bank. . . . No man's land can not be described. It is like the coke oven district around Pittsburgh, only more so. It is the deadest strip of ground I have ever seen."[7]

In the days that followed, Hennie was scared to death much of the time—and so were his comrades. Instead of keeping their feelings bottled up inside, they found that it helped a lot to talk them out each night before turning in. Still, with all the death and dying, it was hard for Hennie to forget his own mortality. "It is a terrible, helpless feeling," he confessed, "to think that any minute may be your last. I know what war is and I am a pacifist."[8]

This daily inferno doubtless seemed a long way from the quiet country atmosphere of Chestnut Hill, and Hennie's thoughts must have turned to home more than once. Yet however frightened he and the others were, they somehow managed to muster enough courage to start out each morning for the trenches. Their worst experience came during a hellish enemy bombardment on 18 and 19 March. Even after a full day back at their shelter, Hennie remained partly dazed and only half able to believe that he was "still alive." He was even more amazed on the twenty-first to learn that the French were awarding him the Croix de Guerre for gallantry under fire.[9] Relief finally came in April when he was invited to enroll in the French Army Transportation School at Meaux. By this time his own country was at war, permitting him to accept a lieutenancy in the French army. Hennie then served for two months as the commander of a trucking unit at Soissons. On learning that his militia battery back home had been called into federal service, he resigned his French commission and returned in August to join them.[10]

Meanwhile, Hennie's cousin Houston Woodward, who, like Hennie, carried their grandfather's first and middle names, was undergoing his own baptism of fire on another section of the front. Houston had gone off to Yale in 1915 where he joined the "Yale Battery," giving him a taste of military life that he much enjoyed. After a year and a half at New Haven,

Houston left college to volunteer, like Hennie, in the American Ambulance Corps.[11]

Of all the Woodward children, Houston had been the most restless and adventuresome, as well as the least interested in books or school. According to his own father, "He was always on the ragged edge of being suspended for something. Out of school he used to take awful chances of breaking his neck by trying stunts," and his father seriously doubted "whether he ever would have graduated from Yale."[12] Like other restless young men of his generation, the seeming romance of war offered Houston an escape from the daily grind of work or school.

Arriving in France about two months after Hennie, Houston's first few weeks there were much like his cousin's. He went out sightseeing whenever possible, talking to the natives as best he could and never failing to be impressed by the stubborn courage and unfailing politeness of the French people. Echoing Hennie's wholly favorable opinion of his hosts, Houston wrote his mother on 13 April, "I love these French people, It's wonderful how kind, patient, and generous they are. . . . They are the most obliging, hospitable, and kind-hearted people that can possibly be imagined. . . . Gentile describes perfectly France, the French, and tout français."[13]

But like Hennie he soon learned that real war was far from romantic. On 21 April he confessed to his mother,

This war seems terribly hopeless to me. I don't see how it can ever be settled in a military way. I hope there will be a revolution in Germany before long. It's the only way I see out. The Allies can push the Boches back a little at a time, but it costs terrifically in lives and munitions, and I can't see that the gain begins to compensate for the loss. . . . The first night of the attack was different from anything I've ever seen. The firing of the French batteries made an incessant unbroken roar from twelve midnight to six in the morning. We rolled through the lines of guns that night, and no lights were needed. It was bright as mid-day, the sky all red and gold, with many star shells and signal rockets adding their brilliant glare with the cannon's flashes. Jets of flame leaped from invisible guns on all sides, shells were landing more intermittently with their brilliant flashes and geysers of mud. Now and then we would come upon a wounded horse, shrieking and dying in agony. Shell-destroyed supply camions lay in the ditches, reserve troops were marching silently, grimly forward, groups of groaning, stooping blessés were struggling gamely backward. It was hell let loose, and seemed like a dream, a delirium. I could hardly believe it was I who was passing through this. One could not think but had to act without thinking, on instinct, and the memory of the whole bloody, foolish business is burned on my mind in such a way that I can never forget it.[14]

With America now in the war, Houston felt duty-bound to get into the fighting himself, but his few weeks at the front left him with few illusions about what awaited him. "Believe me," he confessed to his father, "I don't want to fight, and if I get killed I hope I kill at least fifty of those couchons first."[15]

Houston's fascination with cars and machinery led him to enlist in the French Air Corps, and in the summer of 1917 he began flight training. By mid-August he was utterly enthralled with flying: "Flying is the greatest sport in the world. I love it, and think I ought to get away with it pretty well. I am longing for the time when I can drive my own Nieuport and do all the loops, vrilles, spirals, renversements, barrel turns, and other tricks."[16]

In September Houston "soloed" for the first time, and once in the air he could temporarily forget about the misery and death below. As he climbed higher and higher, he saw the clouds glistening "beautifully in the sun," with the western sky all "pink and red."[17] But the brutal realities of war were never far away, and late December found him back on the front. Bad weather kept him grounded until early January when he had his first dogfight with a German Albatross. Unfortunately, his machine gun jammed just as he was closing in on the kill.

Back on the ground, Houston found that his greatest foe was the damp, penetrating cold: "[I] sleep every night in my two undershirts, two underdrawers, jersey, shirt, sweater-vest, mother's sweater, breeches, socks, and woolen leggings. Over me I have three blankets, peau de picquet coat, overcoat, and combination fourrée."[18] Then, on 6 January he shot down his first German plane, writing a full description of it to his father three days later:

We crossed the lines . . . at 4,000 metres, and soon saw three Albatross mono-planes sailing along at about 3,300 metres. I didn't wait for Parizet, who was lead-ing, to start for them, but picqued on one of them immediately. . . . My Boche made a quick turn, so I redressed and began manoeuvring to get behind and above him. Finally I got him where I wanted him, and picqued steep, shooting all the time. . . . I put my machine in a verticle nose dive, gaining tremendous speed, then redressed, and quickly overtook my fleeing Boche. Got within one hundred metres of him, and sent in a steady stream of bullets. . . . I saw he had been hit, and made a vertical spiral to watch him vrille down to the ground.[19]

Now in the thick of the fighting, Houston found less and less time to write home and finally the letters stopped altogether, the last dated 25 March 1918. The agonizing silence lasted until June when his parents were informed that Houston was reported "missing in action." Through-out the summer and autumn, George and Gertrude hoped against hope that he was still alive somewhere and not until a fellow French flyer located his grave in February 1919 did they know for sure that he was dead. They learned that his plane had been shot down outside the town of Montdidier, his body buried in a shell hole about ten yards from the wreck. Later the remains were transferred to the American cemetery outside Paris at Suresnes.

Like millions of other young men struck down in the "Great War," Houston had just begun to live. The experience in France had forced him to grow up fast and made him realize just how much he wanted to pursue some kind of useful career. In August 1917 he had written his mother, hoping that his life might be spared: "I am beginning to long for some real work," he confided, "and a more or less settled life now, neither of which I have ever wanted before."[20] His parents were doubtless encouraged by Houston's growing sense of maturity and it must have made his death even more difficult to accept.

No sooner had the family begun to absorb the possibility of Houston's death than word came in August that Hennie had been killed. He had returned to France with his militia unit as aide-de-camp to Brigadier General William G. Price, Jr. On 18 August, while walking along a road outside the village of Arcis-le-Ponsart, Hennie was struck by artillery fragments. He died the next day in a local schoolhouse that served as the town's emergency hospital. His body was eventually buried, like Houston's, at the military cemetery in Suresnes.[21]

In their grief, both the Woodwards and Houstons looked for ways to memorialize their fallen sons. Dr. Woodward published a volume of Houston's correspondence, calling it *A Year for France: War Letters of Houston Woodward*. In Chestnut Hill they helped erect a large stone cross of Lorraine at the foot of Germantown Avenue, dedicated to their son and all the other young men from the Hill who had given their lives in the war. And on Chestnut Hill's east side, they built the Watertower Recreation Center in his memory and gave it to the city of Philadelphia. George and Gertrude were also pleased when they learned that Houston would be awarded the French Croix de Guerre posthumously.

In 1921 the Woodwards went to France themselves and erected a stone marker by the roadside outside Montdidier where Houston's plane had fallen. They returned to France in the summer of 1923, accompanied this time by nineteen-year-old Charles and fourteen-year-old Quita. In Paris they were present for the dedication of a monument to American volunteers in the French army who had been killed in the war. They were also invited to a banquet for the families of the American volunteers several days later at the Quai d'Orsay. The Woodwards found themselves the guests of honor, with Gertrude seated to the right of General Mangin who presented Dr. Woodward with the Médaille Militaire in recognition of Houston's sacrifices for France.[22]

The parents and their two children then spent July and most of August touring England, returning to France in time for a memorial service in the village of Rubescourt, just north of Montdidier. Dr. Woodward gave a full account of the day in his "Krisheim News":

When we reached the village there was an arch of flowers across the road with a legend of welcome for us. The mayor and the whole village were waiting, not only for us, but also for the Bishop of Amiens and his attending priests. A young girl read an address of welcome to the Lady [Gertrude] and presented her with a big bunch of flowers. Then the bishop arrived in all his canonicals, and a really fine figure he made. After greeting the mayor, and letting everyone kiss his Episcopal ring, he came across to us and shook hands with each of us. We then all formed a procession back of the clergy and marched to the little new church. The church is St. Martin's, as we saw by the little statue of St. Martin dividing his cloak with the beggar. . . . The Lady of Krisheim gave the clock in the tower and one of the two bells. We were treated with so much gratitude that we began to feel as if we ought to have given the whole church. We were then shown our seats in the chancel and for once attended a Roman Catholic high mass. . . . We were often embarrassed to know when to kneel, when to stand and when to sit down. . . .

After this service we all marched to the village wayside war monument, which the bishop consecrated as he had the church. We then marched to a newly built barn and sat down to an extended banquet. There was course after course, with white wine and red wine and better wine and champagne. . . . After the banquet we walked with the villagers to the cemetery to decorate the war graves and then on to Houston's memorial stone, where we finally said goodbye to these people who certainly had very much touched our hearts.[23]

The Houstons also made a pilgrimage to France in 1920 to see where their son had died. On the road outside Arcis-le-Ponsart where Hennie had fallen, they commissioned a wayside shrine. A wrought-iron cross and crucified Christ in grey metal stood on a raised stone platform. Below, an inscription read, "C'est près d'ici on est tombé pour la France 1st Lieut. Henry Howard Houston, II."[24] And as a gift to the badly damaged village of Arcis-le-Ponsart, his parents helped to restore the parish church, much as the Woodwards were doing at Montdidier. Charlotte gave three bells for the tower, one for each of Hennie's three names. Together she and Sam donated two new altars, a pulpit, baptismal font, and pews. And as a source of safe drinking water for the whole population they installed a new water system and reservoir.[25] Every Christmas they also sent money to the priest at Arcis so that he could give a party and presents to all the children.[26]

Back in Philadelphia Sam Houston encouraged others to help in postwar reconstruction, and he served as local director of the American Committee for a Devastated France. In return for his generosity he was made a chevalier and later an officer in the French Legion of Honor.[27] He also commissioned another wayside shrine in honor of Houston and all the other young men from Chestnut Hill who were killed in the war. Located on the road behind Druim Moir that led down to Valley Green, it was much like the small religious shrines along roads throughout Europe. Under a Gothic canopy was the small bronze figure of a crucified Christ, with a helmetless soldier standing beneath it. (It was removed in 1937 after vandals had damaged it several times.)[28] And in Maine at Falmouth Foreside the Houstons and Woodwards together gave a twenty-five-acre tract to the city as a memorial park to their two dead sons.[29] But perhaps the most appreciated of these memorials back home was the handsome stone building on High Street in Germantown that the Houstons gave to the local American Legion. Named the Henry Howard Houston, 2nd Post, it would serve veterans of several American wars.[30]

There would also be less tangible legacies. A tendency to sympathize with an isolationist foreign policy in the twenties and thirties would be George Woodward's way of trying to save other young men from dying in battle. For his brother-in-law Sam Houston, an interventionist stance in world affairs would make far greater sense.

CHAPTER 9

# State Senator

THERE ARE MANY WAYS to handle grief, but perhaps the healthi-
est way is to throw oneself into some new activity. George Woodward's
decision to run for the Pennsylvania state senate in 1918, followed by an
energetic campaign that autumn, doubtless provided a welcome diversion
during those agonizing months when he and Gertrude were awaiting
more definite news of their son's fate—and in the difficult weeks immediately thereafter. In his *Memoirs* Woodward explained that the independent Republicans of Germantown had first asked him to run for the state
assembly, an offer that he immediately turned down. The following day
they asked him to consider the senate seat from the sixth district and he
agreed. He then sought the endorsement of U.S. senator Boies Penrose,
long the Republican boss of Pennsylvania politics who had recently cast
his lot with the reformers. Woodward insisted on complete political independence and Penrose consented to support him under those conditions.[1]

Just what Woodward's own motives were remain unclear, but his decision to run may have come from a desire to help guide a new city charter
for Philadelphia through the state legislature. Woodward faced a stiff fight
with the Vare machine which had dominated city politics on and off for
over a decade. In order to confuse voters, the Vare faction placed another
George Woodward on the primary ballot, this one a chauffeur from Germantown. Dr. Woodward took the matter to court, claiming that the
chauffeur's petition lacked a sufficient number of signatures and the judge
agreed in time to have the impostor's name removed from the May ballot.[2]
Woodward still had to face incumbent Owen B. Jenkins who had the full

backing of the Vare organization, but he managed to overcome Jenkins on 21 May with 14,571 votes to his opponent's 12,396. Victory in November was now assured, given the continuing Republican domination of Philadelphia politics.[3]

At that time the state legislature only convened every other year, unless the governor called a special session; and even when the legislature met it commonly did not sit for the entire year, with the actual meetings taking up only three days of each week. Senator Woodward would thus have plenty of time to enjoy his home life while attending to his many other interests in Philadelphia.

Woodward's swearing-in for the 1919 legislative session created something of a sensation when he appeared in the senate chamber dressed in his golf knickers and woolen knee socks. He delighted the crowd even more when he vaulted over a brass rail following the ceremony and then dropped into his seat with his legs dangling over the chair arm.[4] Whether amused or irritated, however, Woodward's colleagues in the senate soon learned that he was a serious legislator.

It was soon evident, for instance, that Woodward would use his position in the senate to champion a series of proposals for better government in Philadelphia, many of which required special legislation at the state level. His proposals would also reflect his often random mix of moral and scientific authority.

The first of these crusades was for a new home rule charter in Philadelphia.[5] Woodward agreed with other Philadelphia reformers that the old "Bullitt" Charter of 1885 was woefully insufficient and he eagerly joined a movement to give the city a new frame of government. Above all, Woodward and the others contended that the large and unwieldy bicameral city councils (known as the Common and Select Councils) of 146 elected members had to be altered. Organizing such a large assembly invited and virtually required some sort of boss rule, making it impossible for the reformers to capture and control it. In addition, the machine's numerous seats on the council gave it a continuous source of patronage, as councilmen awarded generous payments to the private contractors who provided most of the city's services.

A movement to reform the councils, as well as many other features of Philadelphia government, was inaugurated at a large dinner on 13 December 1918, where Woodward was named to a subcommittee, headed by veteran reformer John C. Winston, to prepare a framework for city government.[6] The committee enlisted the help of Woodward's Bureau of Municipal Research, completing most of its work by the spring of 1919. Senator Woodward then shepherded the charter through the upper chamber in Harrisburg, an effort that later earned him the name "father of the 1919 charter."[7]

The most important feature of the 1919 charter gave Philadelphia a smaller, unicameral council with twenty-one members, one for each of the state senatorial districts and one additional member for every 20,000 voters. This way local machines could not gerrymander councilmanic districts, while the smaller numbers of councilmen would not be, in theory, so dependent on the machine for organization and direction. Council members would hold office for four years, received $5,000 in annual salary, and were forbidden to hold any other public office simultaneously—a provision that did not exist under the former charter. The city could also pave and repair its own streets and collect its own garbage, thus eliminating some of the kickbacks and political favors to privileged contractors. About 15,000 municipal employees came under civil service, with appointees chosen from the top two candidates on the eligibility lists, while policemen and firemen were forbidden to make political contributions or engage in political activities. All city offices now had to submit their finances to the controller, and the mayor had to provide an annual budget for the council which then held public hearings on it. A department of welfare coordinated social welfare agencies and their activities.[8]

Woodward and the reformers did not get all they had wanted in the charter and only experience would reveal if the machine would succeed in undermining or working around it, but they had assuredly made a move toward better government in Philadelphia. Woodward would spend a considerable part of his three decades in Harrisburg trying to win further reforms in Philadelphia's government, while defending the progress that had already been made. And like a good progressive, he would continue to campaign for honesty, greater efficiency, and essentially nonpartisan solutions to city administration.

He also campaigned against what he saw as schemes to defraud local taxpayers. One of these involved city proposals to buy the Philadelphia Rapid Transit Company (PRT), ostensibly because the citizens were being made to pay far too much for a rundown and mismanaged system. Woodward particularly objected to a requirement that Philadelphia buy the whole system and introduced his own bill that allowed the city to purchase separate segments of the transit combine.[9] His "any or all" provision passed both houses of the legislature, but the city finally bought the entire PRT in 1934 for what Woodward thought an outrageous sum: $84.5 million.

Woodward's opposition to the PRT elicited one of his strongest moral rebukes. Reminding the public that the excessive cost would be borne by generations to come, he urged taxpayers not to condemn their children for the sins of the PRT. "Thou shalt not bow down thyself to them," he warned in quoting from the First Commandment, "for I am a jealous God, visiting the iniquities of the fathers upon the children unto the third and fourth generations of them that hate me."[10] But Woodward's admonitions fell on deaf ears. The city bought the system and renamed it the Philadelphia Transportation Company (PTC).

Yet he approached other urban problems out of a consideration for scientific efficiency. By the early 1930s he especially wanted to abolish the dual city-county government that had plagued Philadelphia since the partial merger of the two units in 1854. The merger had made the boundaries of the city and county coterminous, but it had left all the city and county offices intact, resulting in a wasteful and confusing duplication of effort—not to speak of the greater opportunities for patronage and graft. The so-called county row offices, consisting of the treasurer, auditor, recorder, and eight others, for example, were completely beyond the control of mayor or city council. With 1,800 jobs at their disposal, they were a rich source of political jobbery and patronage for the local machine.

Since county government was mandated by the state constitution, Woodward proposed a constitutional amendment in the spring of 1931 that would merge the city of Philadelphia into the county and greatly simplify the governing machinery. At the head of the newly consolidated unit would be three well-paid commissioners whose generous salaries would attract qualified men to the office. They would establish policy but hire an expert manager to administer the government on a daily basis. This arrangement would save the taxpayers millions while eliminating most of the partisan posturing from government. With a vivid image of how the new apparatus would operate, Woodward asked Philadelphians to "visualize a small round table in a pleasant room, . . . with four men seated comfortably around it. There every day without any legislative pomp and circumstance and speech making and playing to the gallery, these four skillful men [the three commissioners and their manager] will discuss the affairs of Philadelphia. Wise conclusions will be swiftly reached with the minimum of lost motion. Such is the picture of how to do it well and with the least cost and delay."[11]

Under Woodward's merger plan there would be no mayor and no city council, and since the government would be administered by a well-paid, nonpartisan expert, there was also no need for a civil service department. Needless to say, the Philadelphia machine was strongly opposed to the plan, as were numerous state Republicans who rightfully believed that the Woodward plan would weaken their organization in Philadelphia. Woodward was the only member of the Senate Judiciary Committee to vote for the amendment and it died as the 1931 session came to an end. He would propose similar schemes for city-county consolidation in 1933 and 1939; they, too, went down to defeat.[12]

It was also in the 1930s that Woodward began recommending a plan to merge Philadelphia County into a larger administrative district that would include nearby Bucks, Montgomery, Delaware, and Chester Counties. The merger would eliminate a wasteful duplication of services, save money, and permit the entire region to coordinate its approach to transportation and other problems that went beyond boundaries and were common to all. Woodward petitioned the legislature several times on behalf of the plan but no action was taken.[13]

More successful was Woodward's proposal to raise additional revenue for Philadelphia through a tax to be levied against all income earned in the city—whether the recipient lived within the municipal boundaries or not. Woodward drew up the necessary legislation, guided the tax bill through the senate, and in November 1938 the Philadelphia city council levied a 1.5 percent income tax, the first of its kind in the country. The percentages rose in the years to follow, but the tax would help to keep the municipality solvent as thousands of citizens joined the nationwide stampede to the suburbs in the post-World War II period.[14]

With his attention riveted on state and municipal reform during those first years in the senate, Woodward had little to say about federal policies, but his growing opposition to the national prohibition of alcoholic beverages proved an exception by the early 1930s. In concert with many other progressives, he had supported prohibition initially and had voted for the Snyder-Armstrong Act that provided for state enforcement of the Eighteenth Amendment. Yet he could hardly fail to notice that most Philadelphians resented prohibition or that enforcement in the city was uneven and frequently lax. Philadelphia had hundreds of speakeasies, while city breweries operated virtually in the open. A raid on the Philadelphia Cricket Club, which Woodward had purchased in 1925 in order to supply the club with a large development fund, may have also soured him on the "noble experiment." And although the Woodwards did not serve alcohol at Krisheim during these years, both George and Gertrude continued their long habit of having a rum toddy before they went to bed.[15]

Woodward's first open move against the dry laws was his sponsorship of a bill in January 1931 to authorize a statewide referendum on the question. Voters would have a chance to say if they favored a repeal of the Eighteenth Amendment and the state's Snyder-Armstrong enforcement act. They were also asked to consider a modification of the Volstead Act to permit light wines and beer. The legislature approved Woodward's referendum but Governor Pinchot vetoed it.[16]

The prohibition issue also figured in Woodward's decision to seek the Republican nomination for the United States Senate. He came out for the nomination as an avowed "wet" in December 1931 in opposition to incumbent senator James J. Davis. He withdrew before the 1932 primaries, however, citing a number of complex reasons. In reality, he probably failed to generate wide support for his candidacy. He had made far too many enemies over the years with the Vare machine in Philadelphia and with other organization Republicans throughout the state. Nor, according to his son Stanley, did Woodward look forward to spending a large part of his time in Washington where he would miss the pleasant routine at Krisheim.[17]

Woodward's aborted campaign for the U.S. Senate coincided with the first issues of his *Pennsylvania Legislator,* a leaflet that he "published every so often" for the edification of fellow legislators or for anyone who cared to read it. Each issue was printed on heavy blue paper that was folded lengthwise to make a cover and three pages of text. It eventually reached a circulation of around 1,100, with copies going to the press and interested constituents, as well as to brother solons in Harrisburg. The Philadelphia newspapers quoted liberally from it and the *Evening Bulletin* usually carried it verbatim. After the end of each legislative session, Woodward collected the leaflets and published them as a single volume, retaining the title *Pennsylvania Legislator.* Bound in dark green with a gold seal of the state of Pennsylvania stamped on the front cover, seven such volumes appeared between 1932 and 1945.

The avowed purpose of the *Pennsylvania Legislator* was an extension of Woodward's old idea that good government depended upon a dispassionate examination of the facts, and in this regard it harkened back to his days at the Board of Public Health and the Bureau of Municipal Research. His little "bulletin," as he called it, would consider "the major issues in an impersonal manner," giving "the cold facts to the men who have the votes, to knowingly represent their constituents and the people of Pennsylvania." "Real representative government," he continued, "requires the representative to be equipped with facts and to make up his own mind and not have it made up for him by interested parties." Legislators with all the facts, he was sure, would no longer be swayed "by mere public opinion and prejudice."[18] And the first issues of the *Pennsylvania Legislator* were indeed filled with all sorts of facts and figures. As the months passed, however, Woodward increasingly slipped into personal and partisan rhetoric, along with slashing attacks on what he considered to be immoral propositions. As if to mirror his entire career as a reformer, the *Pennsylvania Leg-*

*islator* was often a contradictory amalgam of Woodward's alternatingly moral and empirical approaches to the world around him.

Whatever its shortcomings, the *Pennsylvania Legislator* always made for interesting reading, and fifty years later it still gives fruitful insights into the workings of Pennsylvania state government. At the time it also enhanced Woodward's power and reputation, assuring him regular access to press and public alike. Fellow senators never knew when they might become the target of his pungent wit or the subject for one of his withering political farces that even now make the reader chuckle. Some of Woodward's attacks took the forms of parables or sharply etched allegories that drew liberally on its author's wide knowledge of the Bible, medicine, and secular literature.

The first issues of Woodward's *Pennsylvania Legislator* appeared as the country was slipping deeper and deeper into economic depression. By April 1931 over fifteen percent of Philadelphia's work force was unemployed, and statewide the figure was even higher, reaching a disastrous 37.1 percent by the winter of 1933. At the same time industrial production fell to half its 1929 level. Bituminous coal production declined from 144 to seventy-five million tons over the same period, while pig iron output plummeted from fourteen million to only two million tons. Per capita income, which stood at $775 in 1929, was down to $421 in 1933.

Woodward was sickened by what had happened, referring again and again to 1931 as "this year of our disgrace." On one level his response to the Depression was essentially moral and emotional. Ever the philanthropist, he dug deeply into his own pockets to contribute to the Philadelphia relief drive, headed by Horatio Gates Lloyd. He contributed $50,000 in March 1931 and several times that amount thereafter.[19] Two months earlier he had also put up $5,000 to hire unemployed men to cut down hundreds of dead chestnut trees (victims of a recent blight) along the Wissahickon valley adjacent to Krisheim. Once felled, the trees were split into firewood and given to charitable groups who either gave the wood to the needy or sold it and used the proceeds for relief projects. Additionally, both he and Sam Houston lowered rents on their properties, in some instances forgiving rent payments altogether for particularly hard-pressed tenants.[20]

Woodward was so pleased with the results of his work project that he urged the state of Pennsylvania to establish an "industrial army" to perform similarly useful tasks throughout the commonwealth: The unemployed could enlist for six months at a time, would be fed and housed in camps, and would do such things as clearing land and constructing sewers, public buildings, and water systems. Workers would receive $30 per month in addition to board and room. The idea was not adopted in Pennsylvania, but a very similar arrangement became the Civilian Conservation Corps (CCC) under the New Deal.[21]

It was, in fact, because Woodward knew that private contributions to relief were not enough that he called on the state to act, at the same time challenging other wealthy men and women to contribute their fair share. When some refused or proved stingy in their donations, Woodward became indignant. It infuriated him to read in the newspaper that wealthy New Yorkers had displayed more than two million dollars' worth of clothing and jewelry at the opening of the Metropolitan Opera in 1931, while the unemployed huddled on park benches throughout the city. "Norman Thomas," he advised in the *Pennsylvania Legislator*, "ought to stage a bread line in the shadow . . . of the Metropolitan" to dramatize the callousness of its well-healed patrons.[22] If nothing else, he added, the nation's wealthy should give money to save their own skins from a socialist revolution, a prospect that had haunted some progressives like Woodward since early in the century. Instead, Woodward complained, the millionaires gloat that they have earned their money and "believe that many unemployed are either defectives or plain bums." Unable to face the truth, Woodward wrote, these wealthy cowards had fled South where they sunned themselves after breakfast "with yesterday's newspaper full of the excitement of the starving proletariat rioting at home," the unsavory news only increasing "the serenity of [their] morning game of golf."[23]

Since these unfeeling and selfish men would not give their fair share to relieve the suffering, Woodward believed that the state would have to seize their money through taxation. "The strong arm of the law," he advised, "must take the selfish rich man by the seat of his golf plus fours and shake the money out of his pockets."[24] He recommended a graduated state income tax and was undeterred when he learned that the Pennsylvania constitution would have to be amended to allow for differential rates. A flat two percent rate, he proposed, would soon arouse public opinion and force the constitutional amendment.[25]

On a less emotional level, Woodward thought that the state could and should find ways to help large cities like Philadelphia with their financial woes, pointing out in the *Pennsylvania Legislator* that the state of New York had given New York City more than $83 million in 1929 compared with the mere $3.8 million that Harrisburg had doled out to Philadelphia during the same period.[26] He also believed that a number of functions performed by local government should be turned over to the state, experience having convinced him that there were "many holes . . . in the old armor of local self-government." It was evident to him that state highways were better than township roads or that a state-mandated school curriculum was plainly superior to "the good old days of the little red school house."[27] In Woodward's estimation, officials at the higher levels of government were, likewise, better than local magistrates—at least as a general rule—for only the former were paid enough to attract well-trained and capable men. Most of all, citizens should remember that government was "a science and the practice of government an art."[28]

The emergency of the Depression clearly led Woodward to assign more tasks to government than his political philosophy would have allowed in the earlier decades of the century, but there were limits beyond which he would not go. He generally balked at programs that seemed to violate his belief in economical, scientific, and nonpartisan government, or that threatened to transform government into a paternalistic welfare state.

In 1931, for example, Woodward came out against an old-age pension bill that had been introduced in the Pennsylvania legislature. "Open the door to old age pensions," he warned, "and you open it to unemployment insurance and health insurance. . . . Highway and school costs are inevitable. Welfare costs must be debated. . . . It is the case of Straight Thinking vs. Emotionalism."[29] His stands against pensions proved understandably unpopular among spokesmen for the elderly. Abraham Epstein, national secretary of the American Association for Old Age Security, denounced Woodward by name, while about fifty pickets protested outside his office at the Girard Trust Building in Philadelphia and police had to be called to break them up. Demonstrators also invaded the grounds at Krisheim and were arrested by the local police.[30]

It was during these early days of the Depression that Woodward also turned completely against Governor Gifford Pinchot. A wealthy progressive like Woodward, Pinchot lived on a large and attractive estate in Milford, Pennsylvania. Woodward had known Pinchot at Yale and had applauded his triumphs as chief forester under Theodore Roosevelt. He had also supported Pinchot's first successful run for governor in 1922. But relations between them soured when Pinchot accepted the recommendations of a committee that Woodward had chaired on state government reorganization and then dubbed it the "Pinchot Plan."

Pinchot's reelection in 1930 led to even more ill feeling between the two progressive Republicans.[31] Woodward freely admitted that Pinchot was often right on the issues, but he resented what he saw as the governor's imperious attitude toward the legislature. In one of his comic lines from the *Pennsylvania Legislator,* he likened the governor to a modern movie producer with "a talky film which he has projected for us several times." On another occasion he compared Pinchot to Alice's Queen of Hearts who runs around shouting to the legislators, "Off with their heads!"

Later he called him a would-be Louis XIV who wanted to change the state motto to "L'Etat c'est moi" and wondered if the sage of Milford had not spent too much time reading Machiavelli.[32]

This open break with Pinchot undoubtedly stemmed in part from the clash of two strong-willed men, but Woodward sincerely believed in legislative supremacy and feared powerful executives at all levels of government. For him, it was a simple issue of right versus wrong. Under the circumstances it is not surprising that he became an outspoken critic of Franklin Roosevelt and the New Deal, joining a number of other progressives who turned against an administration that ironically fought for many of their old causes.

To begin with, Woodward believed that a number of New Deal measures were unconstitutional and he bitterly resented pressure from Washington to pass state legislation that was necessary to implement federal programs such as Social Security. He wrote that the central government had been "organized as a necessary condition for these United States. It was not organized to function as a high powered, wasteful institution of philanthropy."[33] He went on to invoke the residual powers clause of the Tenth Amendment in defense of states' rights, convinced that Thomas Jefferson and the other founders would have opposed federal aid to the states. "Let us all become stand-patters on state sovereignty," he implored his fellow legislators.[34]

Even more serious was what Woodward considered the New Deal's unscientific approach to solving the Depression, a common objection among progressives who had spent their lives urging rational organization and greater efficiency in government.[35] In the *Pennsylvania Legislator* Woodward complained that the country was "now witnessing a series of laboratory experiments of trial and error fostered by after-luncheon declarations pleasing to the company gathered around the table with the coffee and cigarettes, but quite disastrous to the hard world of office hours and balanced budgets."[36]

Nor did the New Dealers share Woodward's horror at blatant partisanship. Instead, in Woodward's view, Roosevelt had used the new government programs to create the greatest patronage machine in American history. More alarming, he was using this army of welfare workers to assure himself an unprecedented third term, accompanied by a dangerous expansion of executive authority.[37]

Such fears, however, did not blind Woodward to all New Deal accomplishments. He applauded many of Roosevelt's early measures for economic recovery, as well as Roosevelt's freedom from the sort of hesitation that had thwarted President Hoover's efforts at recovery. And he had nothing but praise for the Civilian Conservation Corps, the Democrats' answer to his own Industrial Army. The CCC had cost the taxpayers plenty of money, he admitted, "but we do have something to show for [it]."[38] Roosevelt's chastisements of dishonest bankers and stock manipulators also appealed to his moral sense. As he put it in the *Pennsylvania Legislator*, "A long overdue spanking has been meted out to the bad side of Wall Street."[39]

Woodward's opposition to the New Deal was thus selective, making it difficult for the observer to determine just what criteria he used for his criticisms. Roosevelt's seeming disregard for states' rights and nonpartisanship, combined with his trial-and-error approach to reform, were clearly major obstacles for Woodward. But beyond these were his worries that the New Deal would completely undermine the private initiative that he and most other Philadelphia reformers had long cherished. A good example is provided by Woodward's attitude toward public housing.

Woodward had been interested in better housing all his life. During the teens and twenties he had attended annual meetings of the National Conference on Housing, and in the early thirties was one of forty-three directors for the Regional Planning Federation of the Philadelphia Tri-State District.[40] But both of these organizations looked largely to private initiative to provide better and more attractive housing.

Even so, Woodward was curious enough about public housing in the late 1930s to visit Philadelphia's Hill Creek project near the corner of Adams Avenue and Roosevelt Boulevard. His first impulse was to applaud. "There was a warm sun shining on the well designed brick buildings," he reported cheerfully in the *Pennsylvania Legislator*. "There were happy children playing and bright flowers blooming. Here, indeed, was a good deed in a naughty world."[41]

Surely, Woodward reasoned, spending public money for decent housing was much better than cash relief, for at least the country had something to show for its expenditures. In Philadelphia he recommended that the state take over "blighted areas" and build dormitories for single people and row houses for the married. This was a clear extension of his own efforts, through the Octavia Hill Association and the Casa Ravello, to provide suitable housing for the poor. Now realizing that the task was far too great for private efforts, he was willing to consider massive state assistance.

Yet for all its good points, Woodward continued to have qualms about public housing. Across the street from the Hill Creek project were solidly built row houses purchased by their hard-working and thrifty occupants who were now taxed to subsidize the somewhat more attractive public dwellings of their neighbors. In the last analysis, Woodward could not break entirely from the "private city's" continuing belief in individual initiative and in his own belief that hard work and thrift were essential virtues. A much better solution, Woodward thought, was a plan worked out in Sweden where families borrowed money from the government to build houses on public land. The owner paid a ground rent to the city, eventually retired his mortgage, and became a proud homeowner. The municipality did not have to give housing subsidies, and it earned a tidy sum from the ground rents. Woodward had learned about the idea in Marquis W. Childs's *Sweden, the Middle Way* (1936) and he heartily recommended the book to readers of the *Pennsylvania Legislator.*[42]

The proper role of government was a question that would continue to plague Woodward for the rest of his political life. Still, much as he enjoyed the give and take of political life, politics would remain only one of his many interests. Unfortunately, it was another family tragedy that absorbed a considerable amount of his energy at home.

*The Henry family, ca. 1900. Left to right: Thomas Charlton Henry, Elizabeth Wolcott Henry (Chatfield), Charles Wolcott Henry, Sallie Houston Henry, and Gertrude Houston Henry (Dodge). CDF collection.*

*Stonehurst, residence of Charles Wolcott Henry and Sallie Houston Henry, Chestnut Hill, Philadelphia. A wedding gift from Henry Howard Houston, designed by McKim, Mead, and White, and completed in 1887. CDF collection.*

*The swimming pool at Stonehurst. CDF collection.*

*"Won't you look at me?" Courting photo of Samuel F. Houston and Edith Atlee Corlies, taken by her father, S. Fisher Corlies, in September 1886 and captioned by him. Dallett collection.*

*Charlotte Harding Shepherd (Brown) Houston, second wife of Sam-
uel F. Houston, in 1920. EHS collection.*

*"Feeding the pigeons in the Piazza, Venice," 1902. Left to right: Henry Howard Houston II, Charlie Brown, an onlooker, and Margaret Corlies Houston (Meigs). Photograph by Edith Corlies Houston (Brown). Dallett collection.*

*The Samuel F. Houston summer house at Clapboard Island, Casco Bay, Maine. Completed in 1898. EHS collection.*

*Samuel F. Houston in his office at the Real Estate Trust Company, Philadelphia, ca. 1925. EHS collection.*

*Samuel F. Houston and the children of Hendren Street, Roxborough, Philadelphia, ca. 1910. Dallett collection.*

*Family portrait in Krisheim library on occasion of Dr. George and Gertrude Wood-ward's fiftieth wedding anniversary, 9 October 1944. George Woodward III, seated beside his grandmother, with his sister Quita Woodward (Horan) on floor to right. Around them (from left to right) are Charles H. Woodward and wife, Elizabeth Gadsden Woodward; Dr. George Woodward; Stanley Woodward and wife, Shirley Rutherford Woodward; and George Woodward, Jr. SW collection.*

*The Woodwards in the garden at Krisheim, ca. 1915: Dr. and Mrs. Woodward, surrounded (from left to right) by Quita, Charles, Houston, Stanley, and George, Jr. EGW collection.*

*Krisheim, residence of Dr. George and Gertrude Houston Woodward, Chestnut Hill, Philadelphia. Designed by Peabody and Stearns and fully completed in 1912. SW collection.*

*Gertrude Houston (Mrs. George) Woodward, ca. 1930. EGW collection.*

*Dr. George and Gertrude Woodward, with dog Mozart, in electric car at Krisheim, ca. 1940. Dallett collection.*

*A set of Dr. George Woodward's quadruple houses, designed ca. 1910 by Durhing, Okie, and Ziegler and built on Benezet Street, Chestnut Hill; and Nippon Street, West Mount Airy, Philadelphia. Photo by author.*

*House in Dr. George Woodward's French Village, Gate Lane, West Mount Airy, Philadelphia. Designed ca. 1925 by Robert Rodes McGoodwin. Photo by author.*

*Dr. George Woodward, ca. 1925. EGW collection.*

CHAPTER 10

# Loss and
# Remembrance

IN MARCH 1934 the Woodwards lost a second child: this time their only daughter, Quita, who died in Zurich, Switzerland, where she had gone to receive treatments for Hodgkin's disease. Her illness and death would prompt both parents to reminisce: Gertrude in a memorial album to Quita and their life together as a family, and George in his wide-ranging autobiography. They would also find much solace in each other, traveling together extensively each year and maintaining a common interest in the welfare of Chestnut Hill.

Quita herself, as Gertrude wrote in her memorial volume, had come as a "special gift": "We had been married 15 years and had four stalwart sons; the general rejoicing over the birth of [a] daughter was very real and, to us, touching in a wide-spread character."[1] The boys felt very much the same way about the arrival of a little sister. In a school composition Stanley wrote, "My favorite pet was given to us on the Twenty-first of April, 1909. Really she is the pet of the whole house and others; she is my sister. . . . She gabbles all the time, and when she sees me she says 'burbur.'"[2] George, Jr., was so taken by her that he named his first yacht *Quita*, frequently treating his sister and her friends to cruises on the Chesapeake Bay or off the coast of Maine.[3]

Quita's unusual name—unusual in an English-speaking country, at least—was a Spanish diminutive meaning "little one." It had come from one of her mother's Bonnell relations, both aunt by marriage and second cousin, whose father, a U.S. naval officer, had probably heard it in a Spanish-speaking port. For the Woodwards, who saw Quita as their own dear little one, the name could not have been better.[4]

Quita went to Miss Landstreet's School in the early grades and then to the Springside School in the autumn of 1918. By all accounts she was a cheerful and outgoing student who made friends easily and excelled in her studies. She loved history the most, a subject that she could explore first-hand during family trips to Europe, almost always with a camera in hand to record their tramps through medieval cathedrals or Roman ruins. Fittingly, her graduation present was an extensive visit to Italy, North Africa, and Greece, undertaken with her parents in the late winter and early spring of 1928.[5]

Quita made her debut at a Krisheim garden party in June 1927. A year later she entered Bryn Mawr College where she continued to enjoy academic life while throwing herself into field hockey and drama. Bryn Mawr was only a half hour's drive from home and Quita often invited her classmates over to Krisheim. On one Sunday afternoon in early March she invited a group for tea and what turned out to be an impromptu supper, the guests having to settle for whatever could be found in the kitchen—in this case, a buffet of bacon and scrambled eggs.[6]

In the summer of 1930 Quita and her college friend, "Jenks," went to Spain and Portugal with Dr. and Mrs. Woodward. She felt fine throughout the trip. But by mid-winter 1931 she was feeling tired and weak much of the time and had to leave Bryn Mawr before the spring examinations. A summer of sailing and rest seemed to restore her—enough, anyway, so that she could make up her exams in the fall and graduate with her class in June 1932. She spent the next summer with her brother, Stanley, and his wife, Shirley, outside Salzburg, Austria, but in the fall she was ill again and Shirley took her to see a specialist in Zurich who recommended x-ray treatments. In early October her parents came over, too. Between treatments, the three of them took a trip on the famed Orient Express. Getting off at Linz, they hired a car and drove along the Danube to Vienna.[7]

Quita responded well to the x-ray therapy and the disease went into remission during the winter of 1933. She was well enough to ski at San Anton and Kitzbühel, remaining in Europe for the time being to continue her medical treatment. She returned to Philadelphia in February to be maid of honor in the wedding of her cousin, Eleanor Houston, and Sam Smith. In July she went to Salzburg for another summer with Stanley and Shirley, and then it was back to Zurich in September where her parents met her. They stayed at the Hotel Dolder, several hundred feet above the lake, and their routine was punctuated by a visit to Stanley and Shirley in Brussels and a Thanksgiving journey to Rome. Quita took a turn for the worse after they got back to Switzerland and her doctor thought it best to put her in the hospital.[8]

From February on, Quita's condition deteriorated rapidly. Her lymph glands swelled and pressed on her trachea, making it very difficult for her to breathe. Dr. Woodward engaged a local carpenter to attach a special strap across her bed so that she could rest in an upright position. Both parents prayed for a miracle, but Quita died on 6 March. They held her funeral at the Anglican church in Zurich, and there was a memorial service a month later back at St. Martin's in Chesnut Hill. Two years later they donated a new wing to the Bryn Mawr College Library in her memory.[9]

In the difficult days that lay ahead, George and Gertrude tried to console themselves through prayer. Dissatisfied with the Episcopal prayer for the dead, they wrote their own, repeating it together every night:

Into thy hands O merciful savior we commend the soul of thy servant departed from the body. Receive her into thy everlasting arms. Keep her in joy and peace against our coming into thy presence, there to dwell with her and all whom we have loved. In our grief without bitterness may we know thy eternal purpose. Send into our hearts thy Holy Spirit to comfort us. Hear us, thy children, for the sake of thy Son who died for us. God our father grant us thy peace.[10]

In addition to the enduring grief, Quita's illness and death had given both her parents many hours to reflect upon themselves and their life together as a family. Gertrude set down her recollections in the memorial album to Quita that was filled with happy photographs of her and the other children, along with accounts of their summers in Wyoming and trips abroad. George's effort, despite the nostalgic childhood tales and abundant good humor, was a very real attempt to take stock of his life.

At age seventy and several thousand miles away from home, he began the autobiography as a way of passing time during Quita's treatments in Zurich. Referring to its self-deprecating title, *Memoirs of a Mediocre Man,* he confessed at the outset that he really preferred to write about a much more important person. But with little off-hand knowledge of any great world figure and with no time to undertake elaborate research, he had little choice but to write about the life he knew best—his own. In any case, he was sure that no one else would care for the job: "If I wait for a biographer, I am certain I shall wait in vain."[11]

Of course, Woodward was an extremely important man in his own corner of the world; and he was moved to admit, a few paragraphs later, that no one's life was truly "mediocre."[12] In any case, it was clear that he wanted to explain himself to others: In the first decade of the century he had written about his reform activities; then in the teens and twenties he had published articles on his housing developments in Chestnut Hill. The *Pennsylvania Legislator* was likewise a conscious bid to make his opinions known to a wider audience, and his decision to bring them out as a series of bound volumes betrayed yet another desire to preserve his thoughts for future generations. Later he would have some of the "Krisheim News" printed in bound volumes under the title *Family Letters*. He seemed to write constantly, scribbling away in the office at Krisheim, at church during a boring sermon, or on the train to Harrisburg, invariably setting down his thoughts with a small silver pencil on yellow legal pads.[13]

Like nearly everything else Woodward wrote, the *Memoirs* are often humorous and engaging. A third of the book is about childhood and youth, with much of the rest given over to his political views, clearly the most rewarding part of his professional life: "Politics, like money and collecting objects," he declared, "never grow stale. A man with a comfortable income, a taste for first editions and a political office to which he can be re-elected ought never to grow old in spirit."[14]

It was evident from the *Memoirs*, too, that Woodward found great happiness in his marriage and home life. "In forty years," he declared, "my wife and I only quarreled once and that was before we were married."[15] They looked forward to each other's company: both found life endlessly interesting and made it a point not to nag or bore the other—qualities that also attracted a multitude of friends to Krisheim. In George's words, "It is our happy lot to keep open house for a large company of friends who find the corner of Mermaid Lane and McCallum Street a pleasant spot to visit."[16]

The *Memoirs* thus gave Woodward an opportunity to look back over an active and largely satisfying life, but it by no means signaled a wish to merely savor the past. At seventy he was still full of restless energy and when he was not in Harrisburg proposing some new scheme for state and local reform, he was riding horses along the Wissahickon Creek or driving around Chestnut Hill in his two-seater electric car to visit friends. When not occupied in Chestnut Hill, he and Gertrude were on another of their frequent trips. They spent August 1935 at Lake George, New York, and were off again in January 1936 for a cruise in the West Indies, with stops in the Virgin Islands, St. Lucia, Trinidad, Caracas, the Panama Canal Zone, and Jamaica. They loved the beach at Montego Bay where Dr. Woodward no doubt swam in his bright red, one-piece bathing suit. He wrote home that it was "the prettiest bathing beach ever advertized anywhere. It has a pretty curve with a background of green palms and grapes, clear white sand, no wind, only a breeze and clear blue water." [17] From Jamaica they sailed to Havana and from there to New Orleans where they bought train tickets to Palm Springs, California, by way of San Antonio, Texas, and the West Coast Mexican Railway. They spent a couple of weeks basking in the sun at Palm Springs. Then it was off for sightseeing in the California desert and a visit to their niece, Grace Dodge, in Tucson, Arizona. Leaving there in early March, they headed by train to Mexico City. Besides exploring the Mayan ruins, they took in an exhibit of Diego Rivera's latest works and were surprised when they liked this avowed socialist's unorthodox depictions of modern life. [18]

George and Gertrude spent the spring of 1936 at Krisheim but were off in July for the Blue Mountain Conference at Chambersburg, Pennsylvania—a combination religious retreat and adult church school. This conference and others like it that they attended at Sweet Briar College in Virginia became the high point of their summer. As usual, George described their experiences in vivid detail:

After dinner we sing hymns in the dell with quite magnificent views of the Allegheny Mountains. There is always an evening meeting, there is compline at 10 P.M. and at 10:30 everyone is supposed to be in bed. The food is better than any restaurant I have met. . . . We have a perfect position to pat ourselves on the back because we have forsaken the world, the flesh and the devil in favor of a spiritual and simple life, but it does make it pleasanter to be good in clean sheets, to breath good air and to eat good food. [19]

Under the circumstances, they could only feel sorry for those dreary resorts where everyone "talks about Katharine Hepburn and Clark Gable" while he and Gertrude were at Sweet Briar discussing Micah and Habakkuk. [20]

In August it was off to New England "to ride horseback over Vermont's back roads," after which they settled down for a couple of weeks at the Bread Loaf Inn and School of English at Middlebury. [21] Both of them loved the rustic Vermont scenery and the fact that the state was "wholeheartedly and forever anti New Deal." Vermonters, Dr. Woodward wrote home, refused federal aid for better roads and "boo[ed]" in the movie theaters whenever "Roosevelt's picture is flashed on the screen." [22] The Woodwards were back in Chestnut Hill by autumn, but right after Christmas they were off again for Jamaica where they spent the early winter of 1937.

George and Gertrude gave up Vermont the next summer to go to England as delegates to an Anglican "Conference on Church, Community and State." Dr. Woodward was amused to find that they were on the same ship with Franklin D. Roosevelt, Jr., who was beginning his honeymoon trip with Ethel Du Pont, daughter of that "economic royalist" Du Pont family that had so recently excoriated the New Deal and funded the Liberty League's strident campaign against Roosevelt in 1936.[23]

Once at the conference in Oxford, Woodward wrote that the town "has 70,000 people and 69,000 bicycles. In spite of these handicaps the colleges and churches dominate. Saturday night we attended the Russian choir of Paris in St. Mary the Virgin. . . . The six Russians sang in minor keys quite beautifully, but my neighbor, a bishop, and I did fall asleep. The bishop dropped things on the floor from time to time which kept him at attention."[24]

In the summer of 1938 they returned to New England, this time staying at Goose Rocks, Maine, where Gertrude enrolled for painting lessons with Eliot O'Hara. She had taken instruction in water colors as a girl and resumed painting after all the children were grown, eventually becoming an accomplished amateur whose canvases reflected her great love of nature. George and Gertrude both liked Goose Rocks very much and returned there annually. The rest of the year generally followed the pattern they had established in the mid-1930s: early summer at a religious retreat, August in Maine, winter in Jamaica, and the spring and autumn at Krisheim.

Back home in Chestnut Hill the Woodwards remained vitally interested in conservation projects, particularly in those that related to the Wissahickon Valley or Fairmont Park. In early 1932 they gave the park a piece of land just north of Lincoln Drive and Allen's Lane. Five years later they ceded two more tracts, one along Lincoln Drive above Springfield Avenue containing about 16,000 square feet and another near the corner of Cresheim Valley Drive and Germantown Avenue that amounted to 4,000 square feet. And in August 1945 they donated thirteen acres more to the park, most of it along St. George's Road in West Mount Airy.[25]

Meanwhile, the Woodwards fought to keep the Wissahickon Valley as natural and unspoiled as possible. When the city proposed to use a grant from the WPA to build picnic pavillions and refreshment stands along the creek, Dr. Woodward, a longtime member of the Friends of the Wissahickon, objected strenuously. Speaking on behalf of the Friends, he told the *Evening Bulletin*, "We are very much against the proposition to erect any kind of shelter in the valley. . . . Such structures would make the valley lose its naturalistic appearance and give it the semblance of an amusement park."[26] In the end, the shelters were built but without the refreshment stands.

Most of all George and Gertrude wanted the public to enjoy the primeval beauty of the Wissahickon gorge. They also delighted in sharing their own beautiful grounds, and on Sundays they opened the Krisheim gates to the whole community.[27] For working-class families on the east side of Chestnut Hill they had built the Watertower Recreation Center, named for an old standpipe at one end of the property. Located near the corner of Ardleigh Street and Hartwell Lane, the facility was built just after World War I and given to the city in memory of their son Houston. The center itself was an attractive stone edifice that contained a gymnasium, auditorium, and meeting rooms. Outside was a large athletic field, as well as playground equipment for the younger children. In 1929 the Woodwards contributed $10,000 toward a new wing at the center. More than sixty years later "the Watertower" continues to serve the Chestnut Hill community.[28]

Such projects brought both of the Woodwards much happiness despite the loss of two children in little more than fifteen years. But as the 1930s came to an end the international scene once again troubled them both.

# CHAPTER 11

# *Brothers-in-Law*

GEORGE WOODWARD AND HIS BROTHER-IN-LAW, Sam Houston, were both deeply worried about the international situation during the late 1930s, though the two of them often held different ideas about what should be done. Foreign affairs, in fact, was not the only area where they failed to agree. While Woodward had grown increasingly doubtful about prohibition, Houston continued to support the Eighteenth Amendment, remaining a strict abstainer after its repeal. And although both men were Republicans, Houston took a much more uncompromising stance against the New Deal. He sincerely believed that Roosevelt's policies were a threat to American liberty: for him Roosevelt was indeed "that man in the White House."[1] In style and appearance, too, the brothers-in-law were worlds apart. Woodward remained a tall and slender man, going about everywhere in his golf knickers, while the more robust Houston always dressed quite conservatively. Despite their differences, the two men got on well enough personally. For other members of the family, however, these years just before, during, and after World War II would bring about some sharp disagreements and hurt feelings.

If George Woodward and Sam Houston held contrary opinions about foreign policy in the 1930s, it was certainly not because either of them wanted to see a newly aggressive Germany or another world war. But Houston, far more than Woodward, took offense at isolationist assertions that the United States should steer clear of Europe's quarrels—whatever might happen "over there." Above all, he could not abide the widespread public belief that American participation in World War I had been a mistake. In an address before the Houston American Legion Post on 12 November 1939, he assured the men once again that they had not fought in vain. It was sad, he said, "to hear even among [some of] the veterans an expression of defeat—a suggestion that it was all useless."[2]

Houston also denounced the American neutrality laws during this period, which restricted trade with belligerent nations, and insisted that they were nothing less than an abandonment of national independence.[3] At the same time, he castigated the government for lack of preparedness and continued to berate the president and Congress for their lack of foresight even after the United States had entered the war.[4] Most of all, Houston believed that German aggression had to be stopped finally and completely if his son's death were to have any meaning at all.

George Woodward also detested everything he saw or read about the new regime in Germany. And, being the writer that he was, it is not surprising that he had far more to say in public than anyone else in the family about the alarming situation in Europe. Hitler's invasion of France in the spring of 1940 filled him with horror, prompting him to support aid for Great Britain and passage of America's first peacetime conscription act. Yet like most other citizens, he hoped that the United States could somehow steer clear of the conflict.[5] He was even more dubious about a war with Japan over the Pacific and Far East, charging that Roosevelt was now trying to extend the Monroe Doctrine to include the Dutch East Indies. The doctrine had already been stretched far beyond its author's original intentions according to Woodward, who believed that it should never be applied outside the Caribbean region.[6]

As for Japan itself, Woodward regretted that Commodore Perry had ever opened the islands to trade and modern influences. The Spanish-American War had also been a mistake so far as he was concerned, leading as it did to annexation of the Philippines in 1898 and the need to defend them from the Japanese.[7] He then sarcastically imagined in the *Pennsylvania Legislator* all the Pacific islands that might fall under American control after a war with Japan and of the patronage bonanza for future presidents. "Think of the political patronage looming all over the Pacific," he remarked. Or think of what it might mean to be "saluted as the Lieut. Governor of Saipan."[8]

The bombing of Pearl Harbor on 7 December 1941 and the subsequent declarations of war against Germany and Japan ended the long debate over entering the war. Woodward, like the overwhelming majority of Americans, supported the cause without question. "No one can be an isolationist, no one ought to be a pacifist," he wrote.[9]

Even so, the reality of sending young men off to fight and die was nauseating. While visiting Atlantic City in August 1942 he and Gertrude saw homesick recruits being drilled, disciplined, and painfully transformed into trained killers—only one example of how the entire nation had thrown itself into the cause. Even the schools were swept into the maelstrom of war, prompting Woodward to think how terrible it was that the "colleges have to scrap the classics and teach young men and women how to drop bombs on innocent civilians." He also reflected bitterly on the deadly role that science and technology were playing in modern warfare. "Harold the Saxon [had] died fighting valliantly against a Norman invader," he noted. "In 870 years we have learned mass production and mass destruction."[10]

But the war was inescapable, and at Krisheim the Woodwards put the whole household on alert. Gertrude ordered blackout curtains and they made their spacious cellar into a bomb shelter, complete with cots and bedding. The night watchman had the additional task of climbing up to the roof to look around for anything suspicious—above or below.[11]

In a world torn asunder by violence, the beauty and peace of Chestnut Hill became more precious than ever before, while the unbroken routine of daily life was a heartening contrast to the horrors that confronted them in the headlines and newsreels. George could still enjoy riding over the rolling hills and, oblivious to the gasoline shortages, rattle about the neighborhood in his trusty electric car. And at Christmas there were the traditional carols outside at Linden Court where sixty "choice spirits" gathered that first Christmas of the war.[12]

As the war continued and particular food items grew scarce, Dr. Woodward helped organize the Food Gardens Association, with himself as vice-president. The group urged Philadelphians to plant "victory gardens," and Woodward persuaded the Fairmount Park Commission to give over certain parcels of park land for planting.[13] Sam Houston meanwhile made undeveloped family properties available for cultivation.[14]

Like certain food items, the *Pennsylvania Legislator* was also a near casualty of the war, as Woodward announced in July 1942 that the pamphlet would be suspended for the duration. He changed his mind the following winter, however, and decided to devote each issue almost wholly to the war and its probable outcome. Above all, Woodward insisted that the war should not become an excuse for enlarging the American overseas empire. "Let us put our fight on the high ground of idealism," he urged, "and not on account of rubber or tin or tungsten."[15] Instead of vying for more islands and spheres of influence, Americans must fight for a "way of life for a Christian and democratic people."[16]

As for the Nazi tormenters themselves, Woodward could "think of no punishment really adequate for these corruptors of men's souls and bodies."

"There were seven hells in Dante's Inferno," he added, "but that was written before the Nazi curse."[17] And upon hearing of the German death camps he asked, "What adequate punishment is there for the men who stripped a little Jewish girl of her clothing, . . . threw her into a closed chamber filled with cyanide gas and cremated her body[?]"[18] Stories like these led him to find much sense in Secretary of the Treasury Morgenthau's plan to turn Germany into a land of subsistence farmers. But Woodward would go further and turn Prussia over to the Jews, exiling the Prussian Junkers to some isolated farm area outside Europe. And every year "Dr. Goebbels would be forced to announce in Yiddish the observance of Yom Kippur in Berlin."[19] Woodward was no doubt only half serious here, but he was sure about the need to de-Nazify Germany and somehow compensate the Jewish people for their monumental suffering.

When it came to peacekeeping after the war, Woodward's isolationist leanings again took the upper hand. He had little faith in an international organization like the United Nations, fearing it would only drag the United States into conflicts that were none of its concern. Such fears, he confessed, had caused him to turn against Wilson's League of Nations, adding, "My oldest son was killed in World War I and I just couldn't see my younger son being shot up to save Armenia."[20] Only the great powers themselves, he asserted, could keep order in the world—a solution adopted at the Congress of Vienna in 1815 that had kept the general peace for nearly a hundred years.[21]

To start with, Woodward advised against a formal peace treaty, for it was impossible "to write a treaty of peace that will not look moth-eaten in less than a year."[22] Nor would he allow much latitude to the smaller countries: they did not have sufficient power to maintain order and their baseless pride would make them difficult partners in any postwar arrangement.[23] Beyond these caveats, he would allow the major nations to arrange a realistic balance of power. Britain would retain its empire, "with an admonishment to behave better to India, Burma, and other exploitees."[24] The Soviets should receive the buffer states in eastern Europe they long had wanted, while the United States should be content with fostering "social and political security south of the Rio Grande."[25] Many of these ideas had come from reading Carl Becker's *How New Will the New World Be,* a book that Woodward recommended highly to fellow legislators in Harrisburg.[26]

Woodward's plans for the Soviet Union have come the closest to being realized, as Soviet forces occupied eastern Europe and secured their long-coveted buffer states. But the British empire collapsed within fifteen years after Hitler's defeat, and the United States has certainly not confined its interventions to the western hemisphere. Yet Woodward's advocacy of great power spheres did come to pass. Despite numerous local wars and the growing threat of nuclear annihilation, there has been general peace for over four decades. And for reasons that Woodward did not foresee, there was no formal peace treaty after the war.

Closer to home, Woodward believed that the country should do something for the returning soldiers who, if nothing else, deserved a decent home for their efforts. Yet he hesitated to help if it meant imposing a massive welfare state, prompting him once again to wonder if there could not be some sort of "middle way between every man for himself and every man controlled by paternal and maternal government apron strings."[27]

Whatever was done, these returning soldiers would face a difficult transition. The end of the war would also mark a turning point in the way all Americans lived. Postwar prosperity, the baby boom, and an avalanche of new cars meant a bonanza for residential building, while high taxes and a dwindling supply of servants signaled a breakup of many large estates. Such changes would ultimately have a strong impact on Houston family properties.

Yet even before the war, forces within the family had led to new development plans. The death of Sallie Henry in June 1938, for example, inevitably raised questions about the future of Stonehurst.[28] The eldest of Henry Howard Houston's surviving children, she and her husband had occupied the second of the family's large residences in Chestnut Hill.

By the time of Sallie's death all of her children were married with children. Her son, T. Charlton Henry, who had died two years before his mother, was married to Julia Rush Biddle, a descendant, as her middle and maiden names proclaimed, of two distinguished Philadelphia families. Sallie's daughter Gertrude had married Donald D. Dodge. The third Henry daughter, Elizabeth ("Bizzy"), had wed William Hayden Chatfield of Cincinnati and had gone to live in his home town.

The two Henry daughters, as well as Charlton's widow, Julia, were also comfortably settled in their own homes at the time of Sallie's death and were reluctant to take over Stonehurst. Julia, a fashionable woman of international renown, was quite contented with her own spacious Chestnut Hill house, Eastdene.[29] Nor were the other two children interested: Bizzy Chatfield, an accomplished horsewoman and lover of the out-of-doors, and her husband, Bill, had no intention of leaving Cincinnati, while Gertrude and Donald Dodge, with a beautiful Chestnut Hill home and plantation in South Carolina, made their permanent home in Rockport, Maine.[30] Since there seemed little point in paying over $10,000 a year in real estate taxes on a property that no one in the family wanted to occupy, the children decided to demolish Stonehurst and divide the fifty acres or so surrounding it into building lots.[31]

The war interrupted any immediate development at Stonehurst. In 1949, however, the Dodges' daughter, Cornelia Fraley, introduced them to architect Oscar Stonorov, in whose offices she was then working. Stonorov presented the Dodges with an exciting residential plan which they accepted with some alterations. After buying out the other heirs and securing all the necessary surveys and building permits, the project was made public in June 1953. Philadelphia newspapers announced that the development would be known as Cherokee, after a street running along the east side of the property.[32]

Both Stonorov and the Dodges wished to do as little damage as possible to existing landscape and foliage: preexisting roads through the property were kept intact, while individual housing units were situated so as to save a maximum number of trees. On the northeastern portion of the grounds, Stonorov designed fifteen two-story structures whose units ranged in size from complete "townhouses" to one- and two-bedroom apartments. Rents were from $100 to $200 a month. The modern-style buildings were either 120 or 240 feet long, with façades of red brick, off-white stucco, and numerous windows of varying sizes. To the south and west of these there were to be a dozen or so single dwellings. Stonorov designed several of the residences himself in a daring contemporary style that gave occupants a dramatic view of the surrounding hills through huge plate-glass windows. Their plain brick exteriors, however, tied them aesthetically with the multi-unit dwellings elsewhere on the grounds. In the mid-1960s a lower section of the former estate, known as Cornelia Place, was also opened for the construction of single-dwelling homes.

The creation of Cherokee did not go without criticism from other members of the extended family. Anticipating the possibility of dissent, Donald Dodge was careful to consult with his wife's Aunt Gertrude Woodward about details and made sure that none of the new units would come too close to the Krisheim boundary.[33] Nevertheless, Gertrude could not help feeling that a subdivision of the Stonehurst grounds was a grievous mistake. Unable to sleep for thinking about it one night, she sat down around 3 A.M. and wrote an unusually frank letter to Donald. The plan, she thought, would "destroy the character of the neighborhood," while lowering property values throughout the area. She also worried that the whole complex might someday be sold to an outside company that would have little regard for local residents. But, worst of all, she thought that her nephew-in-law was violating a family trust: "It does not seem right," she declared, "for one member of the Houston family to do anything which destroys the country character of the region which our father had the vision to create." As if to make her point perfectly clear, she added, "A good name is better than riches." And in answer to the argument that property taxes were a personal burden, she contended that Henry Howard Houston had expected them to be paid out of the generous income from his estate.[34]

Donald was understandably pained by Gertrude's letter, responding a week later to each of her arguments. He denied that the development would hurt property values and reminded her that with an income only one-third as large as her own the real estate taxes were indeed a heavy expense. Besides, no one could expect property in a modern metropolitan area to remain unchanged for seventy to eighty years: "Growth of populations surrounding great cities simply does not stand still; our whole manner of living has been changed . . . by the advent of the automobile." Donald further insisted that even Henry Howard Houston himself, "being [the] practical man" that he was, would understand such changes and the need for appropriate action.[35] Neither correspondent persuaded the other, but the Woodward family became reconciled to the project in the end.

Meanwhile, Sam Houston had been forced to think about developing the thousands of acres of land that remained part of the Houston estate. The Henry heirs in particular regretted that the estate continued to pay large amounts of taxes on this property that produced nothing in return. Some members of the Henry family also believed that a reinvestment of many trust holdings could have generated far greater returns over the years. At the same time they contended that stock dividends on the oil shares should be distributed among the heirs, despite a family agreement in 1915 that they would be retained as principal.

After internal negotiations broke down, the matter was taken before Orphan's Court in the summer of 1941. Council for the Houston estate argued that the investments had remained highly diversified and that the oil stocks in particular had performed very well over the years. The lawyers also pointed out that Henry Howard Houston's will had authorized but not required the trustees to make new investments. On the question of distributing the oil stock dividends, they contended that the plaintiffs themselves had not been a party to the 1915 agreement and were therefore not legally entitled to challenge it. In September 1942 Judge Charles Sinkler upheld the trustees' management of the Houston estate and denied the Henrys' claims for $5 million. As it turned out, the oil stocks would increase in value greatly over the next twenty years—to everyone's benefit. Whether other investments might have done better will, of course, never be known. But at the time there were anger and hurt feelings on both sides.[36]

When it came to the family real estate holdings, Sam Houston had actually been looking for ways to develop various tracts. In the late 1920s the Houston estate had built the Chestnut Hill Apartments, a large stone structure in the 200 block of West Evergreen Avenue.[37] A decade later the estate had also built Tohopeka Court, a charming cluster of small brick houses on West Highland Avenue designed by Robert Rodes McGoodwin.[38]

It was in Roxborough, however, that the great bulk of family land remained. Henry Howard Houston had doubtless wanted to develop Upper Roxborough as an attractive railroad suburb much like Chestnut Hill, but the failure to build the Roxborough railroad in the early 1890s made any further development impossible until the arrival of automobiles on a large scale some twenty or thirty years later. Yet even after the advent of automobile transportation, Roxborough remained relatively inaccessible: a narrow bridge across the Wissahickon at Bell's Mill Road remained the only direct link between Roxborough and Chestnut Hill, while the sole route from Roxborough downtown was along the congested Ridge Avenue which already ran through some of the worst slums in the city. Nevertheless, the Houston estate hoped that wealthy Philadelphians might be persuaded to carve out large country houses on the Roxborough hills. But Roxborough never caught on as a fashionable address, as the "country set" chose to settle in the already exclusive Gwynedd Valley to the east.[39]

By the late 1930s it was abundantly clear that Roxborough would never become another Chestnut Hill. Accordingly, Sam Houston engaged architect McGoodwin to design fourteen semidetached houses on Hendren Street, just a block west of Ridge Avenue. Alternating between red brick and painted cinder block, these units were set off with attractive latticework, much of it arranged in diamond-shaped patterns, around the front entrances. Houston rented these dwellings at very modest rates during the war to women whose husbands were away in the military. One summer day after the war, the children of Hendren Street threw a party for their "Mr. Houston," a delightful affair that he never forgot.[40] McGoodwin designed ten more twins for the Houston estate—to the east of Ridge Avenue on Graykin Lane—that were completed in May 1941. Trimmed with shutters and constructed of red brick and white wooden siding, the small dwellings took on a quaint "colonial look." Entrances were distinguished by the same delicate latticework that had appeared on the Hendren Street houses.[41]

In addition to building these two sets of houses in Roxborough, Houston had also tried to attract several large institutions to the area. In 1921 he failed to interest the city in a site for the nation's sesquicentennial observance, to be celebrated five years later. However, he managed to sell the same tract in 1927 to the Episcopal diocese for a projected cathedral.[42] Resting on one of the highest spots in the city, the cathedral site would be much like Mount St. Albans in Washington where the "National Cathedral" had been rising since early in the century. Houston himself donated the mortuary chapel, but only the chapel and the choir were completed— largely due to declining diocesan interest and a corresponding lack of funds.[43] (In the 1970s the grounds were used to build Cathedral Village, a retirement home affiliated with the Episcopal church.)

Just before World War II, Houston also offered to sell Roxborough land to the Veterans' Administration which had announced plans to locate a new hospital in the Philadelphia area. The project was postponed until after the war when the VA chose a site near the University of Pennsylvania.[44] It was right after the war, too, that Houston tried to sell about 600 acres to the United Nations as a site for their permanent headquarters. While negotiations were pending, John D. Rockefeller, Jr., donated a site along the East River in New York, ending any prospect of the organization's coming to Roxborough.[45] Then in 1947 and 1948 the Houston estate tried to entice Temple University into the area. Temple was thinking seriously about moving from its North Philadelphia campus into a more suburban setting, but decided against it when the state offered substantial funds in exchange for the school's remaining at the old location.[46]

Under the circumstances, the extensive development of small and moderate-sized homes seemed the only solution in Roxborough. Although such a project could not be undertaken until after World War II, Houston hired McGoodwin to make a survey of the Roxborough lands in the summer of 1943. Since property taxes were particularly high on land east of Ridge Avenue, McGoodwin recommended that this area be developed first. Property west of "the Ridge" was taxed at a lower rate because it was hillier and less accessible. He added that a bridge across the Wissahickon Creek, connecting Cathedral Road in Roxborough with Hartwell Lane in Chestnut Hill, would facilitate real estate ventures on both sides of Ridge Avenue and make the properties more valuable. (Because of opposition from residents on the west side of Chestnut Hill, including Houston's nephew, Charles Woodward, the bridge would never be built.)[47]

McGoodwin's findings made even more sense once the postwar building boom became apparent and the city of Philadelphia agreed to widen and extend Henry Avenue. Named for Houston's brother-in-law, Charles Wolcott Henry, the new thoroughfare provided a fast and convenient route between Roxborough and downtown Philadelphia. In 1948 the Houston estate accordingly decided to launch an ambitious residential development on the east side of Roxborough. They named the new neighborhood "Andorra" after a mid-nineteenth-century deer park on the same site, as well as for the Andorra Nurseries that had occupied the premises subsequently. Designed by Philadelphia architect Walter K. Durham, Andorra would include twin houses, single-family dwellings, and apartment buildings, with a shopping center located conveniently on the corner of Cathedral Road and Ridge Avenue. If all went well, around 5,000 residential units would be built, creating a bustling automobile suburb far different from the quiet enclave that Henry Howard Houston must have envisioned six decades earlier.

Ground-breaking ceremonies for Andorra took place on the cold and windy morning of 18 March 1950. An eighty-three-year-old Sam Houston welcomed the small crowd with a brief address, giving a little history of the area and referring specifically to the abortive railroad venture nearly sixty years earlier. Philadelphia Mayor Bernard Samuel then turned the first shovelful of earth.[48]

The Houston estate itself built only a fraction of the projected dwellings, the remainder of the Andorra property being sold to other developers. Sam Houston himself did not live to see the project finished. His wife Charlotte had died in 1940 following a series of strokes that had kept her confined to bed for several years. In 1943, Sam retired as president of the Real Estate Trust but remained active as a trustee at the University of Pennsylvania, where he completed fifty years as a board member in 1948. He continued to visit his alma mater frequently, strolling about campus and usually making a point of dropping by Houston Hall. His auto license plate, with the figures "PA 87," was also a familiar sight around the university. Death came on 2 May 1952 at Druim Moir where Houston had been suffering for several months from cancer of the liver. He was buried beside Charlotte in the unfinished Episcopal cathedral on the peak of the Roxborough hills.[49]

These postwar years also saw George Woodward's retirement from the Pennsylvania state senate after twenty-eight years and seven consecutive terms. He was the oldest man in the senate by then and could claim the longest consecutive service of anyone in the chamber, a distinction that had entitled him to "seat number one" for well over a decade. He gave no official reason for retiring, but at age eighty-three he was worried that his health would not see him through another term. He had recovered quite successfully from the removal of a kidney in 1944, but the operation doubtless came as a signal to slow down a little.[50] His only public regret was having to leave the legislature before "city-county consolidation ha[d] been accomplished."[51] In 1947 the legislative session opened for the first time in nearly three decades without the promise of George Woodward's ready wit and unquenchable thirst for political reform.

Although he was now out of public office, Woodward was not about to abandon all political activity. In early 1947 he was made chairman of a new charter commission in Philadelphia.[52] The eventual result was a new city charter, approved by the voters in April 1951 and put into operation the following year. While it did not abolish the dual city-county government altogether, several of the county "row offices" were disbanded or merged with city departments.[53] The municipal civil service was also overhauled: a stronger merit system was installed, the city council was stripped of all ap- pointive power, and a new civil service commission was created. There would also be a managing director who presided over the ten service de- partments such as police, fire, recreation, health, and welfare. The position was not identical to Woodward's city manager, but it was very similar in concept. Finally, the charter elevated the office of mayor, giving him the authority to veto council legislation along with wide authority to appoint and remove members of his administration.[54]

Woodward himself did not live long enough to pass judgment on the new charter. He died at Krisheim of kidney failure on 25 May 1952, just three weeks after Sam Houston's death. There would be yet another funeral at St. Martin's, with burial in the St. Thomas's churchyard at Whitemarsh.[55]

CHAPTER 12

# The Preservationists

UNLIKE THEIR PARENTS, the surviving grandchildren of Henry Howard Houston had ample time to assume positions of responsibility before their own parents passed from the scene. As is so often the case in Philadelphia families, this third generation became intensely interested in preserving what previous generations had handed down. But to an unusual degree the grandchildren embarked on their own creative ventures—in Philadelphia and in the world beyond.

The oldest of George Woodward's three surviving sons was George, Jr. (1897–1967).[1] His eyes had been badly aligned from birth, disfiguring his face and making it extremely difficult for him to read. School was understandably a torment for him and he dropped out of the Chestnut Hill Academy before graduating. In other ways, too, he was the least attractive of the five Woodward children, having been described by one family member as "tall and gangling."

Perhaps in compensation for his poor eyesight and lack of academic promise, George fell in love with all sorts of mechanical devices, spending much of his free time with miniature steam engines and "mechano sets." He could also devote his talents to mischievous ends. One of his tricks was to insert a penny between a light bulb and lamp socket, blowing a fuse as soon as someone turned on the switch.

From sabotaging the family's lamps he eventually moved to motorcycles. One morning Dr. Woodward awoke to find a bright red Indian motorcycle, complete with sidecar, in the front hallway at Krisheim, doubtless dripping oil all over the Mercer tiles. George had only wanted to give it a safe haven for the night, but his father thought otherwise and banished it to the garage for safekeeping.

Then came a series of automobiles, the first of them a White "steamer." Besides having to fire the kerosene boiler before setting off, George had to worry about replenishing its water supply every twenty-five or thirty miles. For this purpose he carried a long rubber hose that wrapped around the frame of the car to be uncoiled and dropped into the Wissahickon Creek or Schuylkill River for a fresh tank of water.

George's love affair with cars also landed him in several scrapes. A now elderly friend recalled one summer evening when she and several friends went out joy riding with him, "careening around the neighborhood, singing songs, and having a high old time." Their merriment caught the attention of a local policeman who chased after them on horseback blowing his whistle and motioning for them to stop. When George continued, the officer drew his gun, shot into the air, and finally brought the young daredevil to a stop. The girls were all driven home in disgrace and George spent the night in the Chestnut Hill jail for disturbing the peace. A more than irritated Dr. Woodward had to come over and bail him out the next morning.[2]

At other times George's experience with automobiles came in quite handy—as during his stint in the Naval Reserves at Cape May, New Jersey, during World War I. The commander soon recognized George's skill behind the wheel and made him his personal chauffeur.[3]

But even more than driving and tinkering with cars, George loved sailing. Shortly after the war he bought a used, thirty-four-foot power boat called the *Walrus,* which, like his later boats, he kept down at Cape May. With his friend Roy Stuart he cruised from Philadelphia to New York, then up the Hudson River, across to Lake Champlain and the Richelieu River and from there down the St. Lawrence to Quebec. One winter he foolishly undertook a trip to Florida with three friends on a schooner he was later to purchase. They ran into a storm and were blown far out to sea. After two weeks on the water, and nearly out of water and food, they finally made it into Palm Beach and put themselves up at the luxurious Breakers Hotel for a much needed bath and good night's sleep. But a disastrous fire swept the hotel that night and they barely escaped with their lives.

After the sailing schooner he bought a yawl (naming both of them after his sister Quita) and spent a lot of time at the Philadelphia Corinthian Yacht Club. Brother Stanley has described George as a "lighthouse to light-house sailer." He would start out with some lighthouse up or down the coast as his destination, put in to the nearest port for a while, take on supplies when needed, and then sail on to the next coastal beacon. He also entered the two *Quitas* in the Bermuda races, boasting that he finished last in both 1926 and 1930.[4]

Despite such adventures, George never seemed to lack sailing companions. He was likewise quite popular among the younger set back home in Chestnut Hill. These were the "roaring twenties" and George's friends were more than happy to help the decade along. One Saturday morning in the autumn of 1922 his father arrived home from vacation two days early, only to find one of George's weekend house parties in full swing. He soon discovered that there were six young ladies in the third-story guest rooms and about eight young men strewn among the rooms on the second floor, with a matronly cousin playing the role of chaperone. Father George got very little sleep that night, what with "two-somes on the library porch, four-somes in the pantry and a general rally in the billiard room." He managed to drag George, Jr., and some of his friends off to St. Martin's church on Sunday morning, but the peace was shattered as soon as they got back to Krisheim. The party wore on into Sunday evening, leaving Dr. Woodward with the grateful thought that Monday morning could not be too far off.[5]

The house parties came to an end only when George moved into an apartment downtown. Meanwhile he began taking more and more responsibility for the houses at George Woodward, Incorporated. He liked to go out to the construction sites, especially to check up on the plumbing and wiring. In about 1925 he replaced his father as president of the company, releasing the senior Woodward to devote more time to politics and other interests. Soon thereafter George moved the office from the Girard Trust Building downtown to an eighteenth-century stone house at 8031 Germantown Avenue. His mother had spotted the somewhat dilapidated residence, bought it, had it restored, and turned it over to the firm.

As a landlord, George could be most accommodating, especially when he liked his tenants personally. If they wanted an extra room, an extension onto the kitchen, or a patio in the back, he was usually glad to oblige, whatever the expense. And during the Depression of the 1930s he forgave the rent of more than one hard-pressed family. But he also liked to drop by the properties for unannounced inspections, to the dread of unwary tenants. Certain details could also irritate George: broken-down gates among them. Anyone asking for a new gate invited a litany of protest, but the tenant was also likely to be astonished when workmen installed another gate within several weeks.

If George were willing to relent over new gates, he refused to make any concessions on the subject of Franklin Roosevelt. A Republican like his father, George lacked the flexibility that marked Senator Woodward's politics. George seldom passed up a chance to rage against "that man in the White House," prompting even his father to avoid comment on Roosevelt or the New Deal in his son's presence. Brother Stanley, who became a lifelong Democrat, steered clear of political discussion altogether during family gatherings.

Remarkably, George became an admirer of Eleanor Roosevelt after hearing her speak in the late thirties at the present Allen's Lane Art Center in nearby Mount Airy. He was full of praise for her after the meeting, dumfounding his family, who had grown resigned to his anti-Roosevelt diatribes. His sudden liking for Mrs. Roosevelt is even more remarkable in view of her pronounced liberalism. In the last analysis, George's political tastes were probably grounded as much in purely personal factors as they were in partisan labels.

If Eleanor Roosevelt escaped George's verbal wrath, most other public figures did not. Besides attacking FDR every chance he got, George was fond of hurling blasts at most any personality who mildly irritated him. Perhaps these exhibitions of verbal toughness were simply George's way of combatting his own feelings of physical inferiority and self-doubt.

As he grew older, George was also notorious for his disheveled appearance. He bragged to his brothers about wearing the butlers' discarded shoes and thought nothing of wearing old and worn suits to the office. As one in-law put it, "George was determined to be the family character." Always different from his brothers, George's eccentricities may have been his own brave way of admitting these differences to others, while unconsciously trying to face his physical limitations.

In marriage George found happiness as well as sorrow. In 1931 he married Asenath Brooks Thompson of Harwichport, Massachusetts, whose family had long been the proprietors of the Snow Inn there. She suffered a miscarriage early in their marriage and soon thereafter learned that she had a serious heart condition. Her health gradually declined and she died in the spring of 1943. Two years later he wed Laura Leonard, a teacher at the Garland cooking school in Boston, only to lose her in August 1949 after a long bout with cancer. George's third marriage was in November 1954 to Harriet Ellison Hirst of Charlotte, North Carolina. All three marriages were childless.[6]

George's own life came to a painful end in January 1967 when he died of severe burns to the chest and head. He had fallen asleep while smoking one evening and set fire to his shirt. Ever mindful of community needs, he left $1 million in his will to Chestnut Hill Hospital along with smaller bequests to St. Martin's Church and the Chestnut Hill Academy. A life income from the remainder of his estate went to his wife Harriet.[7]

Of Dr. Woodward's three surviving sons, George's personal life was undoubtedly the most difficult. Yet, he was well known for his acts of individual kindness and was genuinely loved by scores of friends. His careful management of the family's real estate business over nearly half a century has also done much to preserve the beauty and tranquility of Chestnut Hill.

But it was George's youngest brother, Charles (1904–1986), who most successfully extended their father's interests in housing and conservation.[8] In fact, Charles turned out to be something of a thwarted architect who discovered his real ambition much too late to make the family's preoccupation with fine housing into a lifetime career. Instead, he had chosen to become a lawyer.

Charles prepared for college at St. George's School in Newport, Rhode Island, and then it was off to Yale and the University of Pennsylvania Law School. St. George's had long been a favorite among well-to-do Philadelphians, while the choice of Yale and Penn were doubtless influenced by family custom. His father, uncle, and two brothers had all gone to Yale before him; and by entering the University of Pennsylvania Law School he became part of a Houston tradition that went all the way back to the eighteenth century.

Even Charles's decision to become a lawyer turned more on family custom and social convention than from any genuine interest in the law. Young men from his background simply became bankers, stockbrokers, lawyers, or, less frequently, Episcopal clergymen. Charles had no interest in banking or business, and he certainly had no intention of becoming a parish priest: that left a legal career. As his father put it, "You'll never go wrong by becoming a lawyer." After graduation from law school in 1929, he went to work with the prominent firm of Hepburn and Norris.

Still a bachelor, Charles shared an apartment downtown for a while with his brother George, but returned to Krisheim when George was married in 1931. It was in the fall of 1933 that he met his future wife, Elizabeth ("Betty") Prioleau Gadsden of Charleston, South Carolina, who had come up to Chestnut Hill to visit her Uncle John and Aunt Mary Sinkler. Originally from South Carolina themselves, the Sinklers belonged to that well-established social and familial network among the upper classes of Philadelphia and Charleston.

This tale of two cities had begun well back in the 1700s when Philadelphia shippers began transporting rice and indigo for Charleston planters. It continued into the next century as Philadelphia bankers, brokers, and insurance agents reached out for southern clients. Shippers, lawyers, businessmen, and brokers, sometimes accompanied by their wives and children, moved back and forth between the coastal cities, particularly in summer, when Charlestonians came north to escape the heat. Friendships were formed, marriages contracted, and children born, welding widely separated peoples into a union of memory and blood. In time, the Charleston-Philadelphia connection took on a life of its own, nurturing itself as successive generations visited each other, fell in love, and settled across sectional lines.

In Betty's case it was Aunt Mary's notion to invite young Charles Woodward to tea and then to dinner that opened up yet another chapter in this continuing story of North and South. Betty was then twenty-one, had made her debut, and was already somewhat bored by the young swains of Charleston. Her departure from Chestnut Hill for home touched off a flurry of letters between her and Charles and soon thereafter a visit from him.

As he was soon to discover, Charleston was in fact a small city compared with Philadelphia, with only 60,000 people in 1930 compared with Philadelphia's nearly two million. Presiding over its social life were several dozen interconnected families whose ancestors had founded the city in the mid- to late seventeenth century. Betty's family, the Gadsdens, were among these earliest settlers. One of them was the rabid revolutionary, Christopher Gadsden, who designed the now famous yellow flag with the coiled snake and uncompromising motto, "Don't Tread on Me." A later ancestor negotiated the Gadsden Purchase from Mexico.

On her mother's side the Chisolms owned a large plantation on the sea islands off Beaufort, South Carolina. Forced to flee from advancing northern troops during the Civil War, they returned home to find everything destroyed. They moved into a former slave cabin for shelter, while the lady of the house sold her ring for enough money to buy a family cow.

Destroyed plantation houses were far from Betty's thoughts as she and her mother discussed her beau's first visit—though Charles's firm northern roots were a matter of some maternal concern. "Oh my God, a Yankee," was her initial reaction, quickly followed by visions of her daughter's living in a cold and snowy climate.

But that was not the "worst of it," Betty warned her family of loyal Democrats. "He's also been speaking on street corners for Herbert Hoover." "And," she explained, "They drink coffee up in Philadelphia after dinner"—a strange custom that nevertheless sent Mrs. Gadsden off to borrow a set of demitasse cups and a silver coffee pot.

Charles himself was a nervous wreck when he finally came to dinner that first afternoon. Sitting down at the table, he immediately took up his napkin and began to polish his silverware. "Are you worried about the silver?" Mrs. Gadsden asked, forcing an embarrassed Charles to explain that it was a bad habit he had picked up from his father who regularly applied his napkin to the silver on the Pennsylvania Railroad as he rode back and forth to Harrisburg. Then as if to redeem himself, Charles made a special point of talking about old Judge Woodward's Democratic politics and unrelenting hatred of President Lincoln.

Whatever they all thought of the meal, Charles began coming regularly each weekend. But the whirlwind trips were not without their toll in lost sleep and train fares, convincing Charles that he ought to ask for Betty's hand—and do it soon. They were married 7 January 1933 at historic St. Michael's Church in Charleston. The bride wore "a beautiful [gown] of white satin made on plain lines," the *Philadelphia Bulletin* reported, "with a veil of tulle extending to the end of her train." [9] After a honeymoon in the West Indies, the newlyweds moved into Krisheim until one of the Woodward houses became vacant. After about six months they moved into the French Village at 415 Gate Lane. It was while there that both of their children were born: Quita in January 1934 and George three years later.

For the new husband there was a return to the weekly rhythm of work. He commuted daily on the train, with lunch downtown at the Philadelphia or Rittenhouse Clubs. He had already begun to grow discontented with legal practice, but family wealth or not, he was expected "to do something," and he put in his long hours like any other conscientious young lawyer. At the same time he became more and more active in local politics.

Dr. Woodward had supposed in his *Memoirs* that Charles was the most likely to succeed him politically and encouraged his son to become involved in public affairs. [10] Charles accordingly joined the Progressive Republican League in Germantown, becoming its president in the early 1930s. At the election of 1932 he spoke out for Herbert Hoover and accused the Democrats of dangerous inflationary schemes to combat the Depression. There was even talk in the spring of 1937 of making him chairman of the Republican city committee, but the organization blocked his selection, citing his lack of wide political experience. Later that year Charles spoke out in favor of his father's amendment to merge city and county government in Philadelphia. [11]

Despite his ongoing support for the Republican party, Charles shared his father's political independence and desire for reform. To the extent that he was a partisan Republican, he clearly sided with the liberal wing of the party as represented by Thomas A. Dewey and then Nelson Rockefeller. Thus when Democrats Joseph S. Clark and Richardson Dilworth challenged the entrenched Republican machine in Philadelphia during the late 1940s and early 1950s, Charles joined with fourteen other like-minded members of his party to form "Republicans for Clark and Dilworth." [12] He enthusiastically supported their plans to reform city government, but also believed that a sweeping Democratic victory was the only way to destroy the old machine and renew the Republican cause. Two decades later he showed few qualms over breaking with his party on Richard Nixon, particularly after Betty appeared on the White House "enemies list" as a result of her generous support for Democratic candidates and her outspoken criticism of the Watergate scandal. [13]

Although Charles worked hard for various candidates, he did not seek elective office himself. In the early years he believed that local voters would balk at supporting two Woodwards, forcing him to stay out of elective politics until his father's retirement from the state senate in 1947. Even then he failed to take the plunge. In the last analysis he probably was not of the right temperament to become a practicing politician. He valued his privacy far too much and doubtless shied away from the rough and tumble of practical vote-getting.

In any case Charles found plenty to do for the city outside of public office. During 1932 he worked to alleviate unemployment by heading up the United Campaign in the Germantown area, part of a citywide project to collect private relief funds. Later in the thirties he led drives for the Germantown YMCA to attract additional money and membership. Such activities were interrupted when World War II began and Charles went to work in contract procurement for the Army and Navy in Philadelphia. [14]

By the time the war ended Charles was a mature man in his early forties whose personal habits and basic temperament were well formed. He could be as outspoken as his father on issues that were important to him, and just as stubborn in wanting to have things his own way. He also inherited much of his father's keen wit, to the delight of everyone around him. People who did not know Charles well could find him aloof, but to family and friends he was a man of great warmth and generosity. He loved to be surrounded by his family, purposely choosing to live near his aging parents, while enjoying the company of his own wife and children. A deeply private man, he would shun publicity all his life, and preferred to make his extensive charitable and civic donations anonymously. Charles had enormous energy and curiosity, combined with a tremendous zest for travel. And, like his parents, he prepared carefully for every trip by reading as much as he could about all the places they planned to visit.

For anyone who liked to travel as much as Charles, the life of a staid Philadelphia lawyer held little appeal after the war, and he decided not to go back to his practice. With no regular job to tie him down, he and Betty decided in 1946 to buy a plantation. They had made numerous visits to

South Carolina over the years and Charles had come to love the land as much as Betty. They looked at every available property around Charleston, finally buying about 500 acres on the Santee River, forty miles north of the city. Called "The Wedge" because of the wedgelike shape of its boundaries, their new winter home had once been a rice plantation belonging to the Lucas family. The Woodwards raised a few head of cattle for beef and sold timber from their heavily wooded estate, but The Wedge was unsuitable for any kind of large-scale cultivation. They also enjoyed horseback riding through the meadows and woods. As a rule they arrived at The Wedge in early January and stayed until April when they returned to Philadelphia.

The acquisition of The Wedge also coincided with another interest that would occupy them both intensely for the next forty years—the restoration of historic buildings. As Betty put it, "Charles was really a frustrated architect." His parents' deep commitment to tasteful architecture had clearly impressed him, and he had loved his fine arts electives at Yale. Years later he would be enthralled by Kenneth Clark's "Civilization" series on Public Television.

Charles's first adventure in architectural design had actually come in 1939 when they decided to build a modern house on Millman Street in Chestnut Hill, directly across from Pastorius Park. They hired Kenneth Day as their architect, but Charles went over the smallest details of the plans and added numerous suggestions of his own even after the house was taking shape, a habit that he would continue over the decades—often to the great annoyance of his architects.

The winters near Charleston seemed to whet his interest in architecture even further. Perhaps it was the novel and exotic beauty of so many Charleston houses that piqued his interest. Whatever it was, their first foray into historical restoration began simply enough. A tall, three-story brick house caught their eye one evening in the late 1950s as they drove down East Bay Street toward the Charleston harbor. The house, Betty discovered, had once belonged to a Gadsden and as they drove by it on successive occasions it began to gnaw away at both of them. "Charles, that house is looking at me," Betty finally said. "And I'm looking at it. I just hate to see it looking so derelict and so pathetic." "Let's buy it," he answered.

The Woodwards not only bought the Gadsden House but completely restored and renovated it. Built in around 1800, the house was typical of the larger city residences built by planters to escape the tropical heat of their plantations during the summer. Tall, deeply shaded porches encircled the house on both the first and second floors to shield the interior from the scorching sun while admitting cool breezes from the harbor below. The porches and other external features were restored to their former elegance, while on the inside the house was divided into three spacious apartments with completely new plumbing and wiring. Once finished, Betty and Charles turned the residence over to the Historic Charleston Foundation which would maintain the structure and use the remaining income to finance other projects. Soon thereafter they bought three very similar dwellings near the Gadsden House and likewise restored them for the foundation.

In the early sixties they took on a much more ambitious project with the old Mikell House at 94 Rutledge Avenue, which in recent decades had been occupied by the Charleston County Free Library. Built in 1853 by planter Isaac Jenkins Mikell, the residence was a massive Greco-Roman edifice that one newspaper writer described as Scarlet O'Hara's "Tara in a metropolitan setting." Actually the Mikell House is a bit more austere than the fictional house in *Gone With the Wind*, with its two-story pedimented portico resting on six massive Corinthian columns. In any case, the Woodwards bought and restored the property, dividing the interior into three spacious apartments. Charles and Betty, who had decided to sell their plantation at The Wedge, took over the middle portion of the house in 1963 and rented the other two.[15]

By 1965 they had salvaged yet another dwelling, this one a "single-style" house at 59 Smith Street that had been built by a Captain Joseph Jenkins in about 1818. Called a "single-style" house because it is only one room wide with its narrow end to the street, such houses had been built by the hundreds during the first half of the nineteenth century. An open gallery along the length of the structure was perfect for keeping out the sun and catching the sea breezes, with the narrow street end minimizing exposure to outside noise.

Next was the Charles H. Drayton House at 25 East Battery, which Charles and Betty bought in conjunction with Mrs. John F. Maybank in April 1971. Constructed between 1883 and 1886, the Drayton House is one of the best examples of flamboyant Queen Anne architecture in Charleston. The wide overhanging roofs, long verandas, and Oriental fretwork on the railings make it look something like a Chinese pagoda from the side, while the narrower street front presents a more familiar Queen Anne façade with a stick-style balcony on the third floor and a carved sunburst under the peak of the sharply slanted roof.[16]

Then in 1973 they sponsored the restoration of an ornate rotunda at the Gibbes Art Gallery. Almost wholly Betty's idea, she commissioned Marguerite Sinkler Valk to redesign it, explaining that she wanted the rotunda to resemble "a precious jewel" when finished. And to many visitors the refurbished space looked much like an emerald, with pale celery walls, "accented by rich dark green velvet panels in each corner."[17]

In the meantime Charles and Betty had tackled the Charleston waterfront itself. In early 1968 they obtained permission from the South Carolina State Port Authority to create a small park at Adger's Wharf, landscaping it with trees, flowers, and walking paths. The transformation seemed miraculous. Once a jumble of weeds, discarded tires, and other debris, Adger's Wharf Park was now an oasis of beauty.[18] But the Adger's Wharf project was only the beginning. Over the next two decades the Woodwards continued to buy up pieces of the Charleston waterfront and turn them over to the city as parks. In 1978 they created the Parklands Foundation to preserve such areas for public use—in Charleston and elsewhere. Throughout these projects Charles and Betty shunned publicity as much as possible and whenever they could gave funds anonymously. But they have not been able to escape the appreciation of thousands of Charlestonians, prompting mayor Joseph P. Riley, Jr., to remark that they had "done as much for Charleston as anyone I've ever met."[19] Wider recognition also came their way when Charles was made a director of the National Trust for Historic Preservation.

Throughout this period the Woodwards were also quite generous in their assistance to Charleston's black community. Their interest had been aroused in the mid-sixties through an article in the Charleston newspaper about St. John's Episcopal Mission on the largely black east side. They visited the mission shortly thereafter and were impressed with what its director, Father Grant, had been able to do on an extremely meager budget. The Woodwards subsequently contributed money to enlarge the building and hire new staff. At Father Grant's suggestion they also helped to salvage a defunct summer recreation site near the city known as Camp Baskerville. Among other activities, the camp offered tutoring to boys who had dropped out of school. At the Woodwards' request girls were later added to the program. Many of these boys and girls have gone on to college and now hold professional jobs. Besides aiding black youths in this way, the Woodwards also built ten housing units on the east side, thereby enhancing the area and providing an incentive for others to repair and maintain their properties.

Yet another area in which Charles and Betty were instrumental in civic projects is Northeast Harbor, Maine, long a retreat for socially prominent Philadelphians, where the Woodwards began spending summers in 1965. Located on the east side of Mount Desert Island, Northeast is surrounded by rocky, forested slopes that plunge into the water below. On the heights above the harbor are summer homes, many of them dating from the late nineteenth century when Mount Desert Island was first "discovered" by a group of proper Bostonians and some Philadelphians, including the family of the first Mrs. Sam Houston.

Charles and Betty first moved into a modest shingle-style house up near the end of the harbor. Later they bought a wooden colonial revival house a bit further down the bay. Just above them on a hill overlooking the length of the harbor was the Asticou Inn. Built by the Savage family in 1902, the rambling, brown-shingled inn was the only hotel left in Northeast by the time the Woodwards arrived and one of the few such establishments remaining anywhere in New England. The Savages had been forced to sell it and there were fears that the Treadway Corporation, which now owned it, might pull it down and build modern apartments.

Fearing the worst, Charles and Betty helped rally other summer residents to save the Asticou Inn. Besides the Woodwards there were Nancy G. Harris, Edward W. Madeira, Jr., Horace D. Nalle, and Peter Godfrey, all of them well known in Philadelphia business or social circles. Forming the Asti-Kim Corporation, they and others bought the inn, made much needed repairs, and did extensive redecorating on the inside. Betty and Nancy supervised the new interior, while fellow salvagers concentrated on the grounds or planned the Thursday night entertainments.[20]

Several years later Charles and Betty moved to preserve a substantial piece of open land belonging to the inn that ran along the road down to the village of Northeast Harbor. They traded their shingle-style house, which lay just below the inn, for the overgrown parcel of land, had it cleared, marked out hiking paths, and turned the property over to the state.

Yet another project at Northeast was the rebuilding of the Jordan Pond House following a disastrous fire. For years it had been a favorite spot for tea following an afternoon of tennis, golf, or hiking. Receiving a plea for money in the mail, Charles decided he would give a generous contribution to rebuild Jordan Pond, provided that work began no later than October. Ground was indeed broken that October, but Charles was very disappointed with the results, finding the low-ceilinged private dining room upstairs particularly offensive. After heated words with the Boston architect, Charles paid to have the whole room done over.

In addition to all their restoration work in Charleston and Northeast Harbor, Charles and Betty managed to carry out a number of building and preservation projects back in Philadelphia. The death of Charles's mother in 1961 and his brother George's passing in 1967 also meant greater responsibility for the family's holdings in Chestnut Hill—along with protracted difficulties in settling the family estate.

Following Dr. Woodward's death in 1952 Gertrude had stayed on at

Krisheim with her servants and a full-time companion. She remained in good health, undergoing a gall-bladder operation at age eighty-seven without the slightest difficulty. Charles, Betty, and the two children continued to come for Sunday dinner when they were in town, but by the late 1950s Gertrude seemed more and more out of touch with the world around her. She died at age ninety-three on 2 October 1961.

In his will Henry Howard Houston had ordered that the principal of his estate be divided among his grandchildren following the deaths of his three surviving children. As the last of the three, Gertrude's passing meant that the estate had to be distributed. According to official court estimates the estate was now worth $145 million, most of it in Standard Oil of New Jersey stocks that had greatly appreciated over the decades.

Settling the estate turned out to be far more complicated than anyone imagined, touching off a series of litigations that took nearly three years to get through the courts. The problem stemmed from the fact that three of Henry Howard Houston's grandchildren had died before their parents—without either children or wills. Sam Houston's son Hennie had been killed in World War I, as had Dr. and Mrs. Woodward's son Houston. And the Woodward's daughter Quita had died of Hodgkin's disease in 1934.

Common sense might suggest that the estate simply should be divided into equal shares among the nine remaining grandchildren, but both state and federal governments stood to collect far more in taxes if it could be held that the three dead grandchildren had in fact inherited a one twelfth share. The three portions would then be held to have passed initially from Henry Howard Houston to the deceased grandchildren, then to their parents, and finally to the nine survivors. Since there were no state or federal inheritance taxes at the time of Henry Howard Houston's death in 1895, revenue authorities could not lay claims against the original estate. But all three grandchildren had died after the enactment of state and federal inheritance taxes, allowing revenue officials to claim that the deceased grandchildren's shares ought to be taxed at the time that they passed to their respective parents and again when they descended to the nine living grandchildren.

In legal terms the decision rested on whether the dead Houston grandchildren had vested or contingent shares in the estate. The state and federal governments argued that the shares were vested—that they would pass on to the grandchildren whether or not they were alive at the time the estate was distributed. The family argued, on the other hand, that the shares were contingent on the grandchildren's being alive to receive them. Judge Charles Klein of the Philadelphia Orphan's court ruled in December 1962 that the inheritance was indeed vested and that the estate had to be divided into twelve equal shares. Those belonging to the dead grand-children would, in fact, be taxed at two different stages. Appeals by the family were rejected, and the original decision was upheld by the Pennsylvania Supreme Court in June 1964.[21]

Charles's legal experience was quite helpful to all three brothers throughout the litigation, but there were plenty of other interests to occupy him in Philadelphia and Chestnut Hill. One was Philadelphia's Fairmount Park system and the incomparable Wissahickon valley along the western borders of Chestnut Hill. His grandfather, Henry Howard Houston, had donated much land along the creek and his parents had added other parcels over the years. He and his brothers had spent happy childhood hours walking the paths, splashing in the creek, and skating on the pond in front of the Valley Green Inn. Charles was determined to join his parents and grandparents in preserving this urban wilderness for generations to come.

An appointment to the Fairmount Park Commission in September 1960 put Charles in an optimum position to act as a guardian over the whole ten-mile strip of parkland—from the Benjamin Franklin Parkway downtown up to Harper's Meadow at the farthest end of Chestnut Hill. Over the next quarter century he continuously fought development plans that would spoil the park's natural beauty, while contributing large sums from his own pocket to round out its borders or to create oases of flowers, shrubs, and trees.

In 1964, for example, Charles successfully opposed a plan to locate a new sports stadium in the park. And as early as 1968 he began pushing for a new Horticultural Hall to replace an earlier one that had been destroyed by a hurricane in the mid-1950s. After ten years of tenacious persuasion and a generous personal donation, the new horticultural building became a reality. Charles Woodward also got behind a drive to rid the city of a cracked and ugly asphalt oval in front of the Philadelphia Museum of Art, replacing it with a symmetrical arrangement of trees, grass, and walkways. Meanwhile Charles began pressuring the city to give the single name "Lincoln Drive" to the confusing array of names that had been given to a contiguous stretch of roadway from the present Kelly Drive into Chestnut Hill, a proposal that was finally adopted, for the most part, in 1984.[22]

The art museum itself was never a particular interest for Charles, but in the mid-sixties he became a major backer of the Pennsylvania Ballet. He gave them two- or three-hundred thousand dollars altogether, paying to have the whole troop perform in Charleston on several occasions. He also loved to go to rehearsals, returning to tell Betty, "I cannot tell you what joy it has brought me!"[23]

Back in Chestnut Hill, Charles gave $100,000 through the Parklands Foundation to repair the fences and roadway along Forbidden Drive. He also purchased two acres of wooded land from the Springside School in 1985, which he donated to the city in order to protect the Wissahickon watershed. And, like his father, he was conscious of the periodic need to clear the Wissahickon forest of fallen trees. Shortly before his death he paid $5,000 to have the trees cleared away, and offered additional funds if they were needed.[24]

In the area of housing, Charles also began to follow in his father and grandfather's footsteps. In 1957 he bought part of the old Cricket Club golf course from the Houston estate and developed large building lots along the gently rolling hills of the present St. Andrew's and Glengarry Roads. Following his brother George's death in 1967 he took over direction of the family real estate interests. Later that year Charles detached his one-third interest to form the Woodward House Corporation, while Stanley's share remained together with George, Jr.'s estate under the old George Woodward, Incorporated. Charles believed that the division would probably help to clarify ownership and responsibility once he and Stanley had died and the properties passed on to their children.[25]

Meanwhile there were no longer any large expanses of land on which to build in Chestnut Hill, but Charles kept a constant watch for small parcels that might otherwise be developed in unsightly or inappropriate ways. In 1965 he bought the former Bracken Garage at Navajo Street and Lincoln Drive and transformed it into an attractive row of apartments.[26] Seven years later he bought the old Lower Springside School which had recently been relocated, along with the Upper School, on what had once been the front lawn of Druim Moir. He was reluctant at first to acquire the Springside building at the corner of Seminole and Willow Grove Avenues, but Betty thought otherwise, reminding him that it was "right in the heart of Woodward territory." In fact, the structure had been built in 1904 by Charles's mother and her sister, Sallie Henry, as Miss Landstreet's School, and Charles himself attended the school in the lower grades. Charles and Betty then bought the property in the fall of 1972 and divided it into four large apartments. They were so pleased with the results that they moved in themselves, their living room occupying the same space where Charles had attended kindergarten nearly seventy years before.

Other acquisitions were more simply attempts to block undesirable developments on the Hill. After a fire at the Atomic Tire shop on Germantown and Willow Grove Avenues, Charles purchased the property, demolished the remaining building, and in 1983 erected a tasteful red-brick structure with shops on the ground floor and apartments above. He similarly purchased and remodeled a building at 7900 Germantown Avenue to keep it from being razed for a Dunkin Donuts franchise. And to head off any city plans for high-rise public housing on a rural tract adjoining the old Krisheim stables, he built two single houses along the Mermaid Avenue side.[27]

Charles's last large housing project was the transformation of Krisheim itself into twelve tasteful apartments. He, Betty, and their two children, Quita and George, had moved into Krisheim after Gertrude Woodward's death in 1961, but they found the place much too large and isolated for their tastes and after a year had moved back to their Millman Street house. George, Jr., had no interest in living at Krisheim, nor did Stanley and Shirley, who had long since settled in Washington's Georgetown section. Wanting to preserve the house while finding some appropriate use for it, the three brothers decided to give it to the United Presbyterian Board of Christian Education as a conference center. The Presbyterians made it into a pleasant retreat with overnight accommodations for fifty and dining space for an additional seventy-five guests.[28] But by the 1980s the Presbyterians were finding Krisheim prohibitively expensive to maintain and decided they would have to sell it.

Not wanting the house to be demolished or the grounds torn up for a closely packed suburban development, Charles bought back the family home and its remaining twelve acres in October 1983. A year later he celebrated his eightieth birthday in the partially renovated house with hundreds of family members, neighbors, and friends. As with all his building projects, Charles went over the plans for Krisheim inch by inch, offering numerous suggestions to both architects and builders as the work progressed.[29] In May 1986, on a brilliantly sunny Sunday afternoon, the family opened a remodeled Krisheim for the benefit of the Chestnut Hill Historical Society. The first-floor rooms, which remain a common area for the tenants, were banked with flowers, while the fireplaces blazed cheerfully to ward off a late spring chill. Once again the house and gardens below echoed with the clink of glasses and the sounds of lively conversation. But Charles was not there to see it. Just a month before he had died of a heart attack in his home in Charleston. Friends and family gathered for a memorial service at St. Martin's Church on 11 April, and that summer his remains were placed in a small clearing at Krisheim overlooking the Wissahickon valley.[30]

Charles's death prompted a flurry of tributes in Philadelphia and beyond. Charleston's mayor, Joseph P. Riley, Jr., wrote:

Few people have done more for Charleston in recent years than Charles Woodward, yet he was unknown to most Charlestonians. He preferred being in the background—in part because his personality was such and his self-confidence so strong that he had no need to be in the limelight; and in part because he was still somewhat self-conscious in Charleston about being a Philadelphian, or as he would laughingly say, "a Yankee." . . .

For many, we can say that death at 81 can be accepted after a full life that had reasonably run its course. This was not so for Charles Woodward. His zest for life, his creativity and forward thinking, charm and personality, his irrepressible smile and his great interest in this community and its people make his death, even at 81, premature. . . .

It is Charleston's extraordinary good fortune that Charles Woodward came to love this city. He was quintessentially a giver. He leaves a legacy to Charleston of enormous contributions, which have immeasurably improved the quality of life of its citizens and added greatly to its beauty.[31]

The Historic Charleston Foundation echoed Mayor Riley's praise in memorializing Charles's "selfless contributions and leadership." "None . . . has been more pivotal and influential in the relatively short and busy life of this Foundation," the trustees proclaimed, "than Charles Woodward."[32]

But perhaps the most telling memorial was a column that Dan Rottenberg wrote for the *Philadelphia Inquirer*—one that Charles in particular would have liked for its wry humor and touches of iconoclasm. Referring to Charles as "the last *de facto* feudal lord of Chestnut Hill," he went on to describe the Houston and Woodward housing developments in some detail. Then of Charles himself he wrote,

George Woodward's son Charles, who died this month at the age of 81 was hardly a Hollywood-movie-type feudal lord. Instead, he was a shy, modest and unpretentious gentleman who worked out of a cramped, threadbare pre-Revolutionary office on Germantown Avenue.

But beneath his self-deprecating façade was a quiet determination to maintain the family's influence on Chestnut Hill. "We're not like General Motors," he told me just six months before his death "but it makes for a nice neighborhood."

European feudalism was undone by the rise of the modern state, and in a sense you could say the same thing is happening today in Chestnut Hill. Real estate taxes—which now gobble up 28 percent of the Woodwards' rental income—have forced the family to drastically increase rents, in some cases by 50 percent or more in the last few years.

As a result, many of the Woodward homes are now renting at close to fair-market prices, with the further consequence that many Woodward tenants have been forced to move elsewhere. The Woodwards, in short, can no longer protect their tenants and their community from the laws of economics.

That isn't necessarily bad. Most of the great civilizations of the world have passed through a feudal period in the course of their history before advancing to bigger and better things; why not Chestnut Hill?

"The Woodwards have done a great deal for Chestnut Hill," says Madeleine Butcher, a former president of the Chestnut Hill Community association. "But it doesn't go on forever." That lesson may ultimately turn out to be Charles Woodward's most valuable legacy to this neighborhood.[33]

CHAPTER 13

# *The Young Diplomat*

CHARLES'S OLDER BROTHER STANLEY (1899–     ) decided that he should find a suitable career outside Philadelphia, for with George, Jr., heading up the family real estate firm and Charles preparing for a career in law, it seemed to Stanley that there were enough young Woodwards in one city to take care of family interests. More importantly, Stanley discovered that he truly loved the outisde world and was attracted by a life in the foreign service.[1] As it turned out, he became a notable American diplomat whose career peaked during and just after World War II, making him an eyewitness to, as well as a participant in, the nation's emergence as a truly global power.

Like Charles, Stanley had spent his high school years at St. George's. From there he went to Yale, graduating in 1922 with a major in English and a minor in History. After graduation he signed up to teach for a year at Yale-in-China. "Ya-Li," as the Chinese called it, had been established a generation before by missionary-minded Yale men. Just outside the city of Changsha—1,000 miles up the Yangtze from Shanghai—they had established a hospital, a school, and a church. Besides a permanent staff of Americans and Chinese nationals, several Yale graduates were selected each year to join the mission. While there, Stanley taught English to elementary school students and himself managed to learn enough Chinese to get around the countryside.

The year in China at an end, Stanley set out for home in the opposite direction from which he had come, determined to travel west and eventually make it all the way around the world. From China he and two college friends, Ward Cheney and Jack Speiden, sailed to Java, Singapore, Burma, and Calcutta. Once in India they went on by train to Benares and Bombay. While on board ship they met an Englishman who arranged a hunting trip for them with the nawab of Bhopal. Put up in style at the nawab's guest house, Stanley suggested a tiger hunt, but they had to settle for antelopes. And instead of setting out on elephants as Stanley had envisioned, they were driven into the field with modern automobiles. Still, there were guides, porters, and bearers to lend authenticity to the hunt, which turned out to be good sport in the end.

From India they traveled through the Red Sea aboard an Italian steamer, but left the ship before entering the Suez Canal in order to take a quick look at Egypt and the pyramids. Under a blazing hot sun they set out on camels to gaze at the ancient tombs, utterly oblivious to the heat and discomfort as only a group of wide-eyed twenty-five-year-olds could be. They rejoined their ship at Alexandria and steamed on to Venice, where Stanley had promised to meet his parents and sister, Quita, more than a year before.

Besides catching up on news of the last year, Stanley had an exciting announcement for the family: he had become engaged to one of the teachers at Ya-Li, a lovely young woman from Toledo, Ohio, named Shirley Rutherford, whom he had first met at Yale during one of her weekend visits from Vassar. The four Woodwards then traveled to Paris where Shirley joined them. Dr. and Mrs. Woodward were delighted at the match and the two were married on 20 October 1923 at the American cathedral in Paris.

While in China Stanley had decided on a career in the foreign service, a choice that his parents heartily approved. In Paris they introduced him to one of Houston's French army friends, Colonel Mercier, who suggested that Stanley enroll in the prestigious Ecole des Science Politiques, an institution that was known for preparing young Frenchmen to enter the diplomatic corps. It would also be a good way for Stanley to become proficient in French, at that time a virtual requirement for diplomats. As Stanley's French was not even good enough for him to make sense of the lectures at first, he hired a tutor for both himself and Shirley. Before long they were both fluent in *la langue diplomatique*.

In the spring of 1924 they returned to the United States and settled in the Georgetown section of Washington, D.C., so that Stanley could take the foreign service examination. He passed easily and found himself among the twenty applicants (out of 200) who were admitted to the new Foreign Service School, created the year before by a congressional act. In fact, there was no "school" in the traditional sense; instead, inductees went through a six-month training program at the State Department. They attended lectures in the morning and in the afternoon visited various offices at State or at other departments and agencies with which they might have contact in the future.

Shirley became pregnant while they were in Washington and the doctor thought it inadvisable for them to travel until after the baby was born. The wife of fellow student David Key found herself in a similar situation. For the time being David and Stanley were given typewriters and sent to the State Department basement to make a card catalog of "local employees" in all American consulates and diplomatic posts abroad.[2] Neither of them could do better than "hunt and peck" with two index fingers, and by the time they got through the list the file was already out of date. Yet despite the tedious work, life was pleasant in Washington, giving both young men and their wives plenty of time to form new friendships, many of which endured for a lifetime.

Finally the babies were born and the wives were ready to pack up and go. Summoning all his courage, Stanley approached Consul General Norton for his assignment. "Are you still here?" Norton asked. "I thought you'd gone out long ago!" Despite Norton's initial astonishment, Stanley, Shirley, and the recently arrived Stanley, Jr., were soon on their way to the American consulate in Geneva, Switzerland.

Stanley was the junior officer in Geneva, in charge of visas, passports, notarial services, and embassy visitors, in addition to managing the office cash. But Consul Pinkney Tuck, Woodward's genial boss, also sent him to observe a variety of meetings at the League of Nations headquarters in Geneva. His reports on these sessions were invariably thorough and concise and doubtless contributed to his being made the American observer to the league's Committee on Traffic in Dangerous Drugs.[3]

While an observer at the league, Stanley also had a chance to see or meet most of the foreign policy leaders of the day, including Britain's Austen Chamberlain, France's Aristide Briand, and Germany's Gustav Stresemann. His stint there also resulted in his growing respect for the league itself, and particularly for Sir Eric Drummond, the league's secretary general. He believed that the organization was performing a number of valuable services, and in his opinion the United States was wrong not to join, but he was never naive enough to suppose that American entry alone could have prevented World War II.

After four interesting years in Geneva—the average length for such assignments—Stanley was promoted to the embassy in Belgium. He already knew Ambassador Hugh Gibson, who had frequently come down to Geneva as the head of the American delegation to league disarmament talks. Gibson had liked Stanley and asked that he be sent to his embassy in Brussels as junior officer. Once there, he and Shirley settled into an attractive house in the fashionable Quartier Leopold where they had an excellent staff and entertained frequently. Their social gatherings were a great aid to the ambassador, helping to keep visiting Americans happy as well as promoting better relations among the diplomatic corps in Brussels. Such efforts were clearly beyond the means of most junior officers and only a generous allowance of $20,000 a year from his parents enabled them to live well during these years and "discharge their duties with élan," as Stanley likes to put it.

Their next assignment was Haiti, yet another French-speaking country, where he and Shirley arrived in 1933. They had come at the end of nearly twenty years of American military occupation and were impressed with the results: new roads and hospitals had been built; Haitian finances had been put on a sound footing; and the marines had created an efficient local constabulary. Stanley was now senior officer at the legation under his good friend Norman Armour, the American minister. They found a beautiful house in the hills above Port-au-Prince and soon became known for their hospitality.

Unfortunately, the move to Haiti was marred by worry over Quita Woodward's continuing illness, and she died while they were in Haiti. Very much wanting to have all their children around them, the senior Woodwards asked Shirley and Stanley to come home after the funeral for an extended stay. Growing concern over Stanley, Jr.'s education was yet another reason to return. Placing him in an American school, they reasoned, might be just what he needed. Stanley accordingly asked the State Department for a year's sabbatical, but was told that such leaves did not exist in the foreign service. Reluctantly, he decided to resign his post after only a year in Port-au-Prince.[4]

Back in Chestnut Hill the Stanley Woodwards moved to the corner of Emlen Street and Allen's Lane, into one of the Norman-style gate houses of Dr. Woodward's French Village, just around the corner from Charles and Betty. As his brother Charles would do nearly thirty years later, Stanley soon obtained an appointment to the Fairmount Park Commission, with a special responsibility for outdoor recreation. Shirley, who had always loved music, meanwhile took full advantage of the world-renowned Philadelphia Orchestra.

By the time Stanley joined the park commission, both Philadelphia and the country at large were beginning to feel the first positive effects of New Deal relief and recovery measures, several of which benefitted the park system directly. The most important of these was the Works Progress

Administration. Grants from the WPA allowed the commission to build additional hiking and riding trails along the Wissahickon, as well as to improve the grounds of Chestnut Hill's Pastorius Park. WPA monies also permitted the commissioners to restore several historic houses that had been acquired along with Fairmount Park land decades before, to build public golf courses, and to make the Wissahickon Creek suitable for fishing. This last project was Stanley's own idea and one in which he took a special interest.

As a commissioner Stanley was at the center of all these projects. He also became immersed in an ongoing dispute with housing contractors in Roxborough who had run raw sewage into the street drains and then into the Wissahickon Creek below. The commissioners first had to hunt down the offending parties and then convince them to install proper sewer lines.[5]

Such efforts on behalf of the park were bound to please Dr. and Mrs. Woodward, whom Stanley now saw quite regularly. Besides discussing park matters, father and son inevitably fell to talking about politics. Stanley freely admitted his warm admiration for President Roosevelt, praising his efforts to restore and then reform the American economy. Dr. Woodward could agree that some constructive work was being done by the Roosevelt administration, but he bitterly complained about the New Deal's flagrant disregard for states' rights. While understanding these objections, Stanley tried to explain that the present emergency simply did not allow for too much concern over state sensibilities. Their arguments over the New Deal were never really heated, and each of them came to respect the other's point of view.

The frequent visits to Krisheim were thus pleasant enough for Stanley, but by 1937 both he and Shirley were eager to get back into foreign service. And just at that time a terrific opportunity opened up for them through the intervention of their old friend Colonel "Pa" Watson, who was now President Roosevelt's military aid. They had known Edwin T. Watson— later General Watson—in Brussels where he was serving as military attaché to the American embassy. The Woodwards liked Pa immensely, and Shirley and Watson's wife, Frances, also shared a love of music. The four of them had managed to keep in touch over the years, visiting each other whenever they could.

Watson himself was a well-informed and genial man to whom Franklin Roosevelt had taken an immediate liking; Pa was soon a member of Roosevelt's inner circle, even to the point of giving advice on appointments. When he learned that the president was dissatisfied with both his chief and assistant chief of protocol, Pa was only too glad to suggest his old friend Stanley Woodward for the assistant's position; for chief he recommended then minister to Panama George Summerlin, whom he knew from their days at West Point.

Stanley eagerly accepted the job as assistant chief of protocol. In nearly every respect he seemed a perfect choice: he was tall, handsome, and amiable, with impeccable manners and a reputation for gracious entertaining. His education at St. George's and Yale, combined with his family's wealth and social prominence, doubtless contributed to a general self-assurance that was essential in dealing with distinguished visitors. Just as important were his past experiences at Geneva, Brussels, and Port-au-Prince.[6]

The Woodwards were off to Washington in September 1937, settling down again in the picturesque Georgetown section. Later they bought an empty lot in the 3000 block of N Street and commissioned William E. Shepherd, a friend and beaux arts architect, to design a red-brick, Georgian-revival house for them. And for a weekend retreat they bought a run-down mountain farm near Charlottesville, Virginia. It was right next door to Jefferson's Monticello and about half a mile from a farm that the Watsons had found several years before. The Woodward place had once belonged to Filippo Mazzei, the Italian *philosophe* whom Jefferson had encouraged to settle in Albemarle County. In imitating neighboring Monticello Mazzei had called his own tract "Colle," or Hill, a name that the Woodwards kept for their own retreat. There William Adams Delano, a distant cousin of President Roosevelt, designed for them another colonial revival house, this one in a style more informal than their Georgetown residence. The Woodwards also owned a country place outside Salzburg, Austria, that they had bought "for a song" during the years in Brussels. They usually spent the late summer there, relaxing and enjoying the famous music festival held in Salzburg annually.

But back in Washington Stanley's most challenging assignment was planning the royal visit of King George VI and Queen Elizabeth in May 1939. They were the first reigning British monarchs to visit the United States, their official purpose being to open the British exhibit at the New York World's Fair.[7]

Stanley drew up the entire schedule for the royal couple, spending "90 days," as he put it, "on a nine-day visit." Thinking that it would be dramatic for the king and queen to approach New York by water on the opening day of the fair, he had them take the train from Washington, D.C., to Sandy Hook, New Jersey, where they boarded a naval destroyer for the trip across the bay to a Manhattan pier. Once out at the fairgrounds, the king and queen were highly amused at director Grover Whalen's outspoken showmanship and general boosterism.

The next day the party was off to President Roosevelt's country estate at Hyde Park for an American-style picnic with the president's family, complete with roasted hot dogs. While Their Majesties spent the night in the main residence at Hyde Park, Stanley stayed at the home of a Roosevelt relative who lived nearby.

Half a century after the event, Stanley remembered the royal couple vividly: "They were just exactly what you expected; they were gracious and poised and friendly." He also reflected on the timeliness of the visit, with war breaking out in Europe at the end of the summer. "They created a great sympathy and interest in Britain," he related—feelings that would benefit both countries immeasurably in the years just ahead.

Such sympathies toward Britain did not immediately translate into American intervention, with public opinion polls in late 1939 and early 1940 indicating that the vast majority of the public was determined to stay out of this last round of European fighting. President Roosevelt shared their desire for peace, but he also had a greater sense of the Nazi peril than most of his countrymen and was increasingly determined to aid Britain in any way he could—short of war itself. The need to help Britain became even more urgent for the president after the Germans conquered France and the Low Countries in the spring of 1940. In late December of that year he went on the radio to pledge that the United States would become the great "arsenal of democracy," wielding all of its industrial might to supply the free world with the weapons to resist Nazi and Fascist tyranny.

American industrialists as well as potential foreign buyers flooded into Washington almost immediately to discover exactly what the speech had meant and how they might "cash in" on the bonanza of war production. It was up to the protocol department to care for the foreign visitors and show them just what the United States could do as "the arsenal of democracy."[8]

An essential part of this task was countering German propaganda. Claiming that they had already won the war, the Nazis insisted that any American aid would be too little and too late. To counter these claims, Stanley and his assistants took interested foreign visitors, most of them from Europe and Latin America, to the more important munitions plants so that they could discover for themselves what was being done. They went to Detroit to see how auto producers were cooperating to turn out more than 100 tanks a week, and then they went on to Buffalo to watch the rapid but precise assembly of Curtis-Wright airplanes, or to shipyards on the two coasts.

As more and more delegations descended on the capital, the protocol office had a difficult time finding enough hotel rooms for entire groups, frequently having to split them up among several establishments. It was

Stanley who struck on the idea of an official government guest house. The building he had in mind was the old Blair mansion just across the street from the White House. He knew that the last occupant, an elderly and infirm widow, had just moved into a nursing home, leaving the house fully furnished and staffed. "I got hold of Percy Blair, who was a bachelor around town," Stanley recalled, "and asked [him] if he'd sound out members of his family [to see] if they'd be willing to rent the Blair House to help us out in this crisis."

A few days later Blair returned with the news that all were in agreement—they would let the department have the house for $100 per day whenever it was needed. This included full use of the premises, with its eight bedrooms, a cook, a housekeeper, and an experienced staff. The arrangement worked so well that Stanley soon got permission from the State Department to attempt to buy the property. Again contacting Percy Blair, Stanley assured him that the government would keep the name Blair House as a permanent memorial to their old and distinguished family. Blair and the others quickly assented to sell everything, including the early nineteenth-century furnishings, Paul Revere silver, Lowestoft and Compagnie des Indes china, French Aubusson carpets, and several valuable portraits. They even left Andrew Jackson's walking stick hanging on the library wall. The State Department got it all for less than $200,000, surely one of the best real estate deals in recent history.[9]

Stanley now found himself the "nation's innkeeper," with full responsibility for the Blair House. It was just the perfect size, he thought, with its eight bedrooms placing a convenient limit on the size of visiting delegations. For that reason he opposed the purchase of the Blair-Lee House next door as a supplementary guest facility and doubted the wisdom of other additions in later years.

Hospitality at the Blair House and elsewhere, along with the numerous visits to weapons manufacturers, did, in fact, help to counter Nazi propaganda about the American capacity to supply arms, but they did nothing in the long run to keep the United States out of the war itself. Stanley and Shirley were having Sunday dinner with the Watsons at their country house in Virginia when the Japanese attacked Pearl Harbor on 7 December 1941. Part way through the meal General Watson received a telephone call from the White House with terse news of the attack and a message that a special car was coming to whisk him back to Washington.

Stanley rode back to the capital with Pa, leaving Shirley and Frances Watson to return later in the day. It was an unseasonably warm Indian summer afternoon as they sped along the highway, with bright sunshine streaming into the car. They listened to the radio throughout the trip, attentive to every additional bit of information about the disaster a third of the way around the world.

By the time they arrived in Washington, Stanley was good and angry, partly because there was simply so little that an assistant chief of protocol could do in the way of decisive action on a late Sunday afternoon. Although 42 years old, Stanley thought of joining one of the military services, but realized after several days that he would only be put into one of their protocol offices at a much lower level than he now occupied, and where he would be much less effective than in the State Department. And, in fact, he had plenty of important work to do in the days just ahead. One of his first tasks was to figure out a way of taking the Japanese ambassador and his entourage into protective custody.

Knowing that Winston Churchill was coming to town at the end of December, President Roosevelt had ordered Secretary of State Hull to get the enemy representatives out of town. Hull passed the assignment on to Chief of Protocol Summerlin who in turn gave it to his capable assistant. Stanley not only had to inform the Japanese that they were going to be removed from the capital, but also had to figure out where to put them until they could be exchanged for the American diplomats still in Tokyo. He knew that the Japanese would be monitoring the treatment of their embassy staff through neutral emissaries in Washington and that they would retaliate against the Americans if any of their nationals were mistreated. Stanley's mission was thus a very delicate one.

Wondering just how he would handle it all, he suddenly remembered that the Chesapeake and Ohio Railroad owned a large resort hotel in West Virginia known as the Greenbriar. It was relatively secluded, was accessible by rail, and was likely to be quite vacant at that time of year. He knew the C & O manager in Washington and they swiftly made the necessary arrangements. Stanley then drove over to the Japanese embassy and told the ambassador and his staff to be ready in 48 hours. "They were scared out of their skins," he recalled, and were "doubtless relieved to be getting out of Washington."

With a couple of limousines for the higher-ranking diplomats and buses for the rest, Stanley, with the help of District police on motorcycles, escorted the Japanese to Union Station where they would board the train for West Virginia. Angry though he was about the bombing, he could not help but feel sorry for Ambassador Nomura whom he had known before the war and whom he regarded as an essentially decent man who had probably been kept largely in the dark about his country's plans to attack the United States. Leaving him at the train, he could only think to say, "I hope you will be comfortable."

Next, there were the German, Italian, Hungarian, and other Axis diplomats to usher out of town, not to mention all the enemy consular officials throughout the country who had to be collected and provided for. Throughout it all, Stanley took some satisfaction from thinking that the Germans, with their professions of racial supremacy, were going to have to share the Greenbriar with their non-Aryan friends, the Japanese. Eventually the Greenbriar filled up, and the State Department took over the nearby Homestead Hotel at Hot Springs to house the continuing arrivals.

The years immediately ahead were also busy ones for Stanley. If anything, the stream of visitors increased during the war, all of them requiring attention from the protocol division. Among them were the duke of Windsor, then governor general of the Bahamas, and French general Charles de Gaulle. Stanley found the duke of Windsor quite easy to please and General de Gaulle among the most complicated, especially when he took up residence at Blair House for weeks at a time, hoping to offer his largely unwanted advice about the war to President Roosevelt. Stanley saw de Gaulle smile only once, sometime later, during a visit to Chicago when Mayor Richard Daley slipped and called Woodward the "Chief of Portico."

*Assistant Chief of Protocol Stanley Woodward, Sr. (far left), with son Stanley Woodward, Jr., and wife, Shirley R. Woodward, at launching of SS George W. Woodward (named for Stanley's great-grandfather) at Fairfield, Maryland, 9 June 1943. SW collection.*

Chief of Protocol Stanley Woodward seated beside President Harry S Truman (in driver's seat) during Truman's visit to Colle, the Woodwards' farm outside Charlottesville, Virginia, 4 July 1948. Immediately left of Woodward is Secretary of the Treasury John Snyder. In the rear seat (left to right) are the president's naval aide and his good friend and military aide, General Harry Vaughan. SW collection.

*Charles H. Woodward, ca. 1965. EGW collection.*

*Lieutenant Henry Howard "Hennie" Houston II in France, 1917. EHS collection.*

*Eleanor Houston Smith in her wedding gown at Druim Moir with her cousin and maid of honor, Quita Woodward (on left), 23 February 1933. EHS collection.*

*Lawrence M. C. Smith (first on left) and Eleanor Houston Smith (first on right) with their six children at Wolfe's Neck Farm near Freeport, Maine, ca. 1950. EHS collection.*

*The Houston clan at Druim Moir, 14 April 1956. Dallett collection.*

# CHAPTER 14

# *Chief of Protocol*

IN JANUARY 1944, following Summerlin's retirement, Stanley succeeded his superior as chief of protocol. Since an often ill Summerlin had delegated more and more work to Woodward as the war progressed, the promotion was more a formality than an actual change in duties. Stanley now saw more of President Roosevelt than in the past, but the burdens of war, in addition to Roosevelt's increasingly frail health, meant that there was less in the way of social activity at the executive mansion, with more of the serious visits taking place at Hyde Park.[1]

President Roosevelt's death in April 1945 saddened Stanley as it did millions across the country. It also meant a new boss, Harry S Truman. Unlikely though it might seem, given their entirely different backgrounds, Truman and Stanley Woodward got along famously and became close friends. No doubt Stanley's easygoing manner helped a great deal, as did his fondness for poker and good bourbon; and for Truman, who had been catapulted into the most powerful office in the world, Stanley's calm and reassuring advice on presidential etiquette must have been quite welcome.

Stanley has always denied that Truman needed any advice on how to behave in office, but it is clear that the president liked to have his chief of protocol nearby, invariably taking him along to his "winter White House" in Key West, Florida. It was down there, as Stanley remembers, that he "really got to know [President Truman] best. . . . He was very fond of playing poker and I'd played a good deal of [it] . . . when I was out west in the summertime . . . and when I was at college. . . . We'd sit around during the free hours [at Key West] and we'd play a game of poker. There were six or seven of us. We didn't play for high stakes, but we had a lot of fun."

Besides the stays at Key West, Stanley went on several foreign trips with President Truman. A swing down to Rio de Janeiro in 1947 for the signing of a new Inter-American Defense pact with the Latin Americans turned into a ten-day visit as the Argentinians decided to hold up the final proceedings until they were satisfied on a minor point.[2] They also traveled together to Canada and Mexico. When the Trumans moved into the Blair House for a year and a half while the White House was being renovated and repaired, Stanley became their landlord of sorts, a relationship about which he and the Trumans often joked. Indeed, once a week or so Stanley would drop by the Blair House around six in the evening to see that everything was going well and to have a little "bourbon and branch" with the president.

Truman and his chief of protocol also shared a love of history. Although Truman had not been to college, he was well-read in history. Stanley remembered that the president invariably would summon up some historical fact or make a pertinent comment about the homeland of a visiting foreign dignitary, a habit that flattered the guest while providing an opening for conversation.

As chief of protocol one of Stanley's duties was presenting new ambassadors to the president. President Roosevelt, he explained, had greatly simplified the process because of his own physical handicaps and the crush of work during the Depression and World War II. Instead of meeting a new ambassador in the White House's diplomatic reception room, attired in striped morning trousers and a black cut-away coat, Roosevelt had the envoy brought to his office, both of them dressed in plain business suits. Stanley typically escorted the ambassador designate to the Oval Office and then introduced him to the president. After a few minutes of informal conversation, he departed with the ambassador for his embassy. The chief of protocol was then commonly invited in for a glass of wine or sherry. After a half an hour or so he returned to his office at the State Department.

These frequent visits to the White House reflected the fact that Stanley, like his predecessors, had a dual role to play: he was both head of protocol at the White House and chief of the protocol division at the State Department. As such he had to determine seating arrangements at official White House dinners and advise the president on the procedural details of state visits. The foreign embassies also turned to him for advice on questions of precedence and rank. And if someone from the staff of a foreign embassy got drunk in public, received too many speeding tickets, or made a general nuisance of himself, it was Stanley's job to approach his ambassador and try to settle the matter before things got completely out of hand.

Stanley also commonly met foreign dignitaries when they arrived in the United States. If friendly crowds were wanted along the route through Washington, he tried to arrange for a motorcade around noon time when thousands of bureaucrats could come out of their offices for a look at the visitor. In some cases the crowds were not so friendly, as when British foreign secretary Ernest Bevin arrived by ship in New York Harbor. Police had to clear a narrow path for the official car to get through the assembled protesters, prompting the chief of protocol to apologize to Bevin for the hostile reception. Bevin, who had been a militant member of the Labor party, replied quite casually, "Don't worry about that. A few years ago I'd have been right down there with them."

Once he had met his high-ranking guests, Stanley had the job of keeping them happy and comfortable. When India's Jawaharlal Nehru came for a visit, Stanley arranged for him to have a few extra days at the end of his trip in New York to see the sights and perhaps attend a couple of serious plays. But when Nehru heard that Stanley had provided him with theater tickets he responded, "What do you think I am, an intellectual?" What he really wanted to do, he admitted, was to see the Rockettes at Radio City Music Hall and take in a performance of *South Pacific*. The Rockettes were easy enough to arrange, but *South Pacific* had just opened to rave reviews and it was sold out for at least six months. In desperation, Stanley telephoned Oscar Hammerstein himself, declaring that Nehru and his entourage simply could not think of returning to India without seeing *South Pacific*. Hammerstein promised to consider the request and call back in five minutes. Stanley got ten tickets to the performance and Nehru was thrilled.

Then there were the embarrassing incidents which even the most careful plans could not avoid entirely. One involved Cuban president Fulgencio Batista who was invited by New York's Cardinal Spellman to dine at the archiepiscopal palace and to attend mass afterwards. Being a staunch Baptist, Batista bluntly refused the astonished cardinal who had assumed automatically that the Cuban president was a Roman Catholic. The fault actually rested with the archdiocesan office: rather than going through the protocol division, which would have informed them of Batista's Protestantism, they had contacted Batista directly.

All things considered, Stanley's job as chief of protocol could be a nerve-wracking responsibility. From state dinners at the White House to the smallest details of a foreign guest's personal habits, he had to make sure that everyone under his care was as comfortable and satisfied as possible. It clearly took a man with Stanley's endless patience and personal charm to keep everything moving smoothly day after day.

Stanley doubtlessly would have stayed on as chief of protocol until the end of the Truman administration, but while at Key West with the president in March 1950 they received word that the American ambassador to Canada, Laurence Steinhardt, had been killed in a plane crash en route from Ottawa to New York.[3] In the discussion that followed Truman asked Stanley whom he thought would make a good replacement and Woodward rattled off several names. Then the president asked, "How would you like it, Stanley?" "I'd love it," the surprised chief of protocol answered, "But don't worry about me. I'm all right where I am." "No," was Truman's response. "Everybody wants to be an ambassador and now it's your turn."

Stanley already knew most of the Senate Foreign Relations Committee and his confirmation sailed through quite easily. He learned from President Truman, however, that former U.S. senator Joseph Guffey had gone to the White House to register a personal protest over the appointment, complaining to Truman that Stanley Woodward's father had frequently called him "Senator Goofey" back home in Pennsylvania. Truman, who had never thought highly of Guffey himself, had several good laughs over the incident.

To prepare himself for the Canadian post, Stanley read widely on Canadian history and current events. Then, in a highly unusual ceremony, he administered the oath of office to himself in the presence of Secretary of State Dean Acheson. One of his jobs as chief of protocol had been to swear in new ambassadors and he knew the words by heart. He and Shirley were then off to Canada where they moved into the large ambassador's residence located in Ottawa's fashionable Rockcliffe section. The house was surrounded by ten acres of beautifully landscaped lawns and gardens that reminded Stanley very much of Krisheim back in Chestnut Hill. Once again they fell into a pleasant routine of entertaining, with all the experience of Geneva, Belgium, Haiti, and the protocol office behind them.

Stanley's only instructions from President Truman before leaving were to try to expedite Canadian-American construction of a seaway that would link the Great Lakes to the Atlantic Ocean via the St. Lawrence River. Such a deep-water passage had been seriously considered as early as 1905, and by the postwar period the Canadians were quite anxious to see it through. The greatest obstacles to this St. Lawrence Seaway were American shipping interests in Boston, New York, Philadelphia, and even Baltimore, who believed that it would divert traffic from their docks to ports on the Great Lakes. Increasingly impatient with such objections, the Canadians were threatening to build the seaway themselves, all of it on the Canadian side.[4]

Under these circumstances, Stanley took it upon himself to assuage American fears about the undertaking. In speech after speech he argued that the seaway would generate more hydro-electric power for neighboring states as well as increased shipping business for everyone, benefitting the Atlantic ports as much as the cities on the Great Lakes. In fact, he spent so much time shuttling back and forth between Ottawa, New York, and other U.S. cities that *Time* magazine dubbed him the "two-way ambassador."[5]

The Korean conflict also presented some potentially difficult negotiations for Ambassador Woodward. Though the struggle was fought under United Nations auspices, more than ninety percent of the money and military forces were supplied by the United States. Secretary of State Dean Acheson accordingly instructed Stanley to approach the Canadians for a larger contribution to the conflict—not an easy task, since the Canadians feared an escalation of the fighting and much preferred their token participation.[6] Nevertheless, Stanley flew off in an embassy plane to see Prime Minister Louis St. Laurent, who was vacationing at his summer residence down the St. Lawrence River. Woodward had a friendly Sunday luncheon with the prime minister and his wife, but made very little headway on the matter of a larger role for Canadian forces in Korea. As Woodward was leaving to fly back to Ottawa, Madame St. Laurent came to the door with a large cake for him, saying "I did not want you to go back empty-handed." The Canadians did eventually contribute more troops to Korea, but not nearly as many as Washington had hoped for.

Back home, Dwight D. Eisenhower's landslide election in 1952 was a clear signal for Stanley to resign his post and return to private life.[7] He had been closely identified with Democratic administrations for more than fifteen years, and he knew that the office-starved Republicans were not likely to keep him on in any significant post. Besides, Stanley had made no secret of his distaste for John Foster Dulles's brand of foreign policy.

Stanley went to the White House in person to turn in his resignation. Once inside, the conversation quickly turned to his own and the president's future plans. Truman told him that he wanted to go back home to Independence, Missouri, but had hesitated for fear that none of his eastern friends would bother to come out and see him. Several had even urged him to settle down in New York, prompting Stanley to joke that he could move into the Waldorf-Astoria with Herbert Hoover.

Stanley, for one, assured the president that he would make a point of visiting Independence regularly, a promise that he tried to keep at least once a year. As for himself, Stanley said he was thinking of going back to Pennsylvania to run for political office. "Don't make a damned fool of yourself, Stanley," Truman shot back. "You'd be as good a politician as I would a diplomat." Both of them laughed, and afterwards Stanley was forced to admit that the president was probably right.

Stanley returned to private life in early 1953, but he by no means gave up all interest in politics. In 1954 the Democratic party, which was still more than $1 million in debt from the 1952 presidential campaign, asked him to serve as party treasurer, with the understanding that he would try his best to restore party solvency.[8] Stanley made good use of Adlai Stevenson, encouraging $100 a plate dinners on his behalf all over the country. He approached individual donors as well, and within a year or so the party was in the black for the first time in years. Having thought that he would quit while he was ahead, Stanley was both flattered and dismayed when the Democratic National Committee refused to consider his resignation, forcing him to work behind the scenes to engineer his own exit a few months later.

Meanwhile the close work with Governor Stevenson had only increased Stanley's admiration for the party's standardbearer, and he actively supported Stevenson's second bid for the presidency in 1956. Stanley doubtless stood to receive an important post in the event of a Democratic victory, but Eisenhower's triumph in November meant at least four more years of private life for the former ambassador and his wife.

If 1956 was a disappointment politically, it turned out to be a most exciting year personally, for in May and June they accompanied the Trumans on a triumphal tour of western Europe. The former president had been to Europe twice before—as an artillery officer in World War I and then for the Potsdam Conference in July 1945. Neither occasion had given him much time to enjoy the sights, and Mrs. Truman had never been there.

The particular timing of the trip was dictated by an invitation from Oxford University for Truman to receive an honorary degree in June. Truman had already been forced to turn down the invitation twice before and he feared that a third time would surely be the last. Shortly after receiving it, he telephoned Stanley from Independence to ask if he and Shirley would help organize the trip and accompany Mrs. Truman and himself to Europe.

The foursome left in early May aboard the SS *United States;* landing in Le Havre, they went by train to Paris. After two or three days of sightseeing in the French capital, they took another train to Italy. From Naples they started up the Italian peninsula "in easy steps," with stops at Rome, Florence, and Assisi. In Florence they rented a car for the drive through

Italian hill towns and then took the train to Salzburg, followed by a restful week at the Woodwards' home there. Next were Paris, London, and finally Oxford.

Everywhere the president and Mrs. Truman were met with great acclaim. For many Europeans he was a hero who had helped seal the fate of Italy, Germany, and Japan and who had later saved them from economic collapse through the Marshall Plan. Stanley thus had to use all the diplomatic savvy he could muster to screen the flood of invitations that awaited them at every stop.

At Naples, for instance, Mayor Loro wanted President Truman to climb Mt. Vesuvius with him and then for Mrs. Truman to join him in a drive along the beautiful Amalfi Drive. The president did not think much of the climb, while Mrs. Truman, who became car sick quite easily, positively blanched at the thought of all the hairpin turns along the famous mountain road. "We'll leave this one to you," the Trumans told Stanley as they went up to their hotel room for a rest. Knowing that Mayor Loro was up for reelection, Stanley decided to offer a compromise: Truman would do a little politicking for the mayor by riding with him in an open car through the streets of Naples. The crowds cheered them wildly and Loro won another term.

In London the two couples were to attend an intimate luncheon at Buckingham Palace with Queen Elizabeth and Prince Philip. Customarily, those who call at the palace must appear several days before the event in order to sign the "Queen's book"; the morning of their arrival, Stanley telephoned one of the queen's equerries in order to ask when they could come by to inscribe their names. They settled on eleven o'clock that very morning, but were advised to come in through the "privy" (or private) entrance in order to avoid the more congested main gate. Realizing what the word "privy" meant in the old days out in Missouri, Stanley decided to have a little fun with Mrs. Truman. "We're to go into the palace through the privy entrance," he told her. "Whaaat?" was her startled reply. And they all had a good laugh.

Two days later the four returned to the palace for their royal luncheon. Before sitting down, Prince Philip offered the president a glass of sherry, which the bourbon-drinking Truman politely accepted. Following drinks they took their places at the table, only to be confronted by a "forest of glasses" around each plate—one for each of the many wines to be served during the course of the meal. Even Stanley, who was used to fine dining all over the world, was a bit intimidated by this display of crystal, carefully lifting each glass out and away from its neighbors before sampling the contents. About ten minutes into the meal Prince Philip himself knocked over one of the glasses, laughed about it, and inadvertently put everyone else at ease for the rest of the afternoon. As they left the table, Queen Elizabeth led them to her priceless collection of paintings. It was a delightful luncheon that the Trumans and Woodwards never forgot.

A second high point of their stay in London was dinner with Prime Minister Anthony Eden at Number 10 Downing Street. Joining them for the evening were the two former prime ministers, Winston Churchill and Clement Attlee, and their wives. After dinner, Churchill asked Shirley to sit with him in the library and he ended up spending the rest of the evening with her, an experience that she and Stanley often spoke about to each other.

Next they went to Oxford, where the weather cooperated beautifully. Truman received his LL.D. degree, and later the four had dinner and spent the night in Oxford, returning to London the next day. With their "mission accomplished," the Woodwards accompanied President and Mrs. Truman to Southampton where they said farewell aboard the SS *United States*. The Woodwards then went back to London and from there to their house in the Austrian hills.

Stanley and Shirley welcomed the narrow Democratic victory in 1960. They had known Jacqueline Kennedy long before her marriage and had met Senator Kennedy several times over the years, yet they were by no means part of the Kennedy inner circle. Stanley, however, accepted a request to organize the Kennedys' inaugural ball, finding it necessary to arrange four balls to take care of the crowds who wanted an invitation.[9] They turned out to be the most financially profitable, if not the most dignified, events of the entire inauguration.

Besides planning inaugural balls, the Woodwards had plenty of other activities to occupy their attention in the early 1960s. Since 1959 they had been absorbed in a highly successful adventure in the arts. They had long lamented the dearth of good paintings in American embassies, a condition that had led many foreigners to suppose that the United States was not capable of truly good art. It was Shirley who hit on the idea of collecting contemporary American paintings and lending them to American embassies all over the world. Calling their project "Art in Embassies," she, Stanley, their friend Betty (Mrs. Lucius) Battle, and a young curator named Henry Geldzahler from the American collection at the Metropolitan Museum in New York began making the rounds to dealers, studios, and art galleries. Over the next two decades they bought about 500 canvases, lithographs, and other objects, all of them by Americans and most falling loosely into the abstract expressionist school that was then in vogue. Among them were paintings by Milton Avery, Robert Rauschen-

berg, Patrick Henry Bruce, Josef Albers, Robert Motherwell, Helen Fran-
kenthaler, Jasper Johns, Georgia O'Keeffe, Frank Stella, and many others.

Upon their appointment, ambassadors were invited to view the
Woodwards' collection and select eight or more works to take along for
display at the embassy residence abroad. An illustrated catalog was then
prepared to accompany the collection, giving information about the artists
as well as descriptions of the paintings themselves. The Woodward Foundation, which Stanley and Shirley had created for that purpose, paid all
costs. The departing emissary had to agree only to return the paintings in
their original containers, again at the foundation's expense.

After nearly twenty successful years, during which ninety-nine separate collections were sent abroad, the Woodwards decided to wind down
their unique program. The abstract expressionist school seemed to have
run its course and some of the paintings were showing signs of wear from
their "foreign service"—both good reasons, Stanley and Shirley thought,
for the canvases and prints to join them in retirement. Besides, the State
Department had been inspired by their example to start its own "Art in
Embassies" program, an initiative that the Woodwards encouraged and applauded. The Woodward collection itself was dispersed among several
museums, including the Metropolitan in New York, the Philadelphia Museum of Art, Yale University, the National Gallery in Washington, and the
Toledo Museum of Art in Ohio, where Shirley had grown up.[10]

Throughout the years, Shirley and Stanley continued to live in their
comfortable Georgetown house—"headquarters," as Stanley called it—
with more and more of their time spent at Colle in beautiful Albemarle
County, Virginia. In the summer they were off to their old Austrian farmhouse and the Salzburg music festival, or to Paris to see their Franco-
American grandson and "pick up a frock or two for the winter," often
accompanied by their good friends, Jimmy and Sue Keith. On three occasions, they extended these trips to the Middle East, traveling through
Egypt, Iran, and Afghanistan with Betty Battle and Henry Geldzahler.

Christmas 1984 was the last that Stanley and Shirley spent together.
They gathered at the Homestead in Virginia with Stanley, Jr., and his family and several friends, making twelve in the party altogether. At eighty-
four Shirley was aging and tired easily but was still her vibrant self and able
to enjoy life quietly. She was pleased when sixteen-year-old Stanley George,
the oldest of their grandchildren, got himself a job as ski instructor on the
Homestead slopes, directly as a result of her insistence that he learn to ski
as a child with the best Austrian instructors.

After Christmas and New Year's 1985, Shirley and Stanley went to stay
at Colle. Stanley, Jr., and his family came with them. On the night of

12 January shortly before midnight, Shirley's heart failed. The rescue squad came with their doctor and worked long and hard but to no avail. It was a quiet ending for one who for so long had been "lovely to look at, and lovely to know," as one of her Vassar College classmates wrote to Stanley afterwards. The brief Episcopal funeral service was held on a bright winter day in the living room at Colle "as Shirley would have wanted it," and her ashes were placed in a grave at the end of the beautiful garden that she had made with her own hands and tended for more than forty years.

For Stanley, the farm and its new vineyard continues to be a source of consuming interest. In 1981, under the direction of an excellent Italian vintner, Gabriele Rausse, he began to grow grapes and marketed his first wine in 1987. By coincidence and good fortune the site is the very one where Filippo Mazzei had set out a vineyard for Thomas Jefferson in 1779. The new vines would doubtless please both Mazzei and his friend next door at Monticello—and, Stanley hopes, a host of others.

# CHAPTER 15

# *Debutante, New Dealer, and Conservationist*

ON THE HOUSTON SIDE OF THE FAMILY, all three of Sam's surviving children—Edith Brown, Margaret Meigs, and Eleanor Smith—had taken up lives and interests of their own. Since none of the sisters wanted to live at Druim Moir after their father's death, they turned it over to the Episcopal diocese in 1953 as a home for retired clergy.[1] It would be administered by a newly created Houston Foundation, endowed by Edith Brown, the eldest of the sisters.[2] As a retirement home, Druim Moir looked much less like the castle that Henry Howard Houston had built seven decades earlier, for during World War II Sam Houston had removed the entire third floor and tower as an economizing measure. The visual approach to Druim Moir would also be altered following Edith and Dr. Henry Brown's gift of the front lawn for a new Springside School.[3]

The Browns resided at Brinkwood, the "honeymoon" house that Henry Howard Houston had built for Edith's father, Sam Houston, back in 1887. First used by the Browns as a summer place, Brinkwood became their year-round residence in 1926.[4] The Browns were famous for their picnics at Brinkwood, and they often invited young physicians from the Pennsylvania Hospital, where Dr. Brown was a well-known surgeon and sometime chief of staff.

In August 1940, as the country was beginning to rearm in earnest, Dr. Brown organized a 750-bed evacuation hospital for the U.S. Army. Just a month after the bombing at Pearl Harbor, Dr. Brown and his unit were ordered to Australia and eventually ended up on a series of Pacific islands where Colonel Brown more than once had to perform surgery at night with the light of a gasoline lantern. After the war he went off to China for several years as a missionary doctor. He died in February 1955; Edith lived on until 1970.[5]

Edith's sister, Margaret Meigs, also settled down in Chestnut Hill after her husband Robert's untimely death in 1932. "Peg," as family and friends called her, eventually located herself in a stuccoed, Georgian-revival house near the corner of St. Martin's Lane and Seminole Avenue that had once belonged to the famous efficiency expert, Frederick W. Taylor. "Boxley," as the estate was called because of its numerous boxwood plantings, had been first occupied by Jean DuBarry, an emigré from Santo Domingo who became a successful Philadelphia merchant. Peg would also die in 1970.[6]

Sam Houston's youngest daughter, Eleanor (1910–1987), had meanwhile been involved in a myriad of activities ranging from Philadelphia to Washington, D.C., and Maine. Eleanor had attended the Springside School and had spent her junior year in Paris. This was actually her second trip to France, the first one having been in 1920 when she and her parents went to Arcis-le-Ponsart to visit the site of her brother Hennie's death in World War I. It was also during this trip that her parents engaged Mlle. Juliette de la Morlais as a governess for Eleanor. To Eleanor she was always "Mademoiselle"—at least until Eleanor's small children had trouble pronouncing the name and shortened it to "Mado." Eleanor would learn to speak French fluently under her new governess, as well as to knit, paint, and work fine needlepoint.

In 1926, Mademoiselle returned to France with the Houstons for "Eleanor's year abroad." They lived at the Plaza Athénée near the Champs Élysées. Through her governess, Eleanor was enrolled at Les Oiseaux, a convent school run by Roman Catholic nuns who, because of the French anticlerical laws, wore long black dresses and lace mantillas in place of regular habits. Eleanor befriended several of the girls at school, two of whom became lifelong friends.

The next year she went back to Chestnut Hill for her last year at Springside. Eleanor loved history and French but hated Latin, and was actually expelled from Latin class one day for reading a magazine under her desk. Following graduation, Eleanor told the Springside yearbook that her greatest wish was to live in Paris.

Eleanor's senior year at Springside was packed with exciting activities. In an undated scrapbook entry for that year she wrote, "Mlle and I went to New York with Renée Claudel the daughter of the French Ambassador and had lunch with her at the Ritz Tower." Eleanor also went to the Penn–Navy football game that year. She and her companions walked around campus after the game, stopping at the Mask and Wig Club to admire the photographs of past performances. Then they went to the Art Alliance downtown where they dressed for dinner and dancing at the Bellevue, ending the evening with a play at the Forest Theater.[7]

For graduation in May 1929 Eleanor's parents gave her a "sky-blue" Packard convertible. The following October she had her "coming out" with a tea and dinner at Druim Moir. It was the week of the stock market crash, with many of the men coming in late after a hectic day downtown at the office. Of course, no one yet knew how serious the economic crisis would become—least of all Eleanor, who spent the next six months caught up in the social whirl of being a debutante. There were teas, thé-dansants, dinners, dinner dances, balls, and theater parties, one right after the other. Mademoiselle was so worried that Eleanor might become physically run-down by the frantic pace that she made her drink a large glass of milk before bed every night. As always, Mademoiselle was Eleanor's chaperone throughout the debutante year, accompanying her to parties, waiting for her, and riding home with her and the chauffeur. If it were an all-night ball at the Bellevue, Mademoiselle took a room in the hotel and was there when Eleanor came up to bed.

One of the most colorful affairs of the year was a ball given partly in Eleanor's honor on 3 January 1930 by the First City Troop, a Philadelphia cavalry unit, now part of the National Guard, that dates back to the American Revolution. According to a particularly vivid newspaper account, the ballroom at the Bellevue was transformed into a "veritable garden of flowers. On either side of the stage, which was massed with pink flowers, were Japanese bridges over miniature waterfalls, and the spaces beneath the boxes had been turned into charming little gardens, six on each side of the . . . room." Members of the First City Troop made a "spectacular entrance at half-past 11," hanging their black and silver helmets on special hooks attached to the ballroom pillars.[8]

It was at one of these balls that Eleanor met her future husband, Lawrence M. C. Smith of Strafford, Pennsylvania. When she came home that evening and told her mother about the wonderful young man she had met, a sleepy Charlotte could only think to say, "Oh no, two Browns in one family are enough; we don't need a Smith." Despite the common surname, the romance blossomed and the two were soon engaged.

Young Mr. Smith was known to his family and close friends as "Sam," a nickname given him by a black gardener who loved to tell stories about "Little Rastus Sambo." Thus, in addition to having a collection of Smiths and Browns in the larger Houston clan, there would now be two Sams, a Sam Houston and Sam Smith, not to mention the children who would carry the name. In order to avoid the inevitable confusion, some family members eventually took to calling Sam Smith by his initials—LMC.

On the Smith side, LMC's ancestors were Quakers who had settled around Upper Darby, Delaware County, in the late seventeenth century. His great-grandfather Smith had been a physician and Pennsylvania state senator. Others in the family, including LMC's father, were lawyers. LMC had graduated from the University of Pennsylvania, then had two years of post-graduate study at Magdalen College, Oxford, before going back to Penn for a law degree. Born in October 1902, LMC was thirty and Eleanor twenty-two when they were married at St. Martin's on 23 February 1933. The principal celebrant was diocesan Bishop Francis M. Taitt. The bride's gown was "of white satin, with V neck, leg of mutton sleeves," and flowing down the aisle behind her was a satin train four yards long.[9] Since the groom's brother was then married to the actress Katharine Hepburn, there was some needless worry that the wedding party would be upstaged at the ceremony.

After a five-week honeymoon in Europe, the newlyweds moved into a modest house on Rose Lane in Haverford. LMC and Eleanor did not stay long on the Main Line. Before their marriage, LMC had briefly left his law firm of Montgomery and McCracken to work for the Home Owners' Loan Corporation (HOLC) in Washington. Now with the New Deal in full swing there were more exciting opportunities than ever for young lawyers in the capital. In August 1933 HOLC director Tommy Corcoran telephoned LMC and invited him to come down and "join the fun." When LMC's firm refused him another leave of absence, he simply resigned and promptly left with Eleanor for Washington. Much to his father-in-law Sam Houston's dismay, they both became staunch New Dealers. LMC was already a Democrat and Eleanor swiftly converted to the party of Franklin D. Roosevelt: "It was a terrible shock to my father," Eleanor recalled. For an orthodox Republican and anti-New Dealer like Sam Houston, his daughter's apostasy was indeed a bitter shock. For the previously sheltered Eleanor, it was undoubtedly part of her personal declaration of independence.

Despite her rebellion, Eleanor's devotion to reform was quite sincere. As a little girl she had often driven with her father in a horse and carriage along the Valley Green Road past a water fountain with the words "PRO BONO PUBLICO" carved above it. Curious then about what it meant, the phrase would always make her feel that everyone had a duty to work for the public good. And as a teenager Eleanor went down to St. Martha's settlement house once a week to teach young girls how to sew. For a while after graduation, in fact, she had wanted to live at St. Martha's as a member of the regular staff—but was discouraged by her parents. She had also been awakened at the Bellevue one morning after a debutante ball by "the shuffling feet of the Bonus Marchers" going down Broad Street on their way to Washington. It was a moving scene for Eleanor, and in many ways it was her first real glimpse of what the Depression meant to millions of unemployed citizens. In the years ahead she would also remember her grandfather Henry Howard Houston's will and his wish that they all continue his habits of generosity. Meanwhile, she and LMC would join scores of other patrician New Dealers, motivated by their own sense of noblesse oblige and Christian charity, and eager to use their superior talents and educations to help reform the American nation.

LMC's first assignment in Washington was with the National Recovery Administration, or NRA, where he helped to draw up codes of fair practice for various industries. When the NRA was declared unconstitutional in 1935 he went over to the Securities and Exchange Commission (SEC). While there, he and a colleague drew up investment trust legislation. Then, in the early months of 1940, he was transferred to the Special Policies Unit of the Justice Department where he oversaw enforcement of the neutrality laws.

Like many other New Deal couples in Washington, the Smiths settled in Georgetown. At first they rented a place at 3306 O Street, a little white house with pillars at the entrance. When Eleanor's mother gave them the furniture from her summer house at St. Andrew's, New Brunswick, they took an unfurnished residence on Bancroft Place. After it was sold from under them, they bought a lot on Reservoir Road and built their own house. Designed by Rudolph Stanley-Brown, it was the earliest modern-style house to be built in Georgetown.

The first of six Smith children was also born soon after the move to Washington. Eleanor loved having the children and especially enjoyed her stays at the hospital. From one window she could see the "Capitol all lit up"; from another "the Washington Monument with the sun setting behind it."

Along with rearing children and working hard to help salvage the nation from mass unemployment and depression, the Smiths also made scores of new friends. Their Christmas Eve parties were especially popular with many friends and acquaintances who found themselves far from home at holiday time. The Smiths were also sometimes invited to large receptions at the White House, but much more enjoyable for Eleanor were Mrs. Roosevelt's pleasant afternoon teas.

The war meant change for the Smiths, as it did for most Americans. And as with the Bonus Marchers during the Depression, Eleanor's first sense of what the war really meant came to her in bed, this time in the hospital just after her daughter Meredith's birth in early May of 1940. Listening in horror to radio reports of one Nazi victory after another, she could not help but compare her children's safe and peaceful world with the terror that now threatened so many children abroad. Eleanor was particularly worried about the children of her friends in France, while LMC remembered comrades from his Oxford days and their families. Under the circumstances they decided to invite all the children they knew from Britain and France to come and live with them. They would even set up cots in the living room, if necessary. In the end, two English children came to live with them: Richard Latham, age eight, and ten-year-old Ann Tyler. Overnight Eleanor and her English nanny had six children instead of four to cope with. During their first summer together the whole family descended on Eleanor's father at Druim Moir. It was not long afterward that Sam Houston removed the entire third floor, prompting Eleanor to joke that he had done it to keep them from coming back the next year.

The day Pearl Harbor was bombed LMC and Eleanor were on the train to Philadelphia for a visit home. Eleanor's half-brother, Charlie Brown, met them at the North Philadelphia station with the terrible news, but they had driven along several blocks in the car before the gravity of it began to sink in. LMC asked Charlie to turn around and take him back to the station so he could return to Washington immediately. Eleanor stayed on to visit and do a bit of Christmas shopping.

Although LMC's work at the Justice Department was important, it was difficult for him to see friends going off in uniform one by one while he remained behind. In 1943 he secured a captaincy in the army, but had second thoughts after so many friends and colleagues argued that he was more valuable to the country as a civilian. Still, it was only after he was promised an assignment overseas that he agreed to give up the idea of entering the military. For the rest of the war he headed up U.S. economic missions, first in French West Africa and then in Switzerland.[10] The neutral Swiss would not sell such items as railroad cars to the American military, but were willing to negotiate with the U.S. government through civilians like LMC. His last overseas assignment was in Sweden, where he bought supplies needed to transfer American troops to the Pacific theater for the final onslaught against Japan.

In 1947 LMC and Eleanor returned to Philadelphia after fifteen years in Washington. They bought a charming Gothic-revival house on School House Lane in Germantown that had belonged to LMC's old boss at Justice, Attorney General Francis Biddle. Upon returning, LMC realized that Philadelphia lacked a radio station devoted solely to classical music. He and Eleanor had invested in such a station while in Washington and now decided to launch their own broadcasting venture. With transmitters on former Houston land in the 8200 block of Ridge Avenue in Roxborough, WFLN would thrive in the decades ahead as "the Delaware Valley's only full-time classical music station."[11]

The return to Philadelphia by no means ended LMC's interest in liberal causes. In 1947 he joined the Philadelphia chapter of the Americans for Democratic Action (ADA). Founded the year before by a group of former New Dealers who wanted to perpetuate the liberal causes that had united them during the Roosevelt years, the ADA would become a major focus of American liberalism during the postwar period. Besides patrician liberals, the ADA attracted labor-union leaders and former socialists.

The Philadelphia ADA became one of the strongest chapters in the country and something of a model for other organizations. In addition to championing liberal programs in general, the Philadelphia chapter was instrumental in obtaining a new municipal charter in 1951, as well as in electing ADA leader Joseph S. Clark, a socially prominent native of Chestnut Hill, as mayor of the city the same year. Clark's victory put an end to the corrupt Republican machine that had dominated Philadelphia for more than sixty years. LMC became co-chairman of the local ADA in 1951 and treasurer of the national organization several years later. He also took an uncompromising and courageous stand against Senator Joseph McCarthy and other Red-baiters who were ruining entirely innocent citizens with charges of Communist subversion.[12]

Meanwhile, LMC continued to use his expertise in foreign trade matters, becoming president of the Panocean Corporation which specialized in export operations and economic development in Central America and Iran. In 1955 he also became chairman of Philadelphia's Board of Trade and Conventions.[13] In just five years under his direction the city's convention revenues nearly doubled from $230,000 to $450,000 per year.[14] Late in 1963 he resigned from the Board of Trade and Conventions to become U.S. vice-chairman of UNESCO, the economic, scientific, and cultural branch of the United Nations.[15] In recognition for his many contributions around the world, Queen Elizabeth II made him an honorary officer of the Order of the British Empire (O.B.E.) in October 1964. And in January 1967 he received Brazil's Order of the Southern Cross.[16] Despite such honors, LMC remained a wholly modest man who liked to describe himself as a generalist. "A generalist is a fellow who does a little of a lot of things," he told the *Evening Bulletin*. "It's a bad rule," he added. "But it's a lot of fun." [17]

At holiday time the Smiths continued to give their large Christmas Eve party. Since most of their Philadelphia friends had families to be with the night before Christmas, Eleanor and LMC invited several hundred foreign students from the University of Pennsylvania's International House, Christians and non-Christians alike. According to International House director Giles Zimmerman, the annual affair was "like going back into Dickens's *A Christmas Carol*." [18] Besides beautiful decorations from all over the world, there was always a festive supper, plenty of wine punch, and Christmas carols led by the enthusiastic host. [19]

Among the Smiths' other varied interests during these years was map collecting. Their fascination with cartography began quite by chance one day in 1958 while visiting Amsterdam's Maritime Museum where they became enthralled with some early maps of coastal Maine. Directed to a local dealer by one of the museum's curators, they bought several maritime maps before returning home to Philadelphia. Over the next decade and a half the Smiths acquired an extensive and valuable collection of maps and globes which Eleanor donated to the University of Southern Maine in 1986.

However, the Smith's most impressive contribution has probably been in the area of conservation. For Eleanor, preservation and improvement of the land was something of a religious duty. They had the right to use the land and its fruits, she told the children again and again, but the earth belonged ultimately to God. They were only trustees and must therefore leave the land as good as or better than the way they found it.

Eleanor's inheritance of a large but undeveloped parcel of Houston land in Roxborough gave her the opportunity to practice these principles. The tract was bordered roughly by Hagy's Mill Road, Port Royal Avenue, the Schuylkill River, and Ridge Avenue. Remembering fondly how she and her father had often walked or ridden over this rolling and largely forested piece of countryside, she was determined to preserve the land as it was. In the spring of 1967, she and her sister, Margaret Houston Meigs, donated 500 acres as a wildlife refuge to be known as the Schuylkill Valley Nature Center. Under the direction of Richard James, the center has become a unique outdoor learning center that thousands of citizens and schoolchildren visit every year. [20] Eleanor donated still other parcels in Roxborough to Fairmount Park.

Eleanor was just as intent on preserving most of their Wolfe's Neck Farm in Maine as open land. After the war she and LMC bought a farm on the coast of Maine near Freeport to use as a summer home. Once there, however, the Smiths felt obliged to use the land to its best advantage. One year they planted a large crop of cucumbers, and in the mid-1950s they began an organic beef farm, raising cattle without insecticides or chemical additives in the feed.[21] They also began to acquire contiguous parcels of land, eventually amassing some 900 acres. Realizing that their land was one of the few undeveloped strips along the entire Maine coast, they decided to set it aside as a park for future generations to enjoy. Before LMC's death at Wolfe's Neck in August 1975 they agreed to establish both Popham Beach and Wolfe's Neck State Parks. In 1985 Eleanor donated most of the remaining acreage to the Farmland Trust, which has given it to the University of Maine as an experimental farm. Eleanor died in Maine at the end of August 1987 after a brief illness.

Before her death, Eleanor had received many awards for her work in conservation. She was given the Nature Conservancy's Green Leaf Award and the Margaret Douglas Medal of the Garden Club of America. She and LMC were also the first recipients of the Environmental Congress Award. In the spring of 1987 the Philadelphia College of Textiles and Science conferred on Eleanor the honorary degree of Doctor of Humane Letters.[22] But probably most satisfying of all, Eleanor had lived up to her own ideals of using the land as she thought God had intended.

# Epilogue

BY THE LATE 1980s there were more than 150 descendants of the Houston and Woodward families, including children who were six generations removed from founder Henry Howard Houston.[1] Living descendants were widely scattered around the nation and abroad, many of them engaged in interests and activities that surely would have pleased their forebears.

Among fourth-generation heirs, who now had reached an age where they could leave a mark of their own in the world, there were several who remained in Chestnut Hill to carry on the family's century-long interest in distinctive housing. On the Woodward side, Quita Woodward Horan and George Woodward III, both children of Charles and Betty Woodward, presided over the Woodward House Corporation, with its forty-eight rental units in Chestnut Hill. They also managed the nine apartments built in the family home at Krisheim. Besides overseeing these properties, Quita is a director of the Friends of Pastorius Park, a neighborhood organization created in 1986 to guide the restoration and preservation of parkland that her grandfather had given to the city three quarters of a century before.

Quita's first cousin, Stanley Woodward, Jr., has been president of George Woodward, Incorporated, since 1983. As such, he is in charge of some 150 houses in Chestnut Hill and West Mount Airy. Following secondary school, Stanley served in the U.S. Army Air Corps during World War II and attended several art schools following his military service. Living in Spain between 1950 and 1982, Stanley has painted, raised Arabian horses, and built yachts. In 1983 he and his wife settled in Chestnut Hill where they live on a property that was once the Krisheim vegetable garden. In addition to raising his Arabian horses, Stanley is committed to maintaining the open land around his Chestnut Hill home.

Similarly devoted to preserving family property is Sallie Smith Kise, daughter of Eleanor Houston Smith and granddaughter of Samuel F. Houston. In response to the Episcopal diocese's decision in the late 1970s to abandon Druim Moir as a retirement home, she and her architect husband, James N. Kise, purchased the family mansion. In the early 1980s they divided the house into three residences, occupying the southernmost dwelling themselves. They have also built a number of attractive townhouses on the grounds that blend very well with Druim Moir's original architecture.[2] In May 1986 a public celebration was held at Druim Moir in honor of its hundredth "birthday."[3] All proceeds went to benefit the Ebenezer Maxwell Mansion on Tulpehocken Street, located just two blocks from the site of Henry Howard Houston's own home in Germantown.

In addition to her continuing interest in Druim Moir, Sallie is a psychiatric social worker. At present she is studying for a bachelor of divinity degree at the Lutheran Seminary in Mount Airy.

Sallie's interest in preservation has been shared by her sister, Mary Minor Smith Lannon, who is a writer and environmentalist in Wiscasset, Maine. She is editor of the book *Maine Forever,* published by the Nature Conservancy. Another sister, Eleanor Smith Morris, has taken up the family's interest in architecture and city planning. Married to a Scotsman and living in Edinburgh, she is associate professor of city planning at the University of Edinburgh and chairman of the Royal Town Planning Institute in Scotland. Her brother, Samuel F. Houston Smith, is a journalist in Washington, D.C., where he and all the older Smith children spent their earliest years.

Dr. Thomas S. Brown, a first cousin of the Smiths and a fellow grandchild of Samuel F. Houston, was one of two Brown sons to follow their father's career in medicine. He served two years with the U.S. Navy during World War II and he has been a family doctor in Lebanon, New Hampshire, since 1957. A lover of nature, like so many others in the family, he has climbed all the major Cascade Mountains.

The Henry cousins, descendants of Sallie Houston and Charles Wolcott Henry, have shared the fourth generation's passion for environmentalism and historic preservation. Among them is Cornelia Dodge Fraley, daughter of Donald D. and Gertrude Henry Dodge, who has worked to preserve open land in Chester County, Pennsylvania. She has also been an active promoter of the arts as a thirty-year member of the Women's Committee of the University of Pennsylvania Museum, and as founder and director of the Yellow Springs Association and its successor, Historic Yellow Springs, Incorporated. She is currently president of the Chester Springs Studio, a county arts facility.

Cornelia's brother Donald D. Dodge, Jr., seems to have inherited the entrepreneurial instincts of several ancestors. Earning a degree in geology from Princeton after his service in World War II, Donald went to work for Texaco in Kansas. In 1956 he moved to Denver, Colorado, and started his own oil and gas exploration company, with operations in the Rocky Mountain area, Indonesia, and Canada.

The Dodges' Chatfield cousins, children of Elizabeth (Bizzy) Henry and William Chatfield, all grew up in Cincinnati, Ohio, where their father was in the papermaking business. Henry Houston Chatfield earned a law degree from Harvard, served for five years in the U.S. Army during World War II, and has been a practicing attorney in Cincinnati since 1947. From 1957 to 1976 he was a member and vice-chairman of the Cincinnati Metropolitan Housing Authority. His brother, John S. Chatfield, also graduated from Harvard Law School. After several years with the New York County district attorney's office, he became interested in business, working as a stockbroker in New York City for E. F. Hutton and then for Dominick and Dominick. Brother Frederick H. Chatfield similarly pursued a career in business. Graduating from Harvard in 1942, he served as a diplomatic courier during World War II. In 1946 he went to work for Mead Paper, retiring in 1972 as group vice-president and director of the Mead Corporation.

The Chatfields' daughter, Helen Chatfield Black, has been active with her husband, Robert, in promoting land conservation. In the mid-1960s they were among the founders of the Cincinnati Nature Center. Helen subsequently served two terms on the Nature Conservancy's board of governors. In the 1980s she and Robert have been helping to preserve Cincinnati's spectacular art deco railroad station. Known as the "Museum Center in the Union Terminal," the station serves as a new home for the city's Natural History Museum and Historical Society.

The two daughters of T. Charlton and Julia Biddle Henry have taken up a variety of interests. Isabel Henry Ault has supported conservation efforts, the Visiting Nurse Service, and the Girls Club of Boston. Her sister, Julia Henry Armour, moved to Chicago following her marriage to Philip D. Armour, Jr., in 1938. She has raised English Springer spaniels and has been an active skeet-shooter and outdoors woman.

Although members of the fourth generation have pursued a number of occupations and interests, at least one individual (and often several) in each main branch of the Houston and Woodward families has been deeply involved in historic preservation or land conservation and environmentalism. For Henry Howard Houston, who gave so generously to Philadelphia's Fairmount Park and who wished to preserve large portions of western Chestnut Hill as open land, there could be no more suitable tribute from his numerous descendants.

The desire for personal achievement and community service has thus continued to burn intensely in many of Henry Howard Houston's and George Woodward's heirs. Houston's great wealth has enabled these capable men and women to obtain good educations at some of the nation's most prestigious institutions. Inherited social status has also given them a platform from which to launch themselves and their proposals for improving the community. Substantial amounts of inherited capital have likewise helped several heirs to finance successful business ventures or to promote philanthropic activities. For some, a sense of religious duty has also remained strong, as they have gone on practicing the social gospel into the late twentieth century. There has also been a sustaining sense of family pride and privilege, which has led fourth-generation descendants to take leading roles in their communities. For them, Philadelphia's reputation as a private preserve—whether they have remained in the Quaker City or have gone elsewhere to seek their fortunes—continues to be at odds with good sense and family values. As the ripples of family enterprise and tradition spread out to embrace future generations, one can hope that the examples of Henry Howard Houston, George Woodward, and their descendants will continue to inspire future generations.

Simplified Map of Lower Chestnut Hill

# FAMILIES OF HENRY HOWARD HOUSTON AND GEORGE WOODWARD

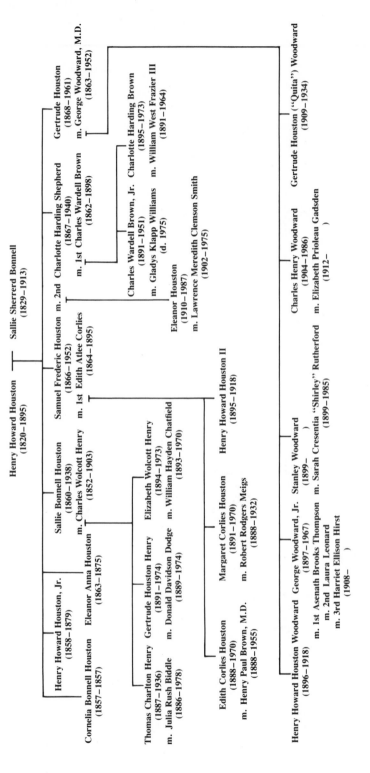

# A Brief Note on Sources

THERE ARE TWO MAJOR manuscript collections that deal with the Houston and Woodward families. The Houston Estate Papers are at the Pennsylvania State Archives at Harrisburg. Special permission is necessary to view any of the materials generated after 1945. The other major manuscript source is the private collection of the late Eleanor Houston Smith. Several smaller collections are in the possession of Stanley Woodward, Cornelia Dodge Fraley, Charlotte Houston Dallett, and the University of Pennsylvania Archives. Much important material was also gathered through lengthy interviews with various members of the family. These are identified in the notes.

George Woodward, M.D., wrote voluminously and brought out a number of his writings in private editions. Most important is his *Memoirs of a Mediocre Man* (Philadelphia, 1935). There are also seven volumes of his *Pennsylvania Legislator,* printed in Philadelphia between 1932 and 1945, as well as two volumes of letters: *Family Letters and Proletarian Essays* (Philadelphia, 1937) and *Family Letters* (Philadelphia, 1946). Following his son's death in World War I, Woodward printed a volume of the young man's correspondence under the title *A Year For France: War Letters of Houston Woodward* (New Haven, 1919). And after the death of their daughter Quita in 1934, his wife Gertrude Houston Woodward wrote and compiled a volume known simply as *Quita.*

A search of Philadelphia newspapers revealed much information on family members, but they were especially helpful in illuminating George Woodward's years as a state senator. The diplomatic career of Stanley Woodward, has likewise been chronicled in magazine and newspaper articles. All of these are listed in the notes.

Public records, such as those in the Philadelphia City Archives, were also helpful, as were the parish registers of the churches that the families attended. The records and papers of the Pennsylvania Railroad were essential to understanding the business career of Henry Howard Houston. Both the board minutes and the railroad's official correspondence may be found at the (Hagley) Elutherian Mills Historical Library near Wilmington, Delaware. The Dun and Bradstreet *Credit Ledgers,* used to evaluate Houston's wealth at several stages, are, similarly, available on microfilm at Elutherian Mills. Houston's personal income tax records for the Civil War period may be found at the National Archives in Washington, D.C.

Biographies, monographs, and other secondary sources were used to shed further light on the lives and times of family members. These, too, appear in the notes.

# *Abbreviations*

| | |
|---|---|
| AAUP | Architectural Archives, University of Pennsylvania |
| AR | Alumni Records in Archives of University of Pennsylvania |
| CDF | Cornelia Dodge Fraley |
| DDD | Donald Davidson Dodge |
| EGW | Elizabeth Gadsden Woodward |
| EHS | Eleanor Houston Smith |
| FJD | Francis James Dallett |
| GHW | Gertrude Houston Woodward |
| GW | George Woodward, M.D. |
| HEP | Houston Estate Papers |
| HHH | Henry Howard Houston (1820–1895) |
| HHHJr | Henry Howard Houston, Jr. ("Howard") (1858–1879) |
| HHH2 | Henry Howard Houston II ("Hennie") (1895–1918) |
| MFL | Mark Frazier Lloyd |
| MWPB | Mary Wickham Porcher Bond |
| *PH* | *Pennsylvania History* |
| *PMHB* | *Pennsylvania Magazine of History and Biography* |
| PRR | Pennsylvania Railroad |
| PSA | Pennsylvania State Archives |

SBH       Sallie S. Bonnell Houston
SFH       Samuel Frederic Houston
SW        Stanley Woodward
UP        University of Pennsylvania
UPA       University of Pennsylvania Archives (general files)

# Notes

*Preface*

1. E. Digby Baltzell, *Puritan Boston and Quaker Philadelphia* (New York, 1979).
2. Sam Bass Warner, *The Private City: Philadelphia in Three Periods of Its Growth* (Philadelphia, 1968).
3. For further insight into this process see E. Digby Baltzell, *Philadelphia Gentlemen: The Making of a National Upper Class* (Philadelphia, 1979).

*Chapter 1: Beginnings*

1. For biographical sketches of Henry Howard Houston, see *The Dictionary of American Biography*, vol. 9, pp. 262–263; *The National Cyclopedia of American Biography*, vol. 35, p. 522; Ellis Paxton Oberholtzer, *Philadelphia: A History of the City and Its People* (Philadelphia, 1912), vol. 4, pp. 254–258; William B. Wilson, *History of the Pennsylvania Railroad Company* (Philadelphia, 1899), vol. 2, pp. 288–299; Frank C. Roberts, Jr., *The Houstons of Philadelphia* (New York, The Newcomen Society, 1954). Among earlier accounts, that of Franklin Ellis and Samuel Evans, *History of Lancaster County, Pennsylvania* (Philadelphia, 1883), pp. 591–592, led to another in *Magazine of Western History*, vol. 9 (1889), pp. 749–751, and to the sketch in *Contemporary American Biography* (New York, 1893), pp. 216–218, all drawn to my attention by Francis James Dallett (FJD). In recent years, Houston has been noticed by E. Digby Baltzell, *Philadelphia Gentlemen;* Nathaniel Burt, *The Perennial Philadelphians* (Boston, 1963); and Russell F. Weigley et al., eds., *Philadelphia: A 300-Year History* (New York, 1982).
2. The Houston family's early history may be found in Ellis and Evans, *History of Lancaster County*, pp. 589–592; in Thomas H. Bateman, *Houston and Allied Families* (New York, 1950), pp. 1–12, a work which requires careful additional use of primary sources; and in a genealogical and biographical memorandum of FJD to the author.

3. On the Wrights see Bateman, *Houston,* 45–47; John Gibson, *History of York County, Pennsylvania* (Chicago, 1886), pp. 14–17, 107, 299, 317, 326, 595–596; John Risser, "Why Columbia, Pennsylvania is not the Capital of the United States," *Susquehanna* (March 1985); *Lancaster New Era,* 21 September 1938; *Philadelphia Inquirer,* 3 October 1974.

4. Carl Carmer, *The Susquehanna* (New York, 1955), pp. 442–443; *Lancaster New Era,* 7 February 1977.

5. Bateman, *Houston,* p. 8.

6. Ibid., pp. 8–9.

7. Gibson, *York County,* pp. 328–334; conversation with Eleanor Houston Smith (EHS), 12 March 1987.

8. Wilson, *Pennsylvania Railroad,* vol. 2, p. 289.

9. Samuel Frederic Houston (SFH), address before the Scotch-Irish Society of Pennsylvania, 23 February 1928, EHS collection.

10. Henry Howard Houston (HHH) to Alfred Huffnagle, 22 March 1843, EHS collection.

11. For an excellent account of life and work at a nineteenth-century Pennsylvania iron furnace see Joseph E. Walker, *Hopewell Village* (Philadelphia, 1966).

12. Aaron J. Davis, *History of Clarion County, Pennsylvania* (Syracuse, New York, 1887), pp. 113–121; Myron B. Sharp and William H. Thomas, *A Guide to the Old Stone Blast Furnaces in Western Pennsylvania* (Pittsburgh, 1966), p. 36.

13. Wilson, *Pennsylvania Railroad,* vol. 2, p. 289.

14. Walker, *Hopewell,* pp. 165–182; Roberts, *The Houstons,* p. 10.

15. Wilson, *Pennsylvania Railroad,* vol. 2, p. 289.

16. On Philadelphia at the time of Houston's arrival, see Elizabeth M. Geffen, "Industrial Development and Social Crisis, 1841–1854," in *A 300-Year History,* ed. Weigley et al., pp. 307–362.

17. George H. Burgess and Miles C. Kennedy, *Centennial History of the Pennsylvania Railroad Company, 1846–1946* (Philadelphia, 1949), pp. 1–40; Philip S. Klein and Ari Hoogenboom, *A History of Pennsylvania* (New York, 1973), pp. 184–188; H. W. Schotter, *The Growth and Development of the Pennsylvania Railroad* (Philadelphia, 1927), pp. 1–32.

18. *National Cyclopedia,* vol. 35, p. 522.

19. Philadelphia Deed Book TH-97, pp. 353–364 (FJD).

20. Mc Elroy's *Philadelphia Directory for 1856,* p. 52.

21. Genealogical data of EHS and CHD. Of the many works, including Bateman, treating the Bonnell family and its antecedents, the most useful is probably J. Robert T. Crane, comp., *The Ancestry and Posterity of Matthew Clarkson (1664–1702),* ed. Harry W. Hazard (Princeton, 1971).

22. Christ Church Parish Register, 1856.

23. Christ Church Parish Register, 1857.

24. Mc Elroy's *Philadelphia Directory for 1859,* p. 334.

25. Bateman, *Houston,* p. 10.

26. Russell F. Weigley, "The Border City in the Civil War, 1854–1865," in *A 300-Year History,* pp. 368–372.

27. On the origins of American suburbs, see Robert A. M. Stern, *Pride of Place* (Boston, 1986), pp. 125–167; Robert Fishman, *Bourgeois Utopias* (New York, 1987).

28. Sidney George Fisher, *A Philadelphia Perspective: The Diary of Sidney*

*George Fisher Covering the Years 1834–1871,* ed. Nicholas B. Wainwright (Philadelphia, 1967), p. 277.

29. For an understanding of Henry Howard Houston's years in Germantown the author is greatly indebted to the extensive research undertaken by Mark Frazier Lloyd (MFL), archivist of the University of Pennsylvania; see also MFL, "The Tulpehocken Street Houses of Henry Howard Houston," *Germantown Crier* (Spring 1980), pp. 40–42.

30. Interview with MFL, 15 September 1986; Mc Elroy's *Philadelphia Directory for 1865,* p. 332; HHH, Alumni Record (AR) file, University of Pennsylvania Archives (UPA). This file, and those of many other members of the family, were extensively augmented by FJD during his tenure as University Archivist.

31. Bateman, *Houston,* p. 10; death certificate, Eleanor A. Houston, Philadelphia City Archives.

32. Cornelius Weygandt, *Philadelphia Folks: Ways and Institutions in and about the Quaker City* (New York, 1938), pp. 272–273.

33. Ibid., pp. 18, 41; Cornelius Weygandt, *On the Edge of Evening* (New York, 1946), pp. 42–43.

34. Gopsill's *Philadelphia Directory, 1881,* p. 799.

35. Weygandt, *Philadelphia Folks,* p. 124.

36. Frank J. Firth, "Memoirs," (family collection), pp. 101–102.

37. Interview with EHS by her daughter Sarah "Sallie" Smith Kise, July 1986.

38. FJD to author, 26 November 1987. HHH exhibited four paintings from his eclectic collection at the Pennsylvania Academy of Fine Arts in 1865.

## Chapter 2: Railroad Entrepreneur

1. Firth, "Memoirs," pp. 41–44.

2. Weigley, "The Border City," pp. 383–394.

3. See James A. Ward, *J. Edgar Thomson: Master of the Pennsylvania* (Westport, Conn., 1980), pp. 123–125.

4. Ibid., pp. 126–128; Burgess and Kennedy, *Centennial History,* p. 345.

5. Ibid., pp. 310–311; Ward, *Thomson,* pp. 127–136.

6. Burgess and Kennedy, *Centennial History,* pp. 243, 324–327; Pennsylvania Railroad (PRR) Board Minutes, 2 December 1863.

7. *National Cyclopedia,* vol. 35, p. 522.

8. These figures were gathered by MFL and were taken from Houston's personal income tax returns from 1863 to 1865, National Archives, Washington, D.C. See HHH, AR file, UPA.

9. HHH to J. Edgar Thomson, 29 June 1867, in PRR Board file no. 8.

10. Ward, *Thomson,* pp. 141–206.

11. HHH, Personal Account Book, EHS collection; Dun and Bradstreet *Credit Ledgers,* vol. 11, p. 63.

12. PRR Board Minutes, 21 October 1868.

13. Ibid., 30 June and 23 November 1870; 27 September 1871.

14. *Theory and Practice of the American System of Fast Freight Transportation* (Philadelphia, 1876), p. 10.

15. Ibid., pp. 23–30.

16. Ibid., pp. 6–21, 30–31.

17. Ibid., p. 39; HHH, Personal Account Book.

18. Allan Nevins, *Study in Power: John D. Rockefeller, Industrialist and Phi-lanthropist,* vol. 1, (New York, 1953), pp. 231–249; Firth, "Memoirs," p. 102.

19. HHH, Personal Account Book.

20. Ibid.; Nevins, *Rockefeller,* vol. 1, pp. 209–211; vol. 2, pp. 5, 7.

21. Minutes of family meeting, 16 November 1961, Houston Estate Papers (HEP), General Correspondence, D–F, Pennsylvania State Archives (PSA), MG-154.

22. HHH, Personal Account Book.

23. Dun and Bradstreet, *Credit Ledgers,* vol. 14, p. 68.

24. HHH, Personal Balance Sheet for January 1884, EHS collection.

25. Wilson, *Pennsylvania Railroad,* vol. 2, p. 292.

26. *A Record of the Class of 1878,* University of Pennsylvania, 1878 to 1898 (Philadelphia, 1899), p. 80.

27. Diary of Henry Howard Houston, Jr. (HHHJr), 20–30 June 1878, EHS collection.

28. Ibid., 1–2 July 1878.

29. Ibid., 3–5 July 1878.

30. HHHJr to his parents, 5 August 1878, EHS collection.

31. Ibid., 29 August 1878.

32. Ibid., 2 September 1878.

33. Ibid., 15 September 1878.

34. Ibid., 23 September 1878.

35. Ibid., 13 October 1878.

36. Ibid.

37. Ibid., 25 October 1878.

38. Ibid., 4, 10, 23, and 25 November 1878; 4 and 22 December 1878; 28 January 1879.

39. *Record of the Class of 1878,* p. 80; *The University Magazine,* 5 June 1879, p. 116.

## Chapter 3: A Planned Community

1. For an understanding of Houston's first venture into church building, the author is again much indebted to Mark Frazier Lloyd.

2. *Case of Christ Church, Germantown* (Philadelphia, 1872), pp. 5–20.

3. See George E. De Mille, *The Catholic Movement in the American Episcopal Church* (Philadelphia, 1941), pp. 65–80.

4. "Christ Church, Germantown," *The Church Standard,* 4 March 1899; interview with MFL, 15 September 1986.

5. "St. Peter's Church, Germantown," *The Church Standard,* 18 March 1899; Theodore S. Rumney and Charles Bullock, *History of St. Peter's Church, Germantown* (Philadelphia, 1897).

6. Interview with MFL, 15 September 1986.

7. HHH, Deed Book, AR file, UPA.

8. Interview with EHS, 11 December 1984.

9. Philadelphia *Evening Bulletin,* 18 March 1950; interview with MFL, 15 September 1986.

10. Willard S. Detweiler, Jr., *Chestnut Hill: An Architectural History* (Philadelphia, 1969), pp. 21–24.

11. PRR Board file no. 8; S. F. Hotchkin, *Ancient and Modern Germantown, Mount Airy, and Chestnut Hill* (Philadelphia, 1889), p. 417.

12. PRR Board minutes, 6 August 1879.

13. PRR Board file no. 8.

14. PRR Board minutes, 16 December 1882.

15. Hotchkin, *Ancient and Modern*, p. 417.

16. PRR Board file no. 8; PRR Board minutes, 8 September 1880.

17. *Evening Bulletin*, 30 August 1879.

18. HHH, Personal Account Book.

19. HHH, Deed Book.

20. HHH, Personal Balance Sheet for 1 January 1884 and 1 January 1885, EHS collection.

21. John J. MacFarlane, *History of Early Chestnut Hill* (Philadelphia, 1927), pp. 18–21; Hotchkin, *Ancient and Modern*, pp. 401–404; Horace M. Lippincott, *Chestnut Hill, Springfield, Whitemarsh, Cheltenham* (Jenkintown, Pa., 1948), pp. 15–19.

22. Dun and Bradstreet *Credit Ledgers*, Pennsylvania, vol. 144, p. 68, contributed by FJD.

23. *Philadelphia Inquirer*, 30 May 1884.

24. Philadelphia *Press*, 1 June 1884.

25. Philadelphia *Public Ledger*, 11 June 1884.

26. *Inquirer*, 27 May 1884.

27. *The Chestnut Hill Local*, 31 May 1984; Hotchkin, *Ancient and Modern*, p. 417.

28. Lippincott, *Chestnut Hill*, pp. 73–75.

29. *Public Ledger*, 2 October 1884.

30. Detweiler, *Chestnut Hill*, p. 27.

31. Helen Moak, "The First Seventy-Five Years," *The Parish News of St. Martin-in-the-Fields Church*, 2 February 1965, pp. 3–8; Hotchkin, *Ancient and Modern*, pp. 424–426; "St. Martin-in-the-Fields, Wissahickon Heights," *The Church Standard*, 30 December 1899.

32. SFH, address on the retirement of the Reverend Jacob LeRoy, St. Martin-in-the-Fields Church, 24 November 1919, EHS collection.

33. Ibid.; Moak, "First Seventy-Five Years," p. 7.

34. *Inquirer*, 4 February 1889.

35. Moak, "First Seventy-Five Years," pp. 14–16. More specific examples of the Houston's generosity may be found in the minutes of the vestry of St. Martin-in-the-Fields Church, 21 October 1895 and subsequent entries.

36. *Public Ledger*, 1 April 1884.

37. Wissahickon Heights Plan, EHS collection.

38. Hotchkin, *Ancient and Modern*, p. 417.

39. HHH, Ledger, AR file, UPA.

40. For example, Summary Exhibits, Estate of Henry Howard Houston, Deceased, 1895 to 1925, pp. 8–10, EHS collection.

41. HHH, Personal Balance Sheet, 1 January 1885.

42. S. W. Bussinger to HHH, 31 August 1891; John McCrea to HHH, 29 June 1891, EHS collection.

43. PRR Board minutes, 9 March, 22 June, 14 December 1892.

44. McCallum Street Bridge contract, EHS collection.

45. Hotchkin, *Ancient and Modern,* pp. 422–423; *Chestnut Hill Local,* 15 May 1986; memorandum from FJD to author.
46. Memorandum from FJD to MFL, HHH, AR file, UPA.
47. George William Sheldon, *Country Seats* (New York, 1887), p. 71.
48. Hotchkin, *Ancient and Modern,* pp. 422–424; *Philadelphia Press,* 25 September 1885; *Chestnut Hill Local,* 15 May 1986. HHH also presented the Village of Connor, County Antrim, with its town hall as a memorial to a Houston covenanting clergyman.
49. Moak, "First Seventy-Five Years," p. 13; J. Wesley Twelves, *A History of the Diocese of Pennsylvania* (Philadelphia, 1969), p. 63; conversation with EHS, 10 February 1987; reminiscences of Sophie Weygandt Harris, as told to FJD and CHD in 1956.
50. Interview with EHS, 11 December 1984; *Pennsylvania Gazette,* February 1952.
51. *Philadelphia Sunday Dispatch,* 27 February 1938.
52. *New York Times,* 12 September 1881.
53. *The Standard-Echo,* 29 June 1895; Horace Mann Bond, *Education for Freedom: A History of Lincoln University* (Princeton, N.J., 1979), p. 460; *Chestnut Hill Local,* 22 February 1979.
54. HHH, AR file, UPA.
55. Interview with EHS, 11 December 1984.
56. Memorandum from FJD to MFL, HHH, AR file, UPA.
57. *Record of the Class of 1878,* pp. 150–152; Charles C. Harrison to HHH, 13 October 1894, AR file, UPA. Houston had commemorated his daughter Eleanor by the gift of the Children's Wing to the Germantown Hospital, on whose board he sat, as he did at the University.
58. *Public Ledger,* 21 December 1894.
59. *Daily Pennsylvanian,* 9 October 1939; *Philadelphia Inquirer,* 7 June 1938.
60. *Public Ledger,* 22 June 1895.
61. Ibid., 25 June 1895.
62. *Evening Bulletin,* 5 December 1961.
63. HHH, Last Will and Testament, Item 57, EHS collection.

*Chapter 4: A New Generation*

1. Interview with EHS, 11 December 1984.
2. St. Peter's Parish Register, 1880–1892, p. 198; *Public Ledger,* 21 November 1884; "Charles Wolcott Henry," privately printed, pp. 13–16.
3. Interview with EHS, 14 November 1986; interview with Cornelia Dodge Fraley (CDF), 5 March 1987; *Public Ledger,* 6 June 1938; memorandum from FJD to author.
4. Memorandum by FJD, SFH, AR file, UPA.
5. Ibid.
6. Interview with EHS, 11 December 1984.
7. SFH, AR file, UPA.
8. Bateman, *Houston,* pp. 11–12; conversation with EHS, 9 January 1987.
9. Ibid.
10. News Bureau, University of Pennsylvania (UP), 11 March 1952, AR files, UPA.

11. *Trip to the Caribbean, 1898,* privately printed, EHS collection.

12. Interview with EHS, 14 November 1986; *Country Life* (April 1925); plans for the Clapboard Island house, Houston Estate file, Architectural Archives, University of Pennsylvania (AAUP).

13. News Bureau, UP, 11 March 1952; AR file, UPA; *Philadelphia Inquirer,* 6 January 1948; *Evening Bulletin,* 2 May 1952.

14. HHH, Last Will and Testament. Recorded in the Office of the Register of Wills, Philadelphia as no. 1059 of 1895. The document was also privately printed.

15. Lease agreement for Andorra Nurseries of 1 April 1895, HEP, General Correspondence, A–C, PSA, MG-154.

16. Hotchkin, *Ancient and Modern,* p. 409; Charles Latham, Jr., *The Episcopal Academy* (Devon, Pa., 1984), pp. 119–120, 129.

17. SFH, Personal Account Book, EHS collection; *Evening Bulletin,* 31 December 1917; *Public Ledger,* 15 January 1928, 31 October 1929; Roberts, *The Houstons,* p. 22; conversation with EHS, 12 December 1986.

18. *Evening Bulletin,* 2 May 1952.

19. Baltzell, *Philadelphia Gentlemen,* pp. 130, 158.

20. *Evening Bulletin,* 4 April 1902; conversation with EHS, 12 February 1987.

21. Conversation with EHS, 31 December 1986.

22. Edith C. Houston to her grandmother, Sallie Bonnell Houston (SBH), 28 December 1902. This and other letters written during the trip are in several family collections.

23. SFH to SBH, 29 December 1902.

24. Ibid., 8 March 1903.

25. Ibid., 22 March 1903.

26. Ibid., 8 April 1903.

27. Ibid., 10 May 1903.

28. Ibid., 11 May 1903; conversation with EHS, 9 January 1987.

29. SFH to SBH, 13 June 1903.

30. Ibid., 4 June 1903.

31. *The New York Times,* 19 June 1903.

32. For an account of Woodward's childhood and youth, see George Woodward (GW), *Memoirs of a Mediocre Man* (Philadelphia, 1935), pp. 13–88.

33. *Diary of Samuel Richards, Captain of the Connecticut Line, War of Revolution, 1775–1781* (Philadelphia, 1909).

34. On Woodward's ancestry see *A Biographical Album of Prominent Pennsylvanians* (Philadelphia, 1889), pp. 87–92; GW, *Memoirs,* pp. 53–54.

35. George Washington Woodward, "Opinions of a Man Who Wishes to be Governor," pamphlet (Harrisburg, 1860).

36. GW, *Memoirs,* pp. 38–39.

37. Nicholas B. Wainright, "The Loyal Opposition in Civil War Philadelphia," *Pennsylvania Magazine of History and Biography* (*PMHB*) (July 1964), pp. 305–308.

38. GW, *Memoirs,* pp. 37, 59–60; "Stanley Woodward," in *A Biographical Album,* pp. 87–92.

39. GW, *Memoirs,* p. 40.

40. Ibid.

41. Ibid., p. 41.

42. Ibid.

43. Ibid., p. 42.

44. Ibid., p. 37.

45. Ibid.
46. Stanley Woodward (SW), to author, 19 March 1986.
47. See George W. Pierson, *Yale College: An Educational History* (New Haven, 1952), pp. 81–83.
48. GW, *Memoirs,* pp. 79–80.
49. Ibid., p. 106; SW to author, 3 March 1986.
50. GW, *Memoirs,* pp. 79–88; *Quarter Century Record, Class of 1887, Yale College,* p. 418
51. GW, *Memoirs,* p. 13.
52. His thesis was entitled "Erythro- and Achro-Dextrins." See GW, *Memoirs,* p. 15.
53. Ibid.
54. George W. Corner, *Two Centuries of Medicine: A History of the School of Medicine of the University of Pennsylvania* (Philadelphia, 1965), pp. 170–175.
55. On Osler see Harvey Cushing, *The Life of Sir William Osler* (London, 1940).
56. GW, *Memoirs,* p. 17.
57. As of March 1986 George Woodward's personal library was still largely intact at Krisheim, his home in Chestnut Hill.
58. GW, *Memoirs,* pp. 19–28.
59. Ibid., p. 29.
60. Ibid., pp. 28–33.
61. Ibid., p. 34.
62. Interview with SW, 18–19 July 1986.
63. GW, *Memoirs,* pp. 95–96.
64. Ibid., p. 98.
65. *Parish News,* November 1961, p. 5.
66. Interview with SW, 21 June 1985.
67. Ibid., p. 22–23, 32–33.
68. Ibid., p. 16.

## *Chapter 5: Progressive Reformer*

1. On Philadelphia during this period, see Lloyd M. Abernethy, "Progressivism, 1905–1919," in *A 300-Year History,* pp. 524–565; John Lukacs, *Philadelphia: Patricians and Philistines, 1900–1950* (New York, 1980), pp. 3–47; Arthur P. Dudden, "Lincoln Steffens' Philadelphia," *Pennsylvania History (PH)* (October 1964), pp. 449–453.
2. Lincoln Steffens, *The Shame of the Cities* (New York, 1904), p. 195.
3. SFH, address before the Men's Club of Holy Trinity Church, Collingswood, New Jersey, 5 April 1914, EHS collection.
4. Interview with EHS, 14 November 1986.
5. SFH, Holy Trinity, 5 April 1914.
6. On SFH's switch to the Republican party see the *Press,* 10 October 1914.
7. On the characteristics of progressive reformers there is Robert M. Crunden, *Ministers of Reform* (New York, 1982), pp. 3–15.
8. Baltzell, *Puritan Boston and Quaker Philadelphia,* pp. 1–15.
9. On Philadelphia municipal corruption during this period and the attempts of reformers to combat it, see Lloyd M. Abernethy, "Insurgency in Philadelphia, 1905," *PMHB* (January 1963), pp. 13–20; Philip S. Benjamin, "Gentile Reformers in

the Quaker City, 1870–1912," *Political Science Quarterly* (1970), pp. 61–79; Robert L. Bloom, "Edwin A. Van Valkenburg and the Philadelphia North American, 1899–1924," *PMHB* (April 1954), pp. 109–127. On urban progressivism in general there are John D. Buenker, *Urban Liberalism and Progressive Reform* (New York, 1973), and Bruce M. Stave, ed., *Urban Bosses, Machines, and Progressive Reformers* (Lexington, Mass., 1971).

10. GW, "The Chemistry of Colostrum Milk," *The Journal of Experimental Medicine* (March 1897); "A Clinical Method for the Evaluation of Breast Proteids," in *Contributions to the William Pepper Laboratory of Clinical Medicine* (Philadelphia, 1900), pp. 447–449.

11. GW, *Memoirs*, p. 36.

12. Ibid.

13. On the campaign against typhoid fever in Philadelphia, see Gretchen A. Condran et al., "The Decline of Mortality in Philadelphia from 1870 to 1930: The Role of Municipal Services," *PMHB* (April 1984), pp. 165–168. Newspaper accounts of Woodward's crusade for filtered water appeared in the *Public Ledger,* 8 October 1897; *North American,* 13, 15, 16, 20, 22, and 25 March 1899.

14. *Press,* 21, 22, and 23 November, 20 December 1904; University of Pennsylvania, *Alumni Register,* December 1899.

15. GW, "A Triumph of the People: The Story of the Downfall of the Political Oligarchy in Philadelphia," *Outlook* (5 December 1905), p. 815.

16. Lloyd Abernethy, "Progressivism, 1905–1919," pp. 543–544.

17. Ibid., 544–545; Clinton Rogers Woodruff, "Progress in Philadelphia," *The American Journal of Sociology* (November 1920), pp. 318, 330–332; *Press,* 2 July 1909.

18. Donald W. Disbrow, "Reform in Philadelphia Under Mayor Blankenburg, 1912–1916," *PH* (October 1960), pp. 379–396.

19. SW to author, 19 March 1986.

20. See Alan F. Davis, *Spearheads for Reform: The Social Settlements and the Progressive Movement, 1890–1914* (New York, 1967); Gwendolyn Wright, *Moralism and the Modern Home* (Chicago, 1980).

21. John F. Sutherland, "The Origins of Philadelphia's Octavia Hill Association: Social Reform in the Contented City," *PMHB* (January 1975), pp. 20–44; Fullerton Waldo, *Good Housing that Pays: A Study of the Aims and Accomplishments of the Octavia Hill Association, 1896–1917* (Philadelphia, 1917).

22. Ibid., pp. 33–34.

23. Ibid., pp. 34–40; Sutherland, "Octavia Hill Association," pp. 38–42.

24. SW to author, 19 March 1986.

25. *Evening Bulletin,* 11 February 1926, 7 May 1927, 26 May 1952; *Quarter Century Record,* p. 419.

*Chapter 6: The Model Suburb*

1. For other accounts of the Houston and Woodward housing developments in Chestnut Hill, see Fishman, *Bourgeois Utopias,* pp. 142–154, and Mary Corbin Sies, "American Country House Architecture in Context: The Suburban Ideal of Living in the East and Midwest, 1877–1917" (University of Michigan, doctoral diss., 1987), pp. 272–362. Both of these works also offer excellent insights into the evolution of nineteenth-century suburbs as a whole. In this regard also see Stern, *Pride of Place,* pp. 125–168.

2. *Arts and Crafts Essays by Members of the Arts and Crafts Exhibition Society,* with a preface by William Morris (London, 1903).

3. Cynthia Ann MacLeod, "Arts and Crafts Architecture in Suburban Phila-delphia Sponsored by Dr. George Woodward" (University of Virginia, master's thesis, 1979), pp. 16–21.

4. GW, *Memoirs,* pp. 105–106.

5. Ibid.

6. Ibid.

7. GW, "Another Aspect of the Quadruple House," *The Architectural Record* (July 1913), pp. 51–55. See also Matlack Price, "Architecture and the Housing Prob-lem: Recent Work of Durhing, Okie, and Ziegler," *The Architectural Record* (Sep-tember 1913), pp. 241–247.

8. GW, "Another Aspect," p. 51.

9. Ibid., p. 52.

10. "English Half-Timber Houses," *The Brochure Series of Architectural Illus-tration* (June 1903), pp. 135–144.

11. Minutes of the vestry of St. Martin-in-the-Fields Church, 5 January, 26 April, 1916, vol. 2, pp. 49, 55.

12. GW, *Memoirs,* p. 106.

13. Interview with SW, 21 June 1985.

14. GW, *Memoirs,* pp. 103–104.

15. See Thomas Nolan, "Recent Suburban Architecture in Philadelphia and Vicinity," *The Architectural Record* (March 1906), pp. 167–193; Stern, *Pride of Place,* pp. 125–167; Edward Teitelman and Betsy Fahlman, "Wilson Eyre and the Colonial Revival in Philadelphia," in *The Colonial Revival in America,* ed. Alan Axelrod (New York, 1985), pp. 71–90.

16. "English Thatched Cottages," *The Brochure Series* (May 1898), pp. 73–82.

17. Gertrude Houston Woodward (GHW), *Quita,* privately printed, p. 17.

18. GW, *Memoirs,* p. 109.

19. Harold D. Eberlein, "Pastorius Park, Philadelphia and Its Residential De-velopment," *The Architectural Record* (January 1916), p. 25. This article contains de-tailed descriptions of the whole Pastorius Park project.

20. Plans and correspondence relating to Pastorius Park may be found in Houston Estate file, AAUP.

21. Ibid.

22. See Christopher Gray, "The French Village," *House and Garden* (De-cember 1983), pp. 82, 84, 86, 88.

23. GW, "Landlord and Tenant," *The Survey,* (11 December 1920), p. 389.

24. Ibid., p. 391.

25. See Collier Stevenson, "The Ice House," *House Beautiful* (March 1910), pp. 91–94.

26. Sies, "American Country House," pp. 206–455.

27. Ibid., p. 229.

*Chapter 7: At Home in Chestnut Hill*

1. HHH Estate, Summary Exhibits, 1895–1925, EHS collection.

2. HHH, Last Will and Testament.

3. Interview with SW, 18–19 July 1986.

4. GW, *Memoirs*, p. 95.
5. Interview with SW, 21 June 1985.
6. Ibid.
7. On the Krisheim gardens, which were designed by the Olmstead Brothers, see "The Garden at Krisheim," *House and Garden* (April 1916), pp. 14–15; *Public Ledger*, 9 April 1930; *Evening Bulletin*, 12 October 1962.
8. See John Lynn Grey, "The Cottage on the Estate," *House Beautiful* (October 1910), p. 135.
9. Interview with SW, 21 June 1985.
10. Ibid.
11. Ibid.
12. SW to author, 29 April 1986.
13. Ibid.; interview with SW, 21 June 1985.
14. Interview with Charles H. Woodward by J. Pennington Straus, Spring 1983.
15. *Evening Bulletin*, 27 July 1918, 1 February 1924.
16. *Parish News of St. Martin-in-the-Fields Church*, 26 May 1935.
17. SW to author, 29 April 1986.
18. Ibid.
19. Ibid.
20. Interview with SW, 18–19 July 1986.
21. GHW, *Quita*, p. 22.
22. Ibid., p. 35.
23. Quoted in Ibid., pp. 62–63.
24. Bateman, *Houston*, p. 11.
25. Interview with EHS, 14 November 1986.
26. This account of EHS's childhood is taken from interviews with the author on 11 December 1984 and 14 November 1986.
27. Interview with SW, 18–19 July 1986.
28. Eugene McWheeler to SFH, 6 October 1933, EHS collection; interview with EHS, 14 November 1986.
29. Ibid.; Alexander Alcan to Mrs. SFH, 28 September 1907; F. T. Ditmars to SFH, 24 September 1934; both letters in EHS collection.
30. Interview with EHS, 14 November 1986; *Evening Bulletin*, 18 October 1918; *House Beautiful* (March 1925), pp. 247–248.

## Chapter 8: *Two Cousins*

1. Interview with EHS, 14 November 1986.
2. Henry Howard Houston II (HHH2) to SFH, 17 September 1916.
3. HHH2, Diary, 2, 3, 4 February 1917, EHS collection.
4. Ibid., 8, 9, 10, 18 February 1917.
5. Ibid., 14 February 1917.
6. Ibid., 11 March 1917.
7. Ibid., 12 March 1917.
8. Ibid., 19 March 1917.
9. Ibid., 20, 21 March 1917.
10. *Evening Bulletin*, 28 August 1918; Twenty-ninth Annual Banquet Program, Houston Post, 12 April 1950.

11. George Woodward, in *A Year for France: War Letters of Houston Woodward* (New Haven, 1919), p. iii.

12. GW, *Memoirs,* pp. 98–99.

13. Woodward, *A Year for France,* p. 57.

14. Ibid., pp. 65–66.

15. Ibid., p. 68.

16. Ibid., pp. 97–98.

17. Ibid., p. 115.

18. Ibid., p. 145.

19. Ibid., p. 148.

20. Ibid., p. 102.

21. Twenty-ninth Annual Banquet Program.

22. GHW, *Quita,* pp. 42–55.

23. GW, quoted in ibid., 51–55.

24. From account of Eleanor Kenner Smith Morris, April 1976, in EHS collection; SFH, letter to his children, 29 December 1926, EHS collection.

25. SFH to children, 29 December 1926; interview with EHS, 11 December 1984.

26. For example, SFH to A. Nemin and A. Thiriet, 11 December 1937, EHS collection.

27. *Atlantic City Gazette,* 6 May 1922.

28. *Evening Bulletin,* 7 August 1921, 15 January 1937, 27 July 1938.

29. Ibid., 21 May 1924.

30. Twenty-ninth Annual Banquet Program.

*Chapter 9: State Senator*

1. GW, *Memoirs,* pp. 113–115.

2. Ibid., pp. 115–116.

3. *Evening Bulletin,* 3 April, 7, 8, 11 May 1918.

4. Ibid., 26 May 1952.

5. For background on the 1919 city charter campaign see Abernethy, "Progressivism," pp. 561–565; Neva Deardorff, "To Unshackle Philadelphia," *The Survey* (5 April 1919), pp. 19–23.

6. *Public Ledger,* 14 December 1918.

7. *Evening Bulletin,* 26 May 1952.

8. Abernethy, "Progressivism," pp. 564–565. See also Laws of the General Assembly of the Commonwealth of Pennsylvania, Passed at the Legislative Session of 1919, pp. 581–638.

9. *Evening Bulletin,* 15 January, 26 March, 4 April 1929.

10. Ibid., 20 May 1936.

11. Ibid., 2 May 1931. See also 22 April, 8 May 1931.

12. Ibid., 6 December 1931, 22 January 1933, 11 November 1939.

13. Ibid., 24 January 1933; *Public Ledger,* 7 February 1933.

14. Philadelphia *Record,* 27 August 1938; *Evening Bulletin,* 25 November 1938.

15. *Evening Bulletin,* 6 February 1925, 24 April 1930; interview with SW, 18–19 July, 1986.

16. *Public Ledger,* 20 January 1931; *Evening Bulletin,* 27 January, 25 February 1931.

17. SW to author, 3 March 1986.
18. GW, *The Pennsylvania Legislator,* vol. 1 (Philadelphia, 1932), pp. 3–4.
19. On private relief efforts in Philadelphia see Bonnie R. Fox, "Unemployment Relief in Philadelphia, 1930–1932: A Study of the Depression's Impact on Voluntarism," *PMHB* (January 1969), pp. 86–107.
20. *Evening Bulletin,* 5 January 1931.
21. Ibid., 17 November 1931.
22. GW, *Pennsylvania Legislator,* vol. 1, p. 128.
23. Ibid., p. 129.
24. Ibid., p. 130.
25. *Evening Bulletin,* 2, 3, 9 November 1931.
26. *Pennsylvania Legislator,* vol. 1, p. 154.
27. Ibid., pp. 190, 192.
28. Ibid., p. 194.
29. Ibid., pp. 67–68.
30. *Evening Bulletin,* 18 March, 29 April, 1933.
31. On Pinchot's second administration, see John W. Furlow, "An Urban State Under Seige: Pennsylvania and the Second Gubernatorial Administration of Gifford Pinchot, 1931–35," (University of North Carolina, doctoral diss., 1973).
32. *Evening Bulletin,* 5 March, 20 March, 13 November 1933.
33. *Pennsylvania Legislator,* vol. 2 (Philadelphia, 1934), p. 109.
34. Ibid., p. 128.
35. See Ronald Feinman, *Twilight of Progressivism and the New Deal* (Baltimore, 1981).
36. *Pennsylvania Legislator,* vol. 3 (Philadelphia, 1936), p. 104.
37. Ibid., pp. 114–115, 148.
38. Ibid., p. 121.
39. Ibid., p. 164.
40. Cynthia Ann MacLeod, "Arts and Crafts Architecture," pp. 17–24.
41. *Pennsylvania Legislator,* vol. 5 (Philadelphia, 1941), p. 231.
42. Ibid., pp. 233–234.

*Chapter 10: Loss and Remembrance*

1. GHW, *Quita,* p. 1.
2. Ibid.
3. Ibid., p. 56.
4. Interview with SW, 18–19 July 1986.
5. GHW, *Quita,* pp. 75–90.
6. Ibid., p. 92.
7. Ibid., pp. 126–128.
8. Ibid., pp. 131–150.
9. Ibid., pp. 133–155; GW, *Memoirs,* pp. 197–209.
10. Ibid., pp. 207–209.
11. Ibid., pp. 7–8.
12. Ibid., p. 8.
13. Interview with Charles Woodward and Elizabeth Gadsden Woodward (EGW), 3 October 1985.
14. GW, *Memoirs,* pp. 145–146.

15. Ibid., p. 89.
16. Ibid., p. 211.
17. GW, *Family Letters and Proletarian Essays* (Philadelphia, 1937), p. 28.
18. Ibid., pp. 12–65.
19. GW, *Family Letters* (Philadelphia, 1946), p. 31.
20. Ibid., p. 30.
21. *Family Letters* (Philadelphia, 1937), p. 75.
22. Ibid., pp. 81, 87.
23. Ibid., p. 114.
24. Ibid., p. 125.
25. *Evening Bulletin*, 13 January 1932, 6 May 1937, 23 August 1945.
26. *Evening Bulletin*, 11 November 1937.
27. *Record*, 9 April 1939.
28. *Evening Bulletin*, 27 June 1923, 14 October 1929.

*Chapter 11: Brothers-in-Law*

1. Interview with EHS, 14 November 1986.
2. SFH, address to the Houston American Legion Post, 12 November 1939, EHS collection.
3. SFH to the editor of the *Inquirer*, 22 May 1941.
4. SFH, Memorial Day Address, Houston Post, 1942, EHS collection.
5. GW, *Pennsylvania Legislator*, vol. 5, pp. 104–105.
6. Ibid., p. 175.
7. GW, *Pennsylvania Legislator*, vol. 7 (Philadelphia, 1945), pp. 51, 101–102.
8. Ibid., 106–107.
9. GW, *Pennsylvania Legislator*, vol. 6 (Philadelphia, 1943), pp. 195.
10. GW, *Family Letters* (1946), pp. 136–137.
11. Ibid., pp. 123–124.
12. Ibid., pp. 122–123.
13. *Evening Bulletin*, 26 February 1943.
14. HEP, General Correspondence, T-V, PSA, MG-154.
15. GW, *Pennsylvania Legislator*, vol. 6, p. 19.
16. GW, *Pennsylvania Legislator*, vol. 5, p. 190.
17. GW, *Pennsylvania Legislator*, vol. 6, pp. 65, 66.
18. GW, *Pennsylvania Legislator*, vol. 7, p. 79.
19. Ibid., p. 92.
20. GW, *Pennsylvania Legislator*, vol. 6, p. 120.
21. Ibid., pp. 48–49.
22. Ibid., p. 174.
23. Ibid., pp. 173–174.
24. Ibid., pp. 51–52.
25. Ibid., p. 52.
26. GW, *Pennsylvania Legislator*, vol. 7, p. 63.
27. Ibid., p. 66.
28. *Record*, 24 January 1936.
29. *Evening Bulletin*, 24 January 1936.
30. Interview with CDF, 5 March 1987.
31. Ibid.; *Evening Bulletin*, 20 November 1941.
32. Ibid., 20 June 1953.

33. GHW to Donald D. Dodge (DDD), 23 August 1949; DDD to GHW, 30 March 1950, CDF collection.

34. GHW to DDD, 23 March 1950.

35. DDD to GHW, 30 March 1950.

36. *Evening Bulletin,* 4 September 1942, 13 August 1962; HEP, General Correspondence, Ma-O, PSA, MG-154.

37. For the plans, see Houston Estate file, AAUP.

38. Conversation with EHS, 13 March 1987.

39. Ibid.

40. Interview with EHS, 11 December 1984.

41. HEP, General Correspondence, In-Ma, PSA, MG-154.

42. J. Wesley Twelves, *Diocese of Pennsylvania* (Philadelphia, 1969), p. 37.

43. Houston Estate file, AAUP.

44. HEP, General Correspondence, T-V, PSA, MG-154.

45. Ibid.; interview with EHS, 11 December 1984.

46. HEP, General Correspondence, T-V, PSA, MG-154.

47. HEP, General Correspondence, In-Ma, PSA, MG-154.

48. *Evening Bulletin,* 18 March 1950.

49. Ibid., 2 May 1952; conversation with EHS, 13 March 1987.

50. SW to author, 3 March 1986; *Evening Bulletin,* 7 June 1944.

51. Ibid., 5 February 1946.

52. Ibid., 3, 5 March 1947.

53. An annotation to Section 1-102 of the Philadelphia Home Rule Charter of 1951 reads, "subsection (2) looks forward to City-County consolidation. . . . Whenever possible each new board and commission to be created is to be attached to a city department." See *Philadelphia Home Rule Charter* (1951), p. 5.

54. For a brief description of the 1951 charter see Joseph S. Clark, Jr., and Dennis J. Clark, "Rally and Relapse, 1946–1968," in *A 300-Year History,* pp. 650–657.

55. SW to author, 3 March 1986; *Evening Bulletin,* 26 May 1952.

## Chapter 12: The Preservationists

1. Unless otherwise indicated, material for George Woodward, Jr., was derived from interviews with EGW on 25 September 1986 and SW on 18–19 July 1986 and from GW, *Memoirs,* pp. 168–170.

2. Mary Wickham Porcher Bond (MWPB) to author, 15 August 1986.

3. GHW, *Quita,* p. 30.

4. Interview of George Woodward, Jr., by MWPB, *Chestnut Hill Local,* 22 October 1959.

5. GW, "Krisheim News," September 1922.

6. *Evening Bulletin,* 4 May 1943, 24 August 1945, 5 August 1949, 7 November 1954.

7. Ibid., 31 January 1967.

8. Unless otherwise indicated, material for the remainder of this chapter was derived from interviews with EGW on 15 and 25 September 1986.

9. *Evening Bulletin,* 7 January 1933.

10. GW, *Memoirs,* p. 175.

11. *Evening Bulletin,* 5 December 1934, 26 March 1937; *Public Ledger,* 9 August 1935.

12. *Inquirer,* 31 July 1951.

13. *Evening Bulletin,* 21 December 1973.
14. Ibid., 7 November 1932, 4 November 1938; *Record,* 23 September 1939.
15. *Charleston News and Courier,* 3 March 1963; *Charleston Evening Post,* 7 March 1963.
16. *News and Courier,* 14 April 1971.
17. Ibid., 10 January 1974.
18. Ibid., 29 February 1968, 16 August 1968; *Evening Post,* 7 January 1969.
19. *Inquirer,* 4 April 1986.
20. *Evening Bulletin,* 15 August 1972.
21. Ibid., 5 December 1961, 26 March, 2, 10, 14 October, 14, 18 December 1962, 28 January, 13 August 1963, 1, 2 June 1964; *Inquirer,* 26 November 1963.
22. *Evening Bulletin,* 21 September 1960, 13 August, 10 November 1964, 10 June 1968, 24 January, 23 September 1969, 9 June 1970, 3 June 1977; Helen Moak, *Chestnut Hill Local,* 10 April 1986.
23. *Evening Bulletin,* 7 May 1970.
24. Moak, *Chestnut Hill Local,* 10 April 1986.
25. Ibid.
26. Ibid.
27. Ibid.
28. *Inquirer Magazine,* 26 December 1965.
29. *Chestnut Hill Local,* 1, 8, 15 March 1984.
30. *Inquirer,* 4 April 1986; Moak, *Chestnut Hill Local,* 10 April 1986.
31. *Charleston News and Courier,* 6 April 1986.
32. Resolution, Historic Charleston Foundation, n.d.
33. *Inquirer,* 30 April 1986.

## *Chapter 13: The Young Diplomat*

1. For a brief biographical sketch of SW see *Current Biography,* 1951, pp. 667–669. Otherwise, most of the material for Chapters 14 and 15 has come from an interview with SW on 18–19 July 1986.
2. *Evening Bulletin,* 2 September 1925.
3. Ibid., 4 February 1927.
4. Ibid., 29 September 1934.
5. Ibid., 2 June 1934; 8 April 1936; 15 October 1936; 12 July 1934.
6. *The Saturday Evening Post,* 27 December 1947, pp. 24–25, 47.
7. *Newsweek,* 19 June 1939; *Time,* 26 June 1939.
8. James MacGregor Burns, *Roosevelt: The Soldier of Freedom* (New York, 1970), pp. 27–29, 35; Robert A. Divine, *The Reluctant Belligerent* (New York, 1967), pp. 104–105.
9. *Newsweek,* 6 July 1942; *The New York Times,* 27 September 1942.

## *Chapter 14: Chief of Protocol*

1. On SW's years as chief of protocol, see *Saturday Evening Post,* 27 December 1947, pp. 24–25, 47; *The New York Tribune,* 29 May 1946; *The New York Times,* 1 December 1946; *Liberty,* (January 1950), pp. 18, 52.
2. Donald R. Mc Coy, *The Presidency of Harry S. Truman* (Lawrence, Ks., 1984), p. 130.

3. *Washington Post,* 23 August 1950.

4. On Canada and the St. Lawrence Seaway, see Blair Frazier, *The Search for Identity: Canada, 1945–1967* (New York, 1967), pp. 67–71.

5. *Time,* 29 October 1951.

6. Frazier, *Canada,* pp. 74–75, 95, 126–127.

7. *Evening Bulletin,* 26 November 1952.

8. Ibid., 3 June 1954.

9. Ibid., 15 January 1961.

10. Ibid., 21 June 1973.


*Chapter 15: Debutante, New Dealer, and Conservationist*

1. Unless otherwise indicated, material for this chapter is based upon interviews with EHS on 11 December 1984 and 16 November 1986, in addition to conversations between EHS and the author on 2, 12, 29, and 31 December 1986 and 9, 12 January, 10, 12 February, and 13, 16 March 1987.

2. *Evening Bulletin,* 22 February 1953; *Inquirer Magazine,* 26 December 1965.

3. *Springside School, 1879–1979,* privately printed, p. 96.

4. SFH, AR file, UPA.

5. *Evening Bulletin,* 26 August 1940, 1 January, 23 March, 18 September 1942, 30 July 1943, 10 May 1947, 21 February 1955, 24 November 1970.

6. Ibid., 22 September 1963.

7. EHS, 1928–1929 scrapbook, EHS collection.

8. *Public Ledger,* 4 January 1930.

9. *Evening Bulletin,* 23 February 1933.

10. Ibid., 12 August 1975.

11. Ibid., 14 May 1949.

12. Ibid., 5 November 1951. See also Hal Libros, *Hard-Core Liberals: A Sociological Analysis of the Philadelphia Americans for Democratic Action* (Cambridge, Mass., 1975).

13. *Evening Bulletin,* 25 January 1955.

14. Ibid., 20 October 1960.

15. Ibid., 17 November, 9 December 1963.

16. Ibid., 7 October 1964, 8 January 1967.

17. Ibid., 23 November 1955.

18. Ibid., 24 December 1959.

19. Ibid., 26 December 1962.

20. Ibid., 12 May 1967.

21. On Wolfe's Neck Farm, see the *Maine Times,* 22 August 1975.

22. *Inquirer,* 30 August 1987 and 4 September 1987; *Maine Sunday Telegram,* 30 August 1987.


*Epilogue*

1. The epilogue contains only the names and activities of fourth-generation descendants who wished to be identified.

2. *Inquirer,* 2 March 1980; *Evening Bulletin,* 29 March 1981; *Chestnut Hill Local,* 24 January, 7 February 1980.

3. *Chestnut Hill Local,* 15 May 1986.

# Index